The Complete Guide to Hunting, Butchering,
   and Cooking Wild Game: Volume 2: Small Game and Fowl
The Complete Guide to Hunting, Butchering,
   and Cooking Wild Game: Volume 1: Big Game
Meat Eater
American Buffalo
The Scavenger's Guide to Haute Cuisine

THE COMPLETE GUIDE TO HUNTING, BUTCHERING, AND COOKING WILD GAME

THE COMPLETE GUIDE TO HUNTING, BUTCHERING, AND COOKING WILD GAME

VOLUME 2: SMALL GAME AND FOWL

STEVEN RINELLA

SPIEGEL & GRAU   NEW YORK

A Spiegel & Grau Trade Paperback Original

Copyright © 2015 by Steven Rinella and Zero Point Zero Production, Inc.

Published in the United States by Spiegel & Grau, an imprint of Random House, a division of Penguin Random House LLC, New York.

Spiegel & Grau and the House colophon are registered trademarks of Penguin Random House LLC.

ISBN 978-0-8129-8705-8
eBook ISBN 978-0-8129-8706-5

Printed in the United States of America on acid-free paper

randomhousebooks.com
spiegelandgrau.com

9 8 7 6 5 4 3

Book design by Christopher M. Zucker

This book is dedicated to all those hunters, and there are many, who fight for the conservation of wild animals and wild places.

CONTENTS

INTRODUCTION

If you're a small game hunter, or have a desire to become one, you're in luck. Right now, here in the first quarter of the twenty-first century, we're enjoying what future generations are likely to regard as the good ol' days of small game hunting. While many big game hunters lament the decreasing access to productive big game hunting grounds and the increasing cost of hunting tags, you seldom hear such complaints from small game hunters. Instead, they are talking about light hunting pressure, long seasons, liberal bag limits, and game populations that are generally thriving. For sure, now is the time to be out there hunting small game.

The fact that I've been doing it for over thirty years is testament to my credentials in compiling this book, and also to my love for the food that small game hunting brings to the table. I remember my own favorite childhood meals of small game—roasted wood duck, broiled Canada goose, rabbit hasenpfeffer, chicken-fried squirrel—far better than I remember all those meals of venison that crossed my plate during the same years. What sticks with me are the endless varieties of flavors, textures, and visual qualities that came from the small game of our local woods and waters. And don't go thinking that I was raised on some sprawling farm or wilderness homestead. I was brought up in a semi-suburban Midwest setting, with a neighbor's house not 50 yards from my front door. Believe me, if I could find small game ranging from fox squirrels to green-winged teal within reach of my home, then you probably can, too.

Beyond all the excitement and great food that have come my way as a small game hunter, I cherish the practical skills that I've picked up as well. I've been lucky enough to hunt big game throughout the United States and beyond, and I've done so with a reliance on skills that l first began to develop as a kid out pursuing critters weighing just a few pounds. All of my foundational skills—stalking, ambushing, calling, wingshooting, rifle marksmanship, skinning, butchering—were born out of experiences with squirrels, rabbits, grouse, and ducks.

But small game hunting should hardly be regarded as simply a training activity for future big game hunters. Some of the best hunters I know, including several who were consulted during the making of this book, are strict small game fanatics who prefer the unique challenges and constant action of small game hunting over the often frustrating and time-consuming world of big game hunting. It's easy for me to see where they're coming from. If I had only two or three weekends that I could devote to hunting every year, I might choose to spend them in a duck marsh or a good patch of rabbit cover rather than waiting on a whitetail deer that might not ever show up. That way, I'd be much more likely to get a good dose of action and excitement—and quite a few tasty meals—from a limited investment of time and money.

Regardless of whether you'll hunt small game a hundred days a year or just one day, you'll find the information that you need for success within this book. It is divided into five primary sections. Section 1 offers a comprehensive overview of firearms, gear, and apparel for the versatile small game hunter. Section 2 covers the basics: how to interpret hunting regulations, identifying potential hunting locations, how to scout for game, and a fundamental overview of the hunting strategies and methodologies used by successful small game hunters. Section 3 covers biology and preferred hunting methods for a wide gamut of small game species, which are subdivided into three categories: furred small game (rabbits, hares, and squirrels), upland birds (grouse, pheasant, quail, ptarmigan, doves, pigeons, etc.), and waterfowl (puddle ducks, diving ducks, and geese). Field dressing and butchering small game is covered in Section 4. Finally, Section 5 provides a collection of beautiful and tasty small game recipes that will help you utilize your kill to its maximum potential.

The organization of this book is pretty straightforward, if I say so myself. But you might find that some pieces of information are missing from where you'd expect to see them. For instance, you might be disappointed to see that turkey decoys are not covered in the gear section. If so, you'll be relieved to learn that the subject of turkey decoys is treated thoroughly in the turkey-specific portion of the species section. Because of these inevitable bits of confusion, I'd suggest that you study this book in its entirety before lamenting any omissions. You'll probably find everything that you need. You'll also learn a lot of stuff that you didn't know you needed. Each page has something to offer for every hunter, regardless of your particular specialty. Even if you're a waterfowl hunter who has zero desire to chase a blue grouse, you're still likely to learn something useful if you read that section. So don't just treat this book like a manual, in which you look up whatever bit of information you need at a given moment. It's best to read it from cover to cover at least once.

You might also be surprised to find contradictory opinions in here. Rest assured that that was my intention. While I am the author of this book, it might best be understood as a giant archive of opinions and strategies that were gleaned from dozens and dozens of hunters throughout the span of my lifetime and then filtered through my own brain before getting poured onto paper. When the opinions of others generally enhance or reinforce my own, I've presented them as coming from the author. In cases where they don't necessarily jibe with my own personal findings, such as

Ron Boehme's spirited argument in favor of using old, break-action shotguns instead of newer models of pump-action and autoloading shotguns, I've been careful to attribute them to the source. But rest assured, everyone who's been given a voice in this book is highly credentialed. Their opinions are no more "right" or "wrong" than my own; instead, they are telling you what has worked for them under the circumstances that they've encountered in their own lives. Do your own personal experimentation to see if these ideas will work for you.

Speaking of personal experimentation, this book is useless if you're not willing to get out there in the woods and subject yourself to failure. I have done some ridiculously stupid things in the woods, but I've managed to get my money's worth out of each dumbass move. I believe that it's hard to understand what works without an equal understanding of what doesn't work. Missed shots, skunked trips, spooked game, cold feet: it all needs to be embraced as the stuff that makes you a better—and better informed—hunter.

So go, get out there. The woods are waiting. There are no excuses.

THE COMPLETE GUIDE TO HUNTING, BUTCHERING, AND COOKING WILD GAME

GEAR

To kick off the gear section, I'll refer to one of my own passages from Volume 1 of *The Complete Guide to Hunting, Butchering, and Cooking Wild Game:* "Gear is like booze. Once you get older, you realize that quality should be regarded more highly than quantity." That basic sentiment holds true for the small game hunter—save your money and focus on getting yourself into a kit of quality gear rather than cutting corners by buying a bunch of subpar junk that brings you lots of frustration and not much game meat. But I'm happy to say that the hunter can equip himself or herself for a generalist approach to small game for a lot less money than it takes to get rigged up for a generalist approach to big

game. The firearms, ammunition, and archery gear for small game are generally cheaper than those intended for big game, and the demands on clothing, backpacks, and cutlery are less severe. The walks tend to be shorter, the animals are smaller, and prime locations are usually a little bit closer to home.

In certain families, equipping a new small game hunter doesn't cost a dime. When I was a kid, I hunted small game successfully for years without ever touching a new piece of gear. I wore hand-me-down clothes and shot hand-me-down guns. I longed for a brand-spickety-new left-handed semi-auto .22, yet I had to settle for an old right-handed bolt-action rifle that my dad had purchased from a nearby summer camp when they discontinued their marksmanship program. At the time, I was embarrassed about that rifle. But now that I'm approaching middle age, with young kids of my own, those days of making do have become a matter of personal pride to me. That old right-handed .22, a Remington Model 581, remains one of my most treasured firearms. As it turns out, it's a real tack driver. I intend for it to serve as my son's first squirrel rifle.

In other words, don't let cost get in the way of your desire to hunt small game. Resident small game licenses are dirt cheap, you usually don't need any special tags (with the notable exception of turkey), and you can get a box of fifty .22 rounds for about five bucks. If you learn to be a deadeye with your .22, that equals ten daily bag limits of squirrels in my home state of Michigan. Or, to put it another way, ten family-sized preparations of hasenpfeffer, a sublime and vinegary dish intended for hares that works great with fox squirrels and gray squirrels as well.

When it comes to selecting hunting gear, it's important to pay attention to the voices of people who have been doing things longer or more successfully than you have. I leaned on

This image of the author and his brother Matt on a camping trip shows that it doesn't take a lot of money to enjoy small game hunts. They are not wearing a stitch of clothing made for the purpose of hunting. The author traded a Husqvarna chain saw and $250 in cash for the "camper" van. The couch that serves as a bed was free.

the expertise of dozens of talented and dedicated hunters while putting this guidebook together. Their impressions of the gear that I discuss (or choose not to discuss) in this section have certainly colored my own opinions. But understand that my recommendations are just that: recommendations. If something here doesn't make sense to you, or if your experiences with a certain product or idea contradict my own, then you should go with what makes you feel comfortable.

FIREARMS

A versatile small game hunter should regard his firearms as the foundation of his hunting gear. I wouldn't say the same for all types of hunting—for versatile big game hunters, apparel and optics are equally as important as firearms. But for small game hunting, it's absolutely true: guns matter, and they matter a lot.

But don't go thinking that you need an arsenal of rifles and shotguns in order to be an effective small game hunter. If you own a vault full of shotguns, that's great, as long as you spend enough time with one of them to learn how to use it. But for you folks who don't have the money or inclination to accumulate a collection of firearms, don't fret. By shopping carefully—either used or new—you can purchase a single shotgun that will cover virtually 95 percent of the small game hunting opportunities that this continent has to offer. If you want to bring your level of preparedness up to 100 percent, that can be easily achieved with the addition of a .22-caliber rimfire rifle.

THE SHOTGUN

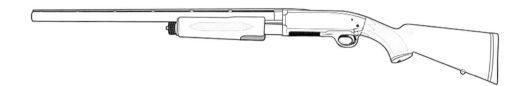

The coolest thing about shotguns is how inherently versatile they are. In a given year, an enterprising hunter might use his or her shotgun to hunt everything from mourning doves weighing 5 ounces to wild turkeys topping out at 25 pounds. If that same shotgun accepts multiple types of barrels—and many do—it might also be used very effectively for whitetail deer. To achieve this level of versatility with a rifle, you'd need a caliber that was ideal for everything from squirrels to moose. (And trust me, it doesn't exist.) While it might seem that a versatile shotgun would be costlier than one with a narrower range of capabilities, the opposite is true. Some of the lowest-priced shotguns on the market carry some of the highest credentials. But first, here's a primer on shotgun terminology and how it applies to you.

GAUGE: Shotguns are sized according to the bore diameter. The smallest shotgun used for hunting purposes is the .410 (rabbits and squirrels, typically), while the largest is the 10-gauge (geese and swans). The .410 is named after its caliber measurement; the diameter of the bore is .410 inch, just as a .308 rifle cartridge is .308 inch. Shotguns that use the term *gauge*, such as 10-gauge, 12-gauge, and 20-gauge, rely on an arcane system that correlates the bore diameter to how many lead spheres of that size it would take to make a pound of weight. A 20-gauge shotgun has a bore diameter of .615 inch, and twenty lead balls of that size would weigh 1 pound. A 12-gauge has a bore diameter of .729 inch; twelve lead balls of that size weigh a pound.

This will piss off a lot of shotgun snobs, including some guys who really know what they're talking about, but the only two gauges worth considering are 20-gauge and 12-gauge. Ammunition for these gauges is widely available and highly versatile, and there's no practical reason to stray into the more esoteric gauges. In recent years there's been a lot of spirited debate about the relative attributes of 12-gauge and 20-gauge shotguns, spurred in particular by advances in ammunition. A person could spend days reading up on these arguments in dedicated firearms magazines, and you're welcome to do so. But here I'm just

From left: .410, 28-gauge, 20-gauge, 16-gauge, 12-gauge, 10-gauge.

going to cut through a lot of the BS and give you a fairly straightforward summation of the information and also a piece of advice. A 12-gauge shotgun has bigger shells than a 20-gauge shotgun, so it throws more pellets and it typically kicks harder. If the bulk of your hunting is going to be for smaller-sized game, such as rabbits, quail, pheasants, et cetera, then feel free to go with a 20-gauge. But if you're also going to be hunting game that's a little larger, such as turkeys, ducks, and geese, go with a 12-gauge.

ACTION: While there are bolt-action shotguns, for practical purposes we'll limit our discussion here to autoloading, pump-action, and break-open shotguns. Each type has its own selling points and liabilities.

AUTOLOADING SHOTGUNS: Sometimes called autoloaders or (incorrectly) automatic shotguns, these harness power from the shotshell in order to eject the spent round, reset the firing pin, and load a new round from the magazine. Autoloaders used to have a reputation for malfunctioning and frequent jamming, but newer models are much more reliable.

AUTOLOADER PROS
- High rate of fire. Every time the trigger is pulled, the gun fires and cycles without the assistance of the operator; most modern semi-auto shotguns will fire as quickly as the shooter is able to pull the trigger.
- Low recoil. Because of gas- or inertia-powered

Top: Autoloader, Remington Versamax 12-gauge. Center: Pump-action, Remington 870 Express 12-gauge. Bottom: Break-open, Tristar Silver II 12-gauge.

cycling systems that harness some of the recoil energy, the felt recoil of the semi-auto shotgun is less than that of pump-actions and break-opens.

• Ease of follow-up shots. Because the semi-auto shotgun cycles without the aid of the shooter, follow-up shots can be made more efficiently due to the lack of operator movement during shooting.

AUTOLOADER CONS

• Versatility. Due to the various cycling systems in semi-auto shotguns, adjustments must be made to most models when switching between various loads and shell lengths.

• Safety. Due to the tension of the recoil spring, a shooter can injure himself or herself when closing the bolt. Also, unintentional shots can be made if the shooter is unfamiliar with the mechanics of the firearm.

• Difficulty of maintenance and assembly. With the various cycling systems available in semi-auto shotguns, the operator must be familiar with all of the internal workings of the weapon when performing basic assembly and disassembly, making the weapons less user-friendly than pump-actions and break-opens.

PUMP-ACTION SHOTGUNS: Sometimes known as slide-action shotguns, these are operated by a manually sliding forearm that ejects the spent shell, cocks the firing pin, and loads a new shell from the magazine. The number-one-selling shotgun of all time is the Remington 870, a pump-action shotgun.

PUMP-ACTION PROS

- Inexpensive. You can get a new pump shotgun that will last a lifetime for a few hundred dollars.
- High versatility. Pumps are manually operated, so as long as the shell is the proper gauge and length, the gun will be able to cycle ammunition ranging from the lightest target loads to the heaviest buckshot or slug loads. Popular models of pump shotguns are easily modified, with literally thousands of available components for customization.
- Capacity. Most pump-action shotguns have a magazine capacity of five shells, plus one in the chamber.

PUMP-ACTION CONS

- Slower rate of fire. Because the operator must manually cycle the weapon, follow-up shots from a pump take longer than with break-open and autoloading shotguns—particularly with inexperienced shooters.
- Slower aiming for follow-up shots. Cycling a pump shotgun throws off the shooter's aim, so follow-up shots need to be consciously realigned.
- Short-strokers beware. First-time users of pump-action shotguns are often guilty of short-stroking, or not working the slide through its entire cycle. Though easily rectified with practice or proper instruction, this can cause jams and misfires.

An autoloading shotgun allows for multiple shots fired in a hurry, with only a minimal amount of adjustment between shots.

BREAK-OPEN SHOTGUNS: Also called break-action shotguns, these have a barrel or barrels set on a hinge so that the gun literally breaks open at the receiver to enable the manual loading of shotshells. Some break-opens have only a single barrel, though those are generally regarded as beginner-level shotguns for kids. Most serious hunting shotguns are fitted with two barrels, mounted either horizontally or vertically. Shotguns with horizontally paired barrels are called side-by-side or double-barrel shotguns, and shotguns with vertically paired barrels are called over/under shotguns. While there is a lot to be said for the old-timey look and feel of a double-barrel shotgun, functional differences between the two are really quite small. It should be said, however, that most serious wingshooters who use break-open shotguns stick to the over/under configuration.

BREAK-OPEN PROS

- Easy handling. Break-open shotguns are generally lightweight and compact. This makes them easier to carry on long walks and easier and faster to handle and shoot in thick brush.
- Mechanically simple. This isn't to say that they are impervious to things such as dirt and ice, but the relative lack of internal moving parts makes them easy to clean and also easy to troubleshoot when you're having problems.
- Safe. Break-open shotguns are a favorite for parents of young shooters, because kids can be instructed to "break open" the action of the shotgun whenever they are not actually shooting. This way, the guardian can tell at a glance, regardless of distance, that the firearm is in a safe position.

BREAK-OPEN CONS

- Capacity. Break-open shotguns limit the shooter to only one or two shots.
- Expensive. Break-opens tend to be costlier than pump-action shotguns.
- Limited versatility. Break-open shotguns are much more difficult to accessorize than pumps and automatics, and are therefore less versatile.

RONNY BOEHME, A MICHIGAN HUNTER, WEIGHS IN ON HIS LOVE OF OLD SHOTGUNS

"Most of the guns that I use for taking game are older than I am, meaning they were produced before 1957. Don't get me **wrong**, there are great guns still manufactured with craftsmanship and quality. But the **bulk** of them, especially the shotguns, are so costly that the average wingshooter (which is what I consider myself to be) cannot justify their purchase.

"Old guns that have passed through **many** hands have a spirit of sorts. They have a story. **The** details of that story may not **be** revealed to us, but **it's** easy to imagine them being shouldered many times to **put** meat on the table. One of my personal favorites is a 109-year-old shotgun made **by Charles** Boswell, **an** English gunmaker. It is sleek, light, and swings on birds as though it's floating in **the** air. Its action opens and closes like an old, well-worn pocket watch. When I am cleaning it, I hold the double barrels by the lug and knock on them with my knuckle. It rings like an old church bell.

"Most hunters have owned at least one pump shotgun. Designed over a hundred years ago, they are reliable and proven. I like to collect old 16-gauge pumps, an oddball gauge. The actions and barrels on these guns are worn down to bare metal

(continued)

in spots, and the walnut stocks are marred and nicked. They carry memories from quail and duck hunts, which were the mainstay of wingshooters back in the early 1900s. The actions slide with an almost effortless motion. The slickness comes from use, sure, but it also comes as a result of being assembled by hand from machined parts that were carefully tested and fitted. I will go out on a limb here and say that all of these old guns came out of the box years ago with no functioning problems. That is not true of guns these days. I've hunted with friends whose brand-new guns broke on the first day of use. Some of these guns have to be taken more than once to a gunsmith for repair before they ever see any real use. I've seen several new double-barrel shotguns that are so stiff you need to use two hands and a knee to open them up.

"Then there's the wood, which is what makes old guns truly special. Synthetic stocks and forearms leave a gun without personality. Plastic has no heart, no soul. Wood, on the other hand, has a fingerprint that is never repeated in nature. It came from a tree that likely harbored and fed animals. When you hold an old gun, it's a handshake with the past. It's like meeting relatives that you never lived near, but when your hands clasp you can feel that you're connected to them."

BARREL LENGTH: A term of obvious definition, barrel length refers to the length of the shotgun's barrel. In general, a longer barrel allows the projectiles to harness more energy from the explosion of the gunpowder and to fall into a truer flight path.

20- to 24-inch barrels. These short barrels are best left to turkey hunters, who are taking careful aim at standing-still birds. They are generally too short for wingshooting, as accuracy suffers. However, many rabbit and grouse hunters who spend their time in extremely thick cover will tout the benefit of a short barrel that doesn't get hung up in the brush.

26- to 28-inch barrels. These are standard barrel lengths that can be used for all shotgun applications, ranging from wingshooting to slug hunting. While a 26-inch barrel is lighter and more maneuverable, a 28-inch barrel is going to be more accurate for long-range shots and should be regarded as perhaps the best all-around barrel length. (Keep in mind that choke selection can mitigate the inherent differences between 26-inch and 28-inch barrels. That is, a 26-inch barrel with a full choke will shoot a tighter grouping than a 28-inch barrel with an improved cylinder choke. See below for detailed information about chokes.)

30- to 32-inch barrels. These longer barrels certainly have their devotees, who use them for all shotgunning applications. However, they are most commonly favored by waterfowl hunters who do a lot of long-range pass-shooting at waterfowl.

CHOKE: A shotgun's choke is a tapered restriction in the muzzle end of the bore. This results in a wider or narrower shot pattern, or "spread" of pellets, as the shot travels downrange. A tightly constricted choke yields a tighter pattern; that is, it concentrates the shot into an overall impact zone of smaller diameter than you'd get from a more open choke at equal distances.

American hunters commonly use five different chokes for hunting purposes. They are:

IMPROVED CYLINDER. Highly versatile choke, used for upland birds, small furred game, and waterfowl. (Safe for slugs.)

MODIFIED. A general-use choke, used for upland birds, small furred game, and for short- to midrange waterfowl shooting. (Safe for slugs.)

IMPROVED MODIFIED. Midrange upland bird and waterfowl shooting. (Not safe for slugs.)

FULL. The most common highly compressed choke. Used for long-range upland and waterfowl shooting. Also good for turkeys. (Not safe for slugs.)

EXTRA-FULL. A highly compressed choke used for specific applications on turkeys and long-range waterfowl shooting. (Not safe for slugs.)

The type of choke you should use depends on the type of hunting you're doing. The tightly restricted extra-full choke that enables you to put an overwhelmingly lethal dose of pellets into the small head of a turkey at 60 yards would be a major handicap when gunning for fast-moving cottontail rabbits in the tight confines of a briar patch. Not only would you miss most of your shots (at 10 yards, your pattern is no bigger than a baseball), but if you did get a direct hit, you'd destroy the bulk of the animal's meat.

If you're shopping for a truly versatile shotgun, it's wise to select a shotgun with screw-in chokes. This makes it a simple matter to change from one choke to the next, something that can be done easily in the field. And you can buy extra chokes for a fraction of what it costs to buy a new gun. (Beware: screw-in chokes are not universal. You need to match chokes to the specific ones designed to fit your gun.) Many older shotguns, however, have either fixed or adjustable chokes. A fixed choke is just that—it cannot be adjusted or unscrewed. Double-barrel and side-by-side shot-

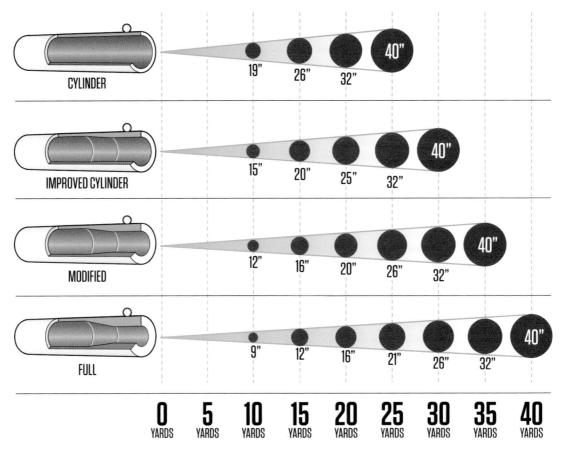

CYLINDER
19" 26" 32" 40"

IMPROVED CYLINDER
15" 20" 25" 32" 40"

MODIFIED
12" 16" 20" 26" 32" 40"

FULL
9" 12" 16" 21" 26" 32" 40"

| 0 | 5 | 10 | 15 | 20 | 25 | 30 | 35 | 40 |
| YARDS | YARDS | YARDS | YARDS | YARDS | YARDS | YARDS | YARDS | YARDS |

*Red circle indicates the diameter of shot spread at said distance.

guns with fixed chokes will usually have a different-sized choke for each barrel—say, a modified choke and a full choke—in order to enhance their versatility. Adjustable-choke shotguns can be adjusted by tightening or loosening a fitting on the end of the barrel. While this style of choke was popular in past decades, it has fallen out of favor with hunters for a number of good reasons and is rapidly becoming a thing of the past.

A good way to understand shotgun chokes is to consider the average percentage of lead pellets from a shotshell that each choke will deliver into a 30-inch circle at 40 yards.

Extra-full: +/- 75 percent

Full: +/- 70 percent

Modified: +/- 60 percent

Improved cylinder: +/- 50 percent

CHAMBER: There are three common chamber lengths for shotguns: 2¾ inches, 3 inches, and 3½ inches. Most modern shotguns are built to accept both 2¾ inches and 3 inches, and many will accept 3½ inches as well. As a general rule of thumb, 2¾ -inch shells are per-

14 · THE COMPLETE GUIDE TO HUNTING, BUTCHERING, AND COOKING WILD GAME

| 10 yards | 20 yards | 40 yards |

The above images show what happens when you shoot a shotgun at varying distances with the same choke and load. Here we have a 20-gauge shotgun with an improved cylinder choke loaded with 2¾ -inch #6 shotshells .

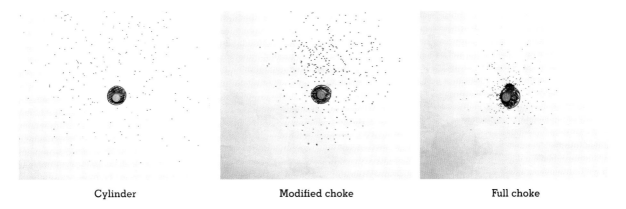

| Cylinder | Modified choke | Full choke |

And here's what happens when you shoot a shotgun with varying chokes at the same distance. We have a 20-gauge shotgun firing at a target that is 25 yards away, using a cylinder choke (not actually a choke, as there is no constriction), modified choke, and full choke.

fectly suitable for all applications up to geese and turkey. And while you can certainly use 2¾ -inch shells for geese and turkey as well, most hunters prefer to jump to a 3-inch shell for these larger birds in order to get a little extra oomph from their shotgun. As for 3½- inch shells, you just have to decide how much abuse your shoulder can take. They give you a few extra pellets and perhaps a tad bit of extra range, sure, but it's debatable whether the advantages outweigh the extra cost, recoil, and risk of jamming.

UNDERSTANDING SHOTGUN SHELLS

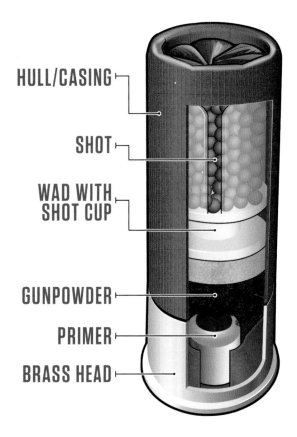

HULL/CASING

SHOT

WAD WITH
SHOT CUP

GUNPOWDER

PRIMER

BRASS HEAD

Shot refers to the pellets, or projectiles, inside a shotgun shell. Shot is categorized with an inverse naming system, in which smaller-sized shot carries a larger number. Though there are smaller shot sizes on the market, #8 is the smallest shot commonly used by hunters. It has a diameter of just .090 inch and is used with great effect by dove and quail hunters. (You can calculate the diameter of shot sizes by subtracting the shot size number from 17 and then dividing that by 100. Hence, 17 − 8 = 9, or .09 inch.)

The numbering system for shot continues up to #1 shot (.16 inch), which is commonly used for ducks and geese, and then it gets weird and confusing. The next-larger shot is called B shot, which is .17 inch, or .01 inch bigger than #1 shot. BB shot is .18 inch. BBB shot is .19 inch. Then it jumps to T shot (.20 inch), followed by TT (.21 inch), F (.22 inch), and FF (.23 inch). Like I said, weird and confusing.

Federal law mandates that only nontoxic (lead-free) shot be used when hunting migratory waterfowl.

LEAD VS. NONTOXIC

For upland birds and small furred game, most hunters regard lead as the go-to material for shot. It's heavy and soft, so it retains energy well and flattens on impact. It drops game very efficiently. However, lead shot is illegal for hunting waterfowl, and for good reason. Ducks and geese will both purposely and inadvertently consume spent pellets while feeding, which can cause lead poisoning. Therefore, what's known as nontoxic shot is federally mandated for all waterfowl hunting. (On the state level, lead restrictions sometimes apply for other forms of hunting as well, so pay careful attention to your state's hunting regulations.) Steel is the most common form of nontoxic shot, though it's lighter and harder than lead and does not work as effectively in side-by-side comparisons. Other nontoxic materials include bismuth and tungsten, which are heavier than steel. However, these metals are more expensive than steel, and also harder. They require a thicker wad to protect the shotgun's barrel from damage, which results in less room for pellets within the shotshell. So what's the hunter to do? Buy the best waterfowl loads you can afford. If that happens to be steel shot, so be it. Far more ducks are taken with steel shot every year than all other forms of nontoxic shot combined.

Here's a general breakdown of the appropriate uses for various shot sizes.

EATERS BEWARE

Hunters may not be crazy about steel **shot**, but it's good business for dentists.

LEAD SHOT

#8, #7½: doves, quail, pigeons, woodcock, small shoreline birds such as rail and snipe

#7½: Hungarian partridge, spruce grouse, blue grouse, and short-range upland birds such as ruffed grouse and woodcock

#7½, #6: squirrel, rabbit, hare, short-range pheasant, long-range grouse, chukar

#6, #4: long-range pheasant, long-range chukar

NONTOXIC SHOT
(STEEL, TUNGSTEN, BISMUTH)

#4, #3, #2: short-range ducks

#2, #1, BB: long-range ducks

BB, BBB: short-range geese

BBB, T: long-range geese

COPPER-PLATED LEAD

#4, #5, #6: turkey

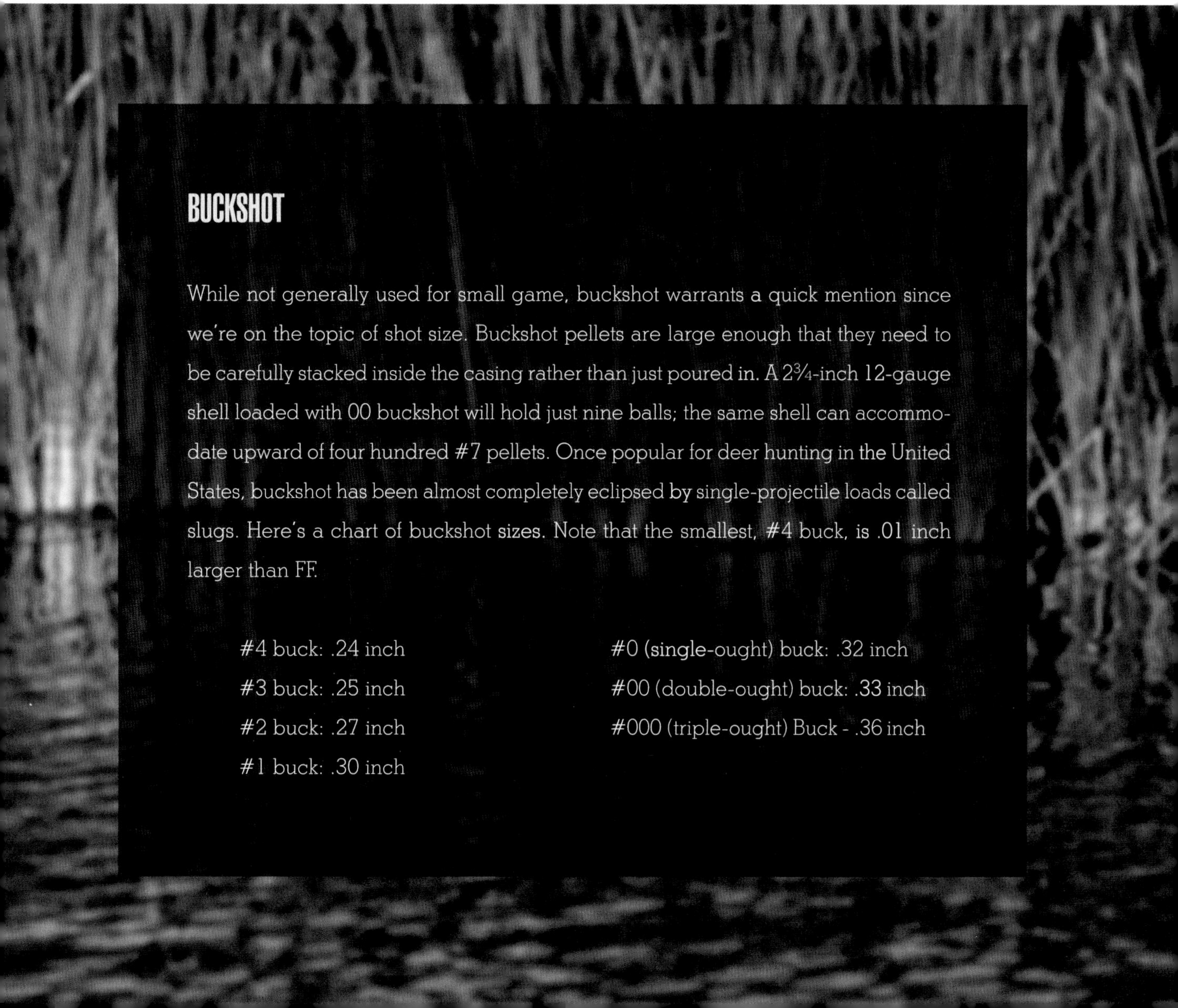

BUCKSHOT

While not generally used for small game, buckshot warrants a quick mention since we're on the topic of shot size. Buckshot pellets are large enough that they need to be carefully stacked inside the casing rather than just poured in. A 2¾-inch 12-gauge shell loaded with 00 buckshot will hold just nine balls; the same shell can accommodate upward of four hundred #7 pellets. Once popular for deer hunting in the United States, buckshot has been almost completely eclipsed by single-projectile loads called slugs. Here's a chart of buckshot sizes. Note that the smallest, #4 buck, is .01 inch larger than FF.

#4 buck: .24 inch

#3 buck: .25 inch

#2 buck: .27 inch

#1 buck: .30 inch

#0 (single-ought) buck: .32 inch

#00 (double-ought) buck: .33 inch

#000 (triple-ought) Buck - .36 inch

Besides the length of the shell and the size and material of the shot, there are two other considerations to keep in mind when buying shotshells: the amount of shot and the amount of powder. Shot is measured in ounces. While 12-gauge loads for general-purpose small game hunting typically carry 1 ounce of lead shot, 12-gauge loads for long-range waterfowl shooting might carry 1⅜ ounces of steel shot.

Powder is measured either in drams or, in a roundabout way, by the muzzle velocity of the discharged load. The dram is an archaic unit of measurement equaling ⅟₁₆ ounce. It long served as the standard unit of measurement for black powder. With the advent of modern smokeless powders, which vary in weight, ammunition manufacturers began describing their powder charges in terms of dram equivalents. That is, a modern shotgun shell listed as having 3 drams of powder actually has a load of propellant equivalent in energy to 3 drams of black powder.

A better way is for ammunition manufacturers to print an estimated muzzle velocity on the box of ammo, as that's the number you're really after. A general-purpose small game hunting load will have a muzzle velocity of around 1,200 to 1,300 feet per second, while a waterfowl load for long-range shooting will have a muzzle velocity in the range of 1,550 to 1,700 feet per second.

A shotshell box top should tell you everything you need to know about the ammo inside. Deciphering the information can be tricky, but it's essential that you learn what everything means in order to select the proper loads for your particular applications.

TURKEY GUNS

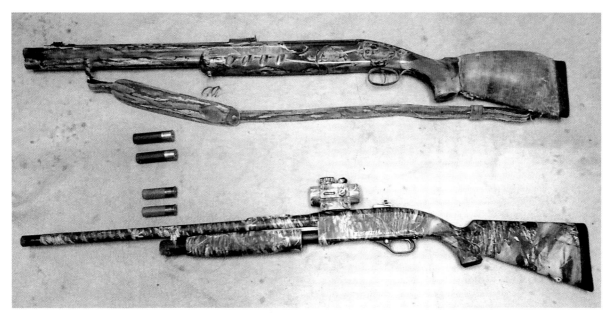

A pair of souped-up turkey rigs. Top: An inexpensive Italian-made break-action over/under shotgun with $800 worth of custom work that turned it into a turkey-specific shotgun. Modifications included polished and lengthened force cones, custom chokes, soldered rifle sights, an elk-leather cheek pad, camouflage paint, and a comfortable sling. Bottom: A Winchester model 1100 pump with a TruGlo red dot scope and an all-weather camo coating.

Rigging up a turkey gun can be as simple or as complicated as you want to make it. For an experienced shooter who limits his shots to 30 or so yards, all you need is your standard 12-gauge shotgun with a full choke and some quality turkey loads. But if you want a gun that's suitable for long hikes and long shots, a few simple modifications can turn your rabbit and grouse gun into a souped-up turkey rig.

TURKEY CHOKES: There are many after-market turkey chokes available. The tight restrictions on these chokes can give you a lot of extra distance, but keep in mind that a tight pattern at long distances means a very tight pattern at short distances. A turkey choke might give you what you need to pepper a bird's head at 60 yards, but it opens up the possibility of missing at 10 yards if your aim is just an inch or two off. Still, turkey chokes are well worth the cost if your shotgun is threaded for screw-in chokes. I've had excellent luck with the Haymaker choke tube from Down-N-Dirty Outdoors. Just make sure to pattern your shotgun before you hunt turkeys (see page 24), and keep a calm head when aiming.

SIGHTS: With a little practice you can hit turkeys very effectively using nothing but the naked barrel of your shotgun and the front

This gun, a Remington 870 with a full choke, was ready to shoot turkeys right out of the box. By a wide margin, this model of shotgun has killed more turkeys than any other shotgun ever produced.

includes a front and rear sight that can be mounted to a standard ribbed shotgun barrel. The company TruGlo has a great line of turkey sights that will fit most any shotgun.

TURKEY BARRELS: If you've got the money, you can solve the issues of chokes and sights with the purchase of a dedicated turkey barrel. Several manufacturers of pump-action and autoloading shotguns produce turkey barrels that can easily be swapped back and forth with your shotgun's existing all-purpose barrel without the requirement of gunsmithing services. The upside to turkey barrels is that they are shorter, which makes them easier to carry and handle, and many come equipped with turkey chokes. Browning produces a turkey barrel for their excellent BPS pump-action shotgun that comes with both a turkey choke and a quality set of permanently attached rifle sights. A downside is cost. A turkey barrel for a Browning BPS costs as much as an entire Remington 870 Express shotgun. And a turkey barrel for the 870 will cost you half as much as you paid for the shotgun in the first place.

bead. But again, if you're looking to stretch your shots out to distances of 50 yards and beyond, it can be a good idea to fit your shotgun with a better sighting system. More and more turkey hunters are using scopes and red-dot sights on their turkey guns, but use of such technologies seems excessive when hunting turkey and risks complicating something that should be very simple. A better bet is to rig your shotgun with a rifle sight system that

SLINGS: Since snap shooting isn't part of turkey hunting, a sling can be a great addition to your turkey gun. It eliminates arm fatigue from toting your gun all day, and it keeps your hands free for working with turkey calls when you're traveling in search of midmorning birds. Most models of shotguns can be fitted with aftermarket sling kits that require little or no permanent alteration of the gun.

TURKEY AMMO

A turkey hunter seldom fires more than one or two shots per season (excluding practice sessions), so there's no need to worry about excessive wear and tear on your shoulder from shooting 3-inch or even 3½-inch shells. As long as your shotgun is chambered for these magnum rounds, it's a smart idea to get as much knockdown power as you can when gunning for these big birds.

Also make sure to stick with dedicated turkey loads. While guys will brag about killing turkeys with nothing but old squirrel loads they inherited from Grandpa, you're better off using turkey loads from reputable manufacturers. Most shotshells designed for turkeys are loaded with lead pellets that have been plated in copper. The heaviness of the lead yields high velocities, while the copper coating prevents the spheres from deforming in the barrel and flying erratically. Turkey loads will also have thicker and deeper wads to protect the metal on tight chokes and to deliver denser patterns at long ranges. Even though wild turkeys are often much bigger than geese, you'll use smaller-sized pellets than you would for goose hunting. For turkeys, #4, #5, and #6 shot all work well, as do "blended" loads that use multiple shot sizes. Some states do not allow shot larger than #4 or smaller than #7½ to be used on turkeys, so, as always, check your local regulations before loading up. The company Hevi-Shot produces one of the best turkey loads out there. It's a nontoxic shot that is very expensive—but in my opinion it's well worth the cost for turkey hunting. The heaviness of the shot allows you to use smaller pellets, which means more pellets in the shell. I have had fantastic luck with their Magnum Blend shotshells loaded with #5, #6, and #7 pellets. When using these rounds, I get more than enough pellets into the bird's head with hardly ever a pellet straying down into the bird's meat.

PATTERNING A SHOTGUN

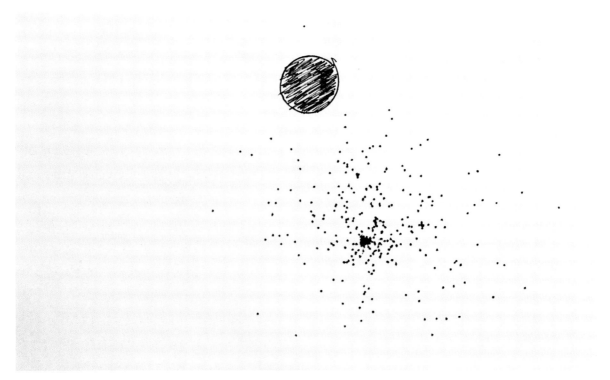

You should always pattern a new shotgun before taking it on a hunt. The shot pattern pictured here has missed its mark. The shooter should experiment with other shells and chokes in order to get better results.

No serious hunter would take a new rifle into the field without testing it at range first. Shotguns should be treated no differently. Before hunting, you should make sure that your shotgun works in harmony with your selected choke and ammunition—and also that it works in harmony with you. This is done through a process known as patterning.

To pattern your shotgun, get two pieces of butcher's paper or newsprint that are approximately 48 inches square. Mark the top of the paper so you remember which side is up, then make a bull's-eye in the center with a marker or duct tape. Next, in a safe shooting location, set the first paper target at a measured distance of 40 yards. Using the choke and ammo that you intend to hunt with, and taking careful aim, fire the shotgun at the bull's-eye. Take that target down, and then fire a round at the second target. For patterning double-barrel or over/under shotguns, make two targets for each barrel and mark them accordingly—left barrel and right barrel, or top barrel and bottom barrel. Then test each barrel independently. Don't make the mistake of thinking that both barrels are in perfect working order just because one of them is.

After shooting, lay the targets side by side on a flat surface, top side away from you, and make a mark at what you determine to be the center of the impact zone on each target—the area with the densest concentration of pellets. (Chances are this mark will not be on the target's bull's-eye.) Now draw a 30-inch-diameter circle around that mark.

Step back and take a look. First, you want to make sure that the two targets look roughly the same. Some differences are inevitable, but if the shot patterns are in wildly different positions, then you may have flinched a shot and accidentally missed your mark. If so, you should consider redoing the experiment.

As long as the positioning of the patterns is similar relative to the location of the bull's-eye, count how many pellets fall inside of each target's 30-inch circle and divide that number by the total number of pellets that were inside the shotshell. (If you can't find this information through the manufacturer's website, you can simply cut open an unfired shell and count the pellets.)

Also take a look at the distance that separates the center of your pattern from the bull's-eye. Ask yourself if it's big enough to cause concern. A couple of inches is not a big deal for wingshooting, but a foot or more difference can lead to some serious frustration in the field when you're missing shots that you could have sworn were dead on. You may need to correct your method of aiming, or else try different combinations of choke and ammunition to see if the problem is correctable in that way.

Finally, and perhaps most important, check your pattern for holes. You want to see a fairly uniform placement of shot radiating outward from the center of the pattern. Large holes or other inconsistencies in your pattern can lead to trouble when wingshooting. Again, correct these issues by experimenting with different chokes and/or ammunition.

PATTERNING YOUR TURKEY GUN

Patterning your turkey shotgun is even more important than patterning a gun for wingshooting, especially if you want the ability to make long-range shots out to 40 or 50 yards or beyond. Either buy a dozen or so turkey patterning targets or draw a 3-inch circle in the center of a dozen sheets of paper. Set the first target at 10 yards and place the rest at 10-yard increments out to 60 yards. From a seated position, with the shotgun resting on your knee, fire at the base of the 3-inch circle or, in the case of turkey targets, at the junction of the head and neck. Now examine each target. Take note of the densities of the shot patterns as well as how many pellets landed in the 3-inch circle or inside the vital head/neck area on the turkey target. One or two pellets inside the kill zone is not what you're looking for; instead, you want to see the head or bull's-eye get nicely peppered with shot. Try different choke and ammunition combinations in order to get different results. And be honest with yourself. Is your shotgun really up to the task of killing birds humanely at 50, 60, or 70 yards every time you pull the trigger? If not, don't take those shots. A patient hunter who knows how to call birds should be able to put a gobbler on the table every year without shooting past 30 yards.

THE RIMFIRE

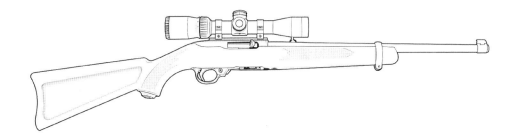

A versatile shotgun will prepare you for 90 percent of North America's small game hunting opportunities. If you want to bring that up to virtually 100 percent, look no further than the simple and ubiquitous .22 LR, affectionately known as the double-deuce.

There are many benefits to owning and shooting a .22:

1. Dirt-cheap guns. You can find great .22s, particularly used models, for under $200.

2. Dirt-cheap ammo. Even with today's inflated ammunition prices, .22 ammo can still be purchased for pennies a round. You can practice the fundamentals of marksmanship as much as you'd like without having to worry about the high costs of ammo. This keeps you honed for big game season, when you need to make shots that really count.

3. A .22 is also a great meat-saving tool. Shotguns can destroy a lot of meat on critters such as squirrels and rabbits, but a .22 won't damage an ounce of usable flesh if you keep your shots where they belong—in the head.

4. A .22 is discreet, perfect for those hunting opportunities that might be described as "fringe." I'm talking about quietly solving a friend's rabbit problem in his or her suburban vegetable garden (and solving your own problem about how to source the primary ingredient for hasenpfeffer).

5. A .22 rifle is also a great way to secure camp meat on backcountry ventures, particularly when weight is an issue. By packing an ultralight .22 on backcountry trips, I've supplemented an otherwise bland diet of freeze-dried backpacking food with a variety of wild meats such as squirrel, rabbit, quail, grouse, and ptarmigan.

Editor and publisher Celina Spiegel on her first hunt. With proper shot placement (head shots only), .22 rimfires do no meat damage.

In my opinion, there are two ways to go with a .22 purchase: you can prioritize accuracy, or you can prioritize weight. The tack driver pictured here is a Ruger 10/22 topped with a Vortex 2–7×32 scope. The lightweight .22, which can easily be slipped into a backpack, is a TC Hotshot. Though suited only for short-range shooting, this rifle is capable of taking a wide variety of small game when in the right hands. It weighs under 3 pounds and measures just 30 inches in total length. It is fitted with an easy-to-use peep sight, perfect for young shooters.

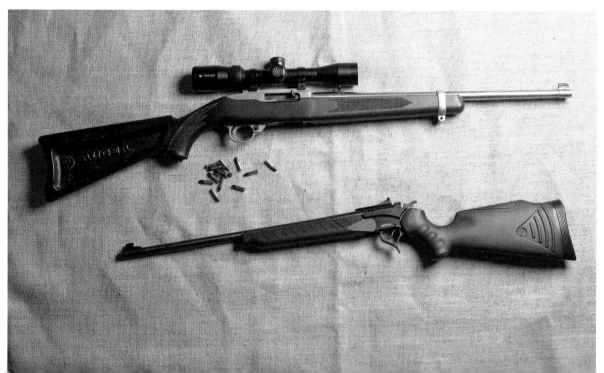

UNDERSTANDING .22 AMMUNITION

Ammunition can be classified into two categories: rimfire and centerfire. Centerfire ammunition has a primer that sits in the center of the casing's bottom, and that's where the firing pin hits. Centerfire ammunition can be reloaded; to replace a primer, simply knock it out of the bottom and seat a new one. With rimfire ammunition, the priming compound is located inside the hollow rim of the casing. The firing pin just needs to strike the rim and smash it enough to ignite the primer. Rimfire ammunition cannot be reloaded, because the firing pin effectively destroys the case. Because the metal on a rimfire case needs to be weak enough to be impacted by the firing pin, there's an inherent limit to the power of rimfire cartridges. They cannot withstand the high pressures that centerfire cartridges can put up with.

The rimfire class of cartridges includes the .17 HMR, .22 Win Mag, and the exceedingly popular .22 LR. The .17 HMR is a very fast and flat shooting cartridge that is borderline too powerful for the small game hunter who hunts for the table. With improper shot placement, it causes too much tissue damage on lightweight game such as squirrels, rabbits, and grouse. The .22 WMR is a suitable small game round, particularly when shooting solid-point bullets. But in the opinion of most serious small

game hunters, the extra yardage that you get with a .22 WMR or .17 HMR does not make up for the extra cost of ammunition and the extra tissue damage that it inflicts on small game.

Rifles chambered for the .22 LR can safely handle a small family of other .22 cartridges as well, including the .22 CB, .22 Short, and .22 Long. For practical purposes, however, let's limit our discussion strictly to .22 LR ammunition, because there's really no great reason for a modern small game hunter to mess around with these alternative ammunitions. (Also, semi-automatic rifles can encounter major cycling problems with .22 CB and .22 Short ammunition.)

Classifications of .22 LR cartridges are based on velocity. There are subsonic-velocity, standard-velocity, high-velocity, and hyper-velocity loads. Subsonic loads have a muzzle velocity less than the speed of sound (1,125 feet per second). The subsonic loads are basically scaled-down versions of the .22 LR; often the propellant for them is nothing more than the primer itself. The greatest advantage to subsonic loads is the reduction in noise, as there is no crack that comes with the breaking of the sound barrier. These loads are most often used for target practice and short-range pest control, but they are great for small game hunters who need to exercise discretion in areas where hunting is legal but might be frowned upon by nearby residents.

Standard-, high-, and hyper-velocity loads are the more common choices for small game hunters. These speedier loads give you a flatter trajectory and increased range. Below, the highly authoritative gun writer Chuck Hawks offers a detailed, technical explanation of the various .22 LR ammunitions that are available.

Read the passage carefully before selecting hunting ammo for your .22—especially the part where Mr. Hawks endorses high-velocity 36- and 37-grain copper-plated hollow-points for general small game hunting. Take some time at the rifle range to shoot ammo from a number of manufacturers in order to find the load that shoots best through your particular rifle.

CHUCK HAWKS, WHO I BELIEVE TO BE THE NATION'S SMARTEST AND MOST REASONABLE GUN WRITER, WEIGHS IN ON EVERYTHING YOU'D EVER WANT TO KNOW ABOUT THE .22 LR

"The .22 Long Rifle (LR) is the most popular and the most highly developed cartridge in the world. The major ammunition producers have put more research and development dollars into this modest little cartridge than into any other. It is used at the highest levels of match target competition, including the Olympic Games. It's strange when you think about it, as the .22 LR is also, along with its predecessors the .22 Short and .22 Long, the most antiquated of cartridges.

"The rimfire principle was used to create the first successful self-contained metallic ammunition. Rimfire cases are constructed with the priming compound spun inside the rim of the copper or brass case, which is crushed by the blow of the firing pin to ignite the main powder charge. This damages the case so that it is useless for reloading and the rimfire design requires a far weaker case rim than the solid head cases used for centerfire ammunition. The permissible maximum average pressure (MAP) for rimfire ammunition is much lower than is possible with centerfire cartridges. Yet the .22 LR endures and prospers, outselling all other sporting cartridges by a large margin every year.

"All current .22 rimfires (except the relatively recent .22 WMR) are ancient black powder designs and use tapered-heel bullets. If you examine a .22 S, L, or LR cartridge, you will see that the case and bullet are the same diameter. The part of the bullet inside of the case (the heel) is reduced in diameter to allow it to fit inside the case. Such bullets are also called 'outside lubricated,' because they are ordinarily waxed or copper plated. In all other modern cartridges, the bullet shank is of constant diameter and the case is slightly larger than the bullet to allow the heel of the latter to fit inside. The old-fashioned term for this design is 'inside lubricated,' as the lubrication grooves of lead bullets are inside of the case.

"The .22 Short is a development of the BB cap using a 29-grain round-nose (RN) bullet in a lengthened case (compared to the BB cap). It was originally powered by four grains of fine black powder (about FFFFg). Strange as it sounds today, the .22 Short was originally developed as a self-defense cartridge for use in a handgun. Today, CCI loads their .22 Short Target ammunition to a muzzle velocity of 830 feet per second for rapid-fire pistol competition.

"The .22 Short is a pretty anemic round, and in 1871 a longer case of the same diameter was developed for the 29-grain Short bullet. This became the .22 Long cartridge, obsolescent but still occasionally seen today. The .22 Long was once chambered in a large number of pistols and rifles. It was originally loaded with 5 grains of very fine black powder and offered a velocity about 100+ feet per second greater than the .22 Short.

"In 1887, the Stevens Arms Co. developed the ultimate in .22 rimfire cartridges, the .22 Long Rifle. This used the .22 Long case with a 40-grain RN bullet loaded to higher velocity than the 29-grain Long bullet. It shot flatter and hit harder than any of the previous .22 rimfires, except the earlier .22 Extra Long, whose performance it essentially duplicated in a shorter case. The .22 LR proved to be more accurate than that cartridge and therefore replaced the .22 Extra Long, which has been obsolete for a long time.

(continued)

"The .22 Long Rifle caught on, was adapted to both rifles and pistols, and became the most popular sporting and target shooting cartridge in the world. After the advent of smokeless powder a high-velocity version of the .22 LR was introduced, which further extended the .22 LR's superiority as a small game hunting cartridge.

"Modern .22 LR target ammunition is loaded to a maximum velocity of about 1,085 feet per second with a 40-grain round-nose bullet, while .22 LR high-velocity cartridges drive a 40-grain copper-plated bullet at a maximum velocity of 1,255 feet per second and a maximum energy of 140 foot-pounds from a rifle barrel. For small game hunters, most manufacturers offer a 36- or 37-grain copper-plated lead hollow-point bullet at about 1,280 feet per second. This load expands nicely and makes for quick kills on small game, given proper bullet placement. The maximum point-blank range (+/- 1½ inches) of typical .22 LR high-velocity loads is about 90 yards when fired from a rifle with a telescopic sight mounted 1½ inches above the bore.

"Because of its popularity, there are many permutations of the .22 LR cartridge. One of the least common is the .22 LR shot cartridge, which fires a pinch of very fine #12 (dust) shot. This load is used, among other things, to collect very small creatures, mice and the like, for museum displays when fired from smoothbore barrels.

"Far more useful are the hyper-velocity .22 LR loads, pioneered by CCI in the form of the Stinger. These use lightweight hollow-point bullets at increased velocity for flatter trajectory and dramatic expansion. Remington followed suit with their famous Yellow Jacket load, and the idea was subsequently picked up by most other manufacturers. The CCI Stinger drives a 32-grain hollow-point bullet at a maximum velocity of 1,640 feet per second with a maximum energy of 191 foot-pounds.

"The .22 LR hyper-velocity cartridges are the varmint loads of choice for those hunting sand rats, gophers, rats, and the like with their .22 rifle or pistol. They kill quickly but are likely to do excessive damage (unless only head shots are taken) to edible small game. The hyper-velocity loads are also the best choice for anyone using a .22 LR firearm for personal protection, as they have demonstrated more stopping power than traditional high-velocity loads.

"For small game hunting with both rifle and revolver, I prefer the .22 LR high-velocity 36- or 37-grain copper plated hollow-point loads from CCI (Mini Mag), Remington

(Golden Bullet), and Winchester (Super-X). I have spent a great many enjoyable hours in the woods carrying my old Marlin Golden 39-A Mountie. That lever-action carbine and I have harvested no end of squirrels together and provided many a meal on camping and hunting trips.

"Somehow I have managed to wear out two firing pins (easily replaced in a Marlin 39) over some fifty years of small game hunting with that old take-down rifle, but it is still a deadly shooter. Manufactured sometime in the 1950s, it had already seen plenty of use when I traded a hunting partner out of it. He had his heart set on a Kodiak .22 WMR rifle I happened to own. However, that is a story for another time."

Chuck Hawks is the owner and managing editor of **Guns and Shooting Online**, www.gunsandshootingonline.com.

AIR RIFLES FOR SMALL GAME

When a lot of hunters think of air rifles, they think of the old Daisy Red Ryders that hurled BBs so slowly that you could watch them leave the barrel. In fact, air rifles have been around a lot longer than the infamous weapon featured in the movie **A Christmas Story**. The Lewis and Clark expedition packed along a Girandoni Repeating Air Rifle on their trip across the American West in the early 1800s. It took about 1,500 strokes from an external

(continued)

pump to fully charge the cylinder, though once it was prepared it could launch up to thirty consecutive rounds of .46-caliber bullets.

There are plenty of air guns on the market today that are perfectly effective on squirrels, rabbits, and whatever game birds happen to be legal for that method of take in your state. California actually allows turkey hunting with air rifles! Rather than the BBs shot from a Red Ryder, air rifles throw cone-nosed lead pellets. You can't get the same shooting distances from an air rifle that you can from a rimfire, but there's still plenty to be said for them. They are quiet, there's essentially no kick, and they are inexpensive to purchase and shoot. What's more, they are safer to use in semi-suburban areas than longer-range rimfire cartridges. Many air rifle shooters are able to work up delicious meals of small game by simply cracking the kitchen window and taking aim at rabbits or squirrels that have become garden nuisances. The neighbors never even know it happened. If you're looking into an air rifle that will be dedicated to hunting, consider the larger .22 and .25 calibers rather than the traditional .17 caliber. Excellent air rifles are offered by Gamo, Benjamin, Beeman, and RWS. When shopping for a small game air rifle, you want to make sure your selected rifle can achieve at least 12 foot-pounds of energy at the muzzle. For a .177-caliber air rifle, that would be a 7.9-grain pellet flying at about 830 feet per second. For a .22-caliber air rifle, that would be a 14.3-grain pellet at about 615 feet per second. Good air rifles are tapped for scope mounts, though be aware that dedicated air rifle scopes have different recoil tolerances than scopes intended for rimfire and centerfire rifles. They are built to withstand vibrations from the pistons and springs. Some are also built to focus clearly on much closer targets.

RIFLE SCOPES FOR SMALL GAME

You can take a lot of game with a .22 rifle fitted with peep or open sights, but to get the full level of versatility from your .22 it's a good idea to top it with a scope. When shopping for a scope for your .22, stick to models that are designed for rimfire rifles. Specifically, this means scopes with a fixed parallax setting for 50 yards. Most scopes have either an adjustable parallax setting or a fixed 100-yard setting, which is less than ideal for the typically close-range shots taken by small game hunters. (For a full explanation of parallax, see Volume 1, on big game.) You don't need a scope with high-power magnification for your .22. Scopes with lower magnification provide a wider field of view, which makes it easier to find moving targets such as a squirrel hopping from limb to limb or a cottontail moving through thick brush. Vortex Optics makes a couple of fantastic variable-power rimfire scopes with 2×–7× magnification. They're affordable and virtually indestructible. You can also go with a simple fixed-power 4× scope. The lack of frills on fixed-power scopes helps to keep them affordable, and you can often find a great fixed-power scope for the same money that you'd spend on a mediocre variable-power scope. If you decide to go with fixed power, check out the rimfire scopes made by Leopold.

RIFLES FOR TURKEY

A lot of well-informed turkey hunters disagree with this management policy, but multiple states allow the harvest of turkeys with rifles during spring and/or fall seasons. Those who oppose rifle turkey seasons have a few arguments against them: (1) it gives hunters an unsportsmanlike advantage, as the birds can be sniped from hundreds of yards away; (2) wound loss is too great, due to poor shot placement; and (3) long-range rifles are dangerous to other turkey hunters, particularly in the spring, when multiple hunters might be pursuing the same gobbler—all wearing camouflage, using stealth

(continued)

tactics, and hunting on the ground rather than from the relative safety of elevated platforms.

But if you have your heart set on a rifle turkey hunt and you have a safe place to do it, keep in mind that some of the states that do allow rifles for turkeys do *not* allow rimfire cartridges because of the even greater risk of wound loss. In these cases, consider small-caliber centerfire cartridges such as the .22 Hornet, .22-250, and .223. But before you try it, see the turkey-hunting portion of Section 3.

GETTING ZEROED

Before chasing small game with your .22, make sure it's zeroed. The results are well worth the effort.

Sighting in a high-power rifle can be painful for your shoulder, ears, and wallet, but zeroing a .22 is so much fun and so inexpensive that you'll want to spend hour upon hour at the range as you familiarize yourself with the capabilities of your rifle. For general small game hunting purposes, it's good to zero your .22 at 50 yards. This will keep your bullets within

½ inch of your point of aim at any distance between 10 yards and 60 yards.

Here's how:

1. Fire three shots at the bull's-eye of a large paper target placed at a distance of 50 yards. If you're lacking a commercially produced target, you can use a large sheet of paper (waxed butcher paper works well) with a piece of duct tape measuring 1 inch by 1 inch stuck to the middle. (Note: If your first shot misses the paper entirely, move the target to a distance of 10 yards and complete the following process until your bullets are hitting close to the bull's-eye. Then move the target back to 50 yards and continue zeroing the rifle.)

2. Mentally average the center of your three shots, and measure the horizontal and vertical distances that separate that point from the bull's-eye. Remove the turret caps on your scope and make the necessary adjustments. Moving the turret in the up direction, as depicted on the turret, moves the bullet's point of impact in the corresponding direction. Same with the left and right arrows on the turret that control horizontal movement. (Most scopes are adjustable in increments of ¼ MOA. 1 MOA equals 1 inch at 100 yards; ¼ MOA equals ¼ inch at 100 yards.)

3. Shoot another three shots. You should notice that the center of your three-shot group has moved toward the bull's-eye—and ideally has hit it. If the bullet's point of impact hasn't moved according to your adjustments, carefully repeat step 2. If you still have problems, you're likely dealing with an accuracy issue that could come from user error, equipment malfunction, or both. If the center of the group has gotten closer but is still not on the bull's-eye, measure the new distances and adjust the scope turrets again. Repeat as necessary.

4. Once your bullet is hitting dead center, fire a series of three rounds to make sure that the gun is grouping well. At 50 yards, a quality .22 rifle (with a good marksman) should shoot a three-shot group that can be covered with a quarter.

5. Experiment with your rifle at a variety of distances, starting at 10 yards or less and moving out at 10-yard increments to 100 yards or beyond. Find out exactly where the bullet hits at each distance, so you can confidently and consistently place shots in the bull's-eye by aiming slightly higher or lower as necessary.

6. If you're not happy with your rifle's performance, ask yourself the following questions. If the answer to any of these is yes, try to remedy the situation. If you still can't figure out the problem, it might be time for a visit to the gunsmith or a marksmanship clinic.

- Am I flinching in anticipation of the firearm's noise and kick? (A flinching shooter will never shoot consistently.)
- Is my form improper? Am I jerking the trigger rather than squeezing it? Am I putting

unnecessary torque on the grip or forearm in an effort to hold the rifle on target? Am I altering the position of my cheek on the stock from one shot to the next?

- Is my shooting rest unstable? Does the rifle feel wobbly while I'm aiming?

Once you've ruled out shooter error, ask a few questions about your rifle.

- Is the bore of my rifle excessively dirty? (A dirty barrel causes erratic shooting. See "Routine Rifle Cleaning," opposite.)

- Is my scope damaged? Is there a loose reticle? Is the scope's body badly dinged or dented? Did it take a serious blow?
- Is my scope poorly mounted? Are the rings or mounts loose or improperly installed? Do I feel any wiggle or turning when I put pressure on the scope or try to spin it?
- Does the rifle shoot equally poorly with different ammo? (Often a rifle might shoot horribly with one brand of ammo and then shoot much better with another brand.)

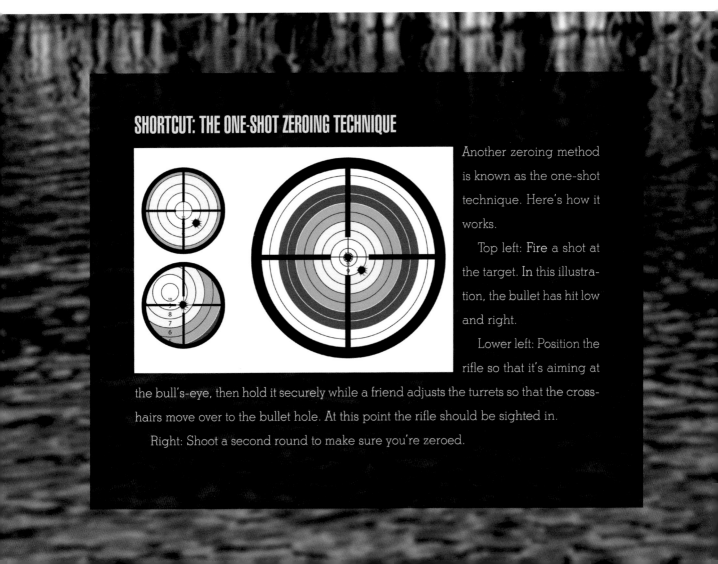

SHORTCUT: THE ONE-SHOT ZEROING TECHNIQUE

Another zeroing method is known as the one-shot technique. Here's how it works.

Top left: Fire a shot at the target. In this illustration, the bullet has hit low and right.

Lower left: Position the rifle so that it's aiming at the bull's-eye, then hold it securely while a friend adjusts the turrets so that the cross-hairs move over to the bullet hole. At this point the rifle should be sighted in.

Right: Shoot a second round to make sure you're zeroed.

ROUTINE RIFLE CLEANING

Dirty barrels are probably the number one reason that otherwise good shooting rifles turn bad. Getting a barrel truly clean requires a few tools and products that are widely available, plus a lot of work.

- Gun cradle/vise. By securing the rifle in a vise or cradle, you have a solid work surface and two free hands. (Most cradles also offer a convenient place to store your cleaners and tools.)
- Coated cleaning rod. Coated cleaning rods have a protective surface that will not damage the bore of the rifle. The best cleaning rods also have free-spinning handles that allow the rod to turn with the barrel's rifling.
- Nylon or brass brush for loosening powder residue.
- Brass jag, used for holding and pushing cleaning patches through the barrel.
- Cleaning patches made from material that's 100 percent cotton or a blend.
- Bore guide. Essential for keeping the rod true and preventing cleaning products from dripping back into the action.

- A powder solvent such as Hoppe's No. 9.
- Copper solvent such as Sweet's 7.62.
- Lightweight gun oil such as Rem Oil.

Here's the procedure:

1. Using a cleaning rod and jag, run a few solvent-soaked patches through the bore. Follow these with a dry patch, then alternate between solvent-soaked patches and dry patches until the patches are coming out clean. This may take twenty or more repetitions on a really dirty rifle.

2. On approximately every fifth cleaning, follow step 1 using a copper solvent. Copper solvents should be used in strict accordance with the manufacturer's specifications.

3. Run a patch that's been lightly oiled with Rem Oil through the barrel. For long-term storage, the barrel is now done. If you're heading out to the range or on a hunt, run one last dry patch through the bore to remove excess oil.

4. Spray the bolt with the powder solvent and wipe with a paper towel or rag. A toothbrush works great to loosen any caked-on crud.

TIPS FOR GUN CARE IN THE FIELD

1. Keep an oiled lint-free cloth in your gun case at all times and use it to wipe down your weapon after it has been exposed to moisture.

2. Never leave a wet firearm inside a case for an extended period of time.

3. Carry lens wipes and a lens brush for cleaning your rifle scope.

4. Always bring along a BoreSnake or similar product to clear any mud or snow that might get packed into the bore. (Which shouldn't happen, since you're supposed to keep your muzzle capped with tape or latex finger cots.)

FIREARM ACCESSORIES FOR THE SMALL GAME HUNTER

SHOOTING STICKS: Oftentimes the window of opportunity is very narrow when it comes to shooting at small game such as squirrels and rabbits. Since you won't always have time to find a good resting position, and since you'll often be shooting at upward angles when hunting for squirrels, a shooting stick can be invaluable. This can be a commercially produced shooting stick such as the monopods made by Stony Point, or simply a forked walking stick that you cut on location with the saw of your multi-tool. Just make sure that the stick is sturdy and thick enough for your hand to grip comfortably.

SCOPE COVERS: Protect your scope. For one thing, scopes are expensive, and you don't want the lens to get scratched. For another, it's nearly impossible to aim when your lens is obscured by snow or excessive moisture. When conditions warrant, keep your scope covered until you're ready to shoot. Neoprene "scope socks" are a great bet, because they're inexpensive, are long-lasting, and provide a bit of protection against impacts to the scope body. Rubber "bikini-style" scope covers are great at keeping out moisture, but they tend to fall apart. Same with flip-cap scope covers. If you're sitting in a blind, these are fine. But

Slings are as good for shotguns as they are for rifles. A properly fitting sling prevents fatigue and frees up your hands for working game calls, opening gates, or handling decoys.

hunters who put a few miles on their boots often find that flip caps are easy to demolish.

SLING: A sling lets you carry the weight of your rifle (or shotgun) on your shoulder, which frees up your hands for glassing, ducking limbs, and other tasks. Since .22 rifles are generally lighter and smaller than high-power centerfires, you can get away with using a more slender and therefore less obtrusive sling than you might need to use on your deer rifle. A sling made from a 1-inch strip of leather or nylon webbing will usually suffice. However, insist on quality hardware for all of your rifle slings. You don't want to risk the integrity of your fine-tuned double-deuce just to save a few dollars on a sling.

TRAVEL CASE: A good travel case protects from dings and scratches incurred during travel. Besides the cosmetic angle, this ensures that your scope doesn't get knocked out of zero. I prefer hard-sided cases from Boyt and Pelican, but these might be regarded as overkill for a .22. Soft-sided cases are a good bet as well, but they do not offer enough protection for airline travel. Airlines require firearms to be cased inside a hard-sided, lockable case.

ARCHERY FOR SMALL GAME

Unlike big game hunting, where there are typically separate seasons for firearms and archery equipment, there are no legal incentives to hunt small game with a bow. (There are a few exceptions to this rule, including an archery-only duck hunt on a coastal refuge in the vicinity of Anchorage, Alaska. That alone should make you interested in archery equipment!) Instead, the decision to hunt small game with a bow typically comes down to personal aesthetics. Some hunters value a challenge as much as or more than they value wild meat, and the thrill of hitting (or trying to hit) a flying bird or running rabbit with an arrow is too much to resist. My father was such a guy. Over the years, he managed to kill many cottontails, squirrels, and grouse with his bow, as well as pheasants and ducks hit in midair.

MONTANA HUNTER MATT RINELLA WEIGHS IN ON THE ETERNAL GUN VS. BOW CONUNDRUM

"Although I've always been a highly committed bowhunter, I've never been any good at it. Several years ago I decided to see if redoubling my efforts to improve my abilities might help me transition from poor to mediocre at my chosen pastime. More than anything, I was intent on reducing the frequent missing and occasional wounding that had always plagued my archery hunting career. I got a new bow shortly after big game season and shot it almost daily all winter. By the time spring turkey season drew near, my confidence had increased a smidge, so I decided to leave the shotgun home and take my bow after gobblers. Turkeys screaming into a call or decoy give me acute-onset arrhythmia, and I figured if I made good shots on toms while experiencing stroke-like symptoms, this would be a good indication I'd earned my yellow belt in bowhunting.

"Leaving the shotgun home was a big move for me because I love wild turkey meat and pride myself on consistently bagging the two birds per year allowed hunters in my home state of Montana. I began to think I'd made a huge mistake when it took me three days of hard hunting to get a tom in range, only to miss him at 5 yards. I couldn't believe it. At that distance, he appeared so huge that shooting around him seemed to require more skill than arrowing him would have. A deep sense of self-loathing instantly settled over me. My chance at redemption came unbelievably quickly, however, as a second tom came trotting into the decoys before the missed tom was even out of sight. My self-disgust must have had a calming effect, because I made a perfect shot on the second tom. I've never seen a game animal go from healthy to dead as quickly as that bird . . . he tipped over without a single kick. We can only hope for so painless an undoing.

(continued)

"In terms of assessing my archery hunting abilities, I became a bit confused. Was the second bird more indicative of my current abilities and the first bird a fluke, or vice versa? I needed more data. A week later I made another perfect shot on a tom and thought this settled the matter. I now believed I was finally coming of age as a bowhunter. A number of years and tons of bowhunting have transpired since the spring I arrowed the two toms, and I've realized that the optimism I felt at the time was naive. Sure, I've had some successes since then, but I've also continued to make poor shots and other mistakes as well. The spring with the toms is emblematic of where I'm at, where I've always been, as a bowhunter. I'm consistently inconsistent. The thing I've learned is that mistakes can happen at any time, so there is little sense in jacking up my ego when things go well or donning sackcloth and ashes when things go poorly. I like to think lessons learned through my successes and failures are gradually making me more confident and capable, but I know my bowhunting skills will always remain a work in progress."

My personal philosophy on bow selection is identical to my philosophy on rifles and shotguns. That is, I'm looking for a versatile hunting tool that can handle a wide variety of species under ever-shifting sets of circumstances—be it calling javelina in the desert, perched high in a midwestern oak tree for whitetail deer, or still-hunting a northern spruce forest for snowshoe hares. Nothing will meet all of these challenges as efficiently as a fast-shooting compound bow. What's more, by using the same bow for both big game and small game hunting, you'll be practicing for big game hunting while chasing small game, and vice versa. But if you're considering a bow purchase strictly for small game, and more particularly for flushed rabbits and game birds, you should consider going with a traditional recurve or longbow that will allow you to make snap shots at fast-moving game. (A compound bow must be held at full draw to aim and fire; this takes time and prevents snap shooting.) Here are some additional pros and cons to consider when purchasing a bow that you'll use for small game hunting.

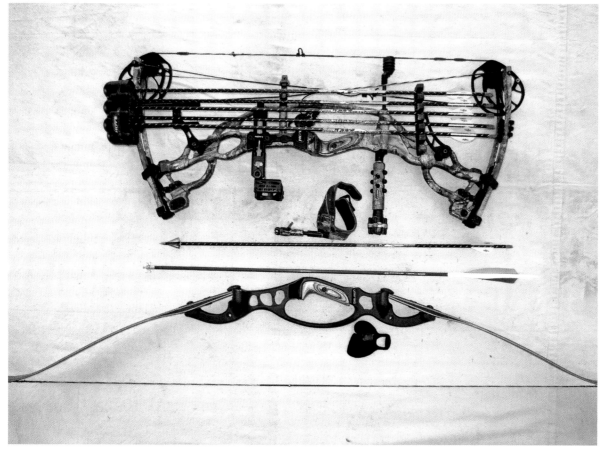

Top: Compound bow. This is a Hoyt Carbon Spyder with Easton Full Metal Jacket arrow and a Wasp Archery fixed blade broadhead. Bottom: A traditional bow. Shown here is a Hoyt Tiburon recurve with High Plains Hunter arrow and Judo small game point.

COMPOUND BOW

Pros: More accurate than traditional bows at longer ranges. It's far easier to gain a comfortable level of proficiency with a compound than it is with a traditional bow.

Cons: The increased speed of the arrow causes greater damage to the arrow as it deflects off the ground and rocks after a miss, which can be common with small, fast-moving targets. Compounds are heavier than traditional bows, and they can become a burden on long hikes. Compound bows have many moving parts and require more maintenance than traditional bows.

TRADITIONAL BOW

Pros: Light and easy to carry. Because the arrow is traveling slower, it can absorb the impact from errant shots and be used again. Shots can be fired very quickly.

Cons: Difficult to master. Limited efficacy at longer ranges.

ARROWS AND HEADS

It's been said that a good arrow will fly true out of a bad bow, but a bad arrow cannot be made to fly well from even the best bow. Arrows must be straight and have proper stiffness, weight, and length to work with any given bow. All of these factors combined determine the characteristics of the arrow's flight. For instance, pick the wrong length of arrow for your bow setup, and you could have an arrow that fishtails through the air rather than flies like a dart. Arrows are made from wood, aluminum, graphite, carbon fiber, and combinations of these materials. By far, the best-shooting and most practical arrows are made primarily from carbon fiber (which can be used both as a core and as a coating). Shooters of traditional bows who choose to use wooden arrows are doing so for aesthetic purposes—tradition for the sake of tradition. Several manufacturers have gone so far as to make carbon-fiber arrows with a faux wood finish. This allows traditional archers to *look* old-timey while still enjoying the performance of space-age materials. Besides flight performance, carbon-fiber arrows are far more durable than other options. That's an important thing to keep in mind with small game hunting, where you need arrows that can be fired again and again without breakage.

The weight and diameter of your arrows (and the weight of your broadheads) are crucial considerations for big game hunting, where good penetration of bone and muscle is key. For small game hunting, these details are far less important. Instead, you should feel free to use whatever arrows fly best from your particular bow, regardless of weight and flight speed.

Nowadays, most arrows are fletched with synthetic veins made of plastic-like composites. However, some traditional shooters prefer either real feathers or fake feathers that look like the real thing. Like wood, feathers are an aesthetic choice. Some guys just love the look and feel of a wooden arrow with real turkey feathers, and there's nothing wrong with that. But for practical purposes, you'll have far fewer headaches when using solid synthetic veins.

Aerial shooting is a major exception to this rule. Your chances of retrieving an arrow with standard fletching that's been fired into the air after a flushing pheasant or an incoming mallard are pretty much nil. For these purposes, you want to use flu-flu arrows—basically a standard arrow fletched with four or more oversized veins that spiral around the shaft of the arrow. This creates increased drag that rapidly slows the arrow after a short flight of around 30 or so yards. The rapid deceleration and short flight distance means you can watch the arrow reach its final destination and then retrieve it easily.

Standard field points, or target points, can certainly be lethal on small game, but they are not a great choice. The odds of simply wounding the animal despite a clean pass-through are quite good with field points, and so is the risk of losing a lot of arrows after they burrow under the grass and brush. Broadheads designed for big game hunting are much more lethal, but they tend toward overkill, causing meat loss due to excessive damage. And they are also quite expensive.

A better option is to use either Judo points or one of many variations of the popular "blunt" design. Judo points, which are made by a com-pany called Zwickey, have small springs en-circling the tip that catch on brush and grass in order to prevent the arrow from burrowing in. Usually a Judo point will cause the arrow to hop end over end upon impact, making re-trieval very easy. While many hunters use these points strictly for "stump shooting" as a form of target practice, they are highly effective small game points. Despite the springs, they pack a wallop and will penetrate game quite well.

Blunt tips come in many designs, from sim-ple steel spheres to fluted squares with scal-loped edges to points that look like the tip of Grandpa's cane. Like Judo points, most blunt designs will resist the arrow's urge to burrow

From left: Snaro bird point, Judo small game point, Bludgeon small game point, Hammer small game blunt, round blunt point.

under vegetation, and they won't lodge into wood—which is a very good thing for anyone who shoots at squirrels or birds up in trees. Two of the best blunt designs were given very graphic names by their manufacturers: Hammer and Bludgeon. If you're hunting for birds and are aiming for the head and neck area, it's worth your time to experiment with Snaro Bird Points. Some hunters love them; others think the points are ridiculous.

ARCHERY GEAR FOR TURKEYS

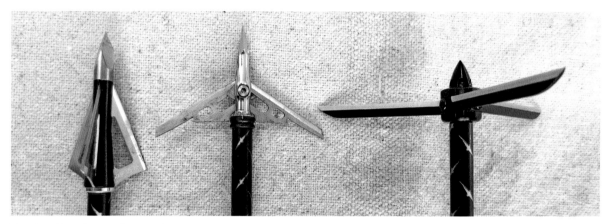

From left: Wasp Archery Hammer, Rage Hypodermic, Magnus Bullhead.

It's certainly possible to kill turkeys with traditional bows; thousands are taken every year that way. But before you attempt it, make sure that your shooting skills are absolutely top-notch, and don't be tempted by birds that are at the outer limits of your comfortable shooting range. Turkeys are a hell of a lot tougher to kill with a bow than you might think.

It's safer to attempt your first archery turkey with a compound bow. Not only are compounds much faster and more forgiving with regard to form (they can be shot easily from crouched, sitting, and kneeling positions), but the let-off of the draw weight allows you to pull your bow when the bird passes behind a tree or decoy or other obstacle; then you can comfortably hold the bow at full draw while you wait for the bird to step clear and present you with a shot. The difficulties of getting a wary gobbler to hold still at 15 yards while you go through the draw cycle on a recurve forces many traditional archers to hunt from inside a pop-up ground blind—something that I regard as an unwelcome man-made barrier that diminishes the rawness of being up close and personal with a large, wild bird.

The various small game arrowheads mentioned above are inadequate for turkeys. To a lesser extent, many popular big game broad-heads are also frowned upon by serious turkey hunters. That's because a lot of big game broadheads have relatively small cutting diameters of around 1¼ to 1½ inches. These are meant to minimize energy loss upon impact and maximize penetration through muscle and bone in order to reach the heart and lungs of big game animals. When it comes to turkeys, the heart/lung area is much smaller and harder to hit, yet the bird's feathers and bones are far easier to penetrate than a deer's shoulder blade. Therefore, shot placement on a turkey can be as much about structural damage to bone and muscle as it is about organ damage. In other words, you'd never try to kill a deer by disabling both of its legs with a broadhead. But it's very possible to bring down a turkey by shattering the bones at the base of its wings.

Still, I'm sad to report that there's little consensus among dedicated turkey hunters about which turkey broadheads are best. There are at least three schools of thought on the issue. In random order, one school argues that archers should ignore the body of the turkey and shoot for the neck or head with a extra-wide three-blade broadhead such as the Magnus Bullhead, which is designed to decapitate the bird. A direct hit leads to an instant and humane death for the turkey. Another school argues that there's a heightened chance of a miss with a neck shot, since you have very little room for

horizontal error. They say that the best approach is to aim for the body with an expandable head such as the Rage Hypodermic broadhead, which boasts a cutting diameter of 2 inches. That way, even if you miss the chest cavity, you'll still do enough damage to bones and muscle to slow the bird down at least enough to catch it. Finally, you've got the third school, which maintains that wide-cutting expandable heads are too prone to failure or outright breakage upon contact with the wing and leg bones of turkeys and that you should ignore much of the above information and stick to a fixed-blade broadhead such as the Wasp Hammer and not take a shot unless you're absolutely sure that you're going to put that arrow into the proper location on the turkey's body for a quick, clean kill. So who's right? What broadheads should you buy? I think that all schools have a valid point, though the second makes the most sense to me.

Whichever approach you take, carry a range finder when bowhunting for turkeys. Don't think of this as a technological crutch; think of it as a tool for responsible hunting. Range finders help turkey hunters rule out the uncertainty of gauging target distances, especially on birds that are straddling the border between close enough and too far. You can misjudge the distance on an elk by 10 yards without it necessarily causing you to miss the kill zone, but the smaller target of a turkey is much less forgiving.

BOWHUNTING FOR SMALL GAME IN THE WATER

When I was growing up, we always thought of hunting and fishing as slightly different versions of the same thing. When someone asked us what we liked to do, we said *huntin'n'fishin'* as though it was one word. Of course there are some major and obvious differences, especially when it comes to catch-and-release fishing. But if there's one practice that seamlessly combines the two disciplines, it's bowfishing. In most states, bowfishing opportunities are limited to a class of fish commonly known as "rough fish" or "non-game species." These include carp, gar, suckers, various species of shad, and sometimes bullhead and catfish. Other states have added some surprising additions to this list: northern pike in Alaska, tilapia in Texas, rays, flounder, and shark in the coastal states of the Southeast—the list goes on. Granted, many of these fishes are not as universally tasty as members of the salmon and perch family, but a competent chef can turn each into worthy table fare. (Hint: Fried fish cakes are the American bowfisherman's best friend.)

Most bowfishing is done in clear water ranging in depth from around 2 to 4 feet, usually along the edges of deeper water or near escape cover provided by aquatic vegetation or overhanging trees and shoreline vegetation. The water needs to be

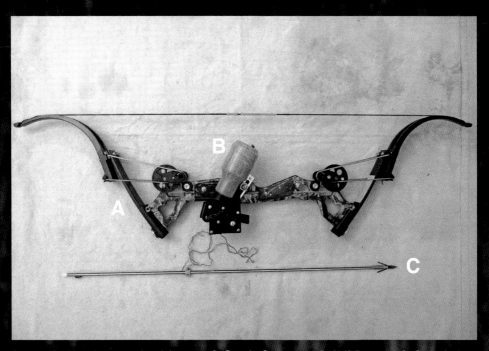

A very reliable and **accurate** bowfishing rig. **A: Oneida** Osprey bow. B: AMS Retriever. C: Cajun **Archery** Yellow Jacket fish arrow.

clear enough for you to see the fish and shallow enough that your arrow can pen-etrate the fish. (Water is much denser **than** air and slows the arrow dramatically; you can literally catch an arrow once it's traveled through about 8 feet of water.) Silence is important, as the sound of feet scuffling on a boat will spook fish and send them fleeing for cover or deep water. Excessive waves and loud talking can make things tough as **well**. A quick **mind** and body **are** also important, as often there's just a couple of seconds' **worth** of a shot opportunity between the moment you see the fish and the moment it disappears. The **ability to make** snap **decisions** translates to an ability to get fish. By far, though, the most difficult aspect of bowfishing is dealing with refraction. As light passes from one medium to another—air to water, in this case—it bends or refracts. Just think of how a fishing rod appears to bend abruptly at the waterline when you stick the end into the water. This means that submerged fish aren't where they seem to be from the bowfisher's perspective as he looks into the water. I'd say that about 98 percent of all bowfishing misses are fired over the fish's back. You have to aim low to hit them, but determining just how low can be tricky.

(continued)

One rule of thumb is that you should **aim** about 10 inches lower **than** where you want to hit the fish. (The best shot placement is in the front half of the fish, along the midline; ideally, you'd punch all your fish through the gill plate.) This is a decent piece of advice, as that would correct a significant portion of the misses that occur. But to really start hitting fish, it's best to keep in mind a rule sometimes described as 10-4. If the fish is 10 feet away and 1 foot below the surface, aim 4 inches low. If you double the distance or depth, double how low you aim. Thus, on a fish that's 20 feet away and 1 foot below the surface, lower your aim 8 inches. If it's 20 feet away and two feet below the surface, aim 16 inches low. If it's 15 feet away and 1 foot below the surface . . . well, you get the point.

OPTICS: BINOCULARS

Binoculars are important to many kinds of small game hunting; don't leave them behind. Here, Janis Putelis is wrapping up a Tennessee squirrel hunt where he used binoculars to locate squirrels hiding up in the treetops. Notice that he wears a bino harness to protect his investment. FHF Gear, out of Belgrade, Montana, makes custom bino harnesses to fit almost any binocular style. They also make superb pouches for GPS units, range finders, and other valuable tools and equipment.

Optics aren't nearly as integral to small game hunting as they are to big game hunting, but if I had to choose between bringing my pants or my binoculars on a small game hunt, I'd have a hard time deciding. Not only do I use my binoculars to scan for small game and to identify suitable habitats at a distance, but I also like to have them around my neck for observing non-game wildlife and scouting for future big game hunts.

Before I get into the technical aspects of binoculars, I'm just going to come right out and say that a pair of 8×32 roof prism binoculars are hard to beat for all-around small game hunting. Now, if you care to know what that means and why I feel the way I do, read on.

Binoculars are usually described with two numbers separated by an ×. For instance, you might see binoculars described as 8×32, 8×40, 10×40, or 12×50. The first number, the one that precedes the ×, refers to magnification. A pair of 10× binoculars, for example, produces an image as if you were ten times closer to the object, while 8× magnification produces an image as if you were eight times closer. The amount of magnification you need depends on what you're doing. My go-to big game binoculars are 10×, especially when hunting open country where I'm able to mount my binoculars on a tripod in order to stabilize them. But I much prefer a set of 8× binoculars for the up-close detail work of small game hunting, particularly when looking for rabbits in thick brush or trying to pick out a squirrel that's hiding on top of a tree limb in the canopy of an oak. The lower magnification of 8× binos creates a steadier sight picture than you get from 10× binos, which are strong enough to betray every little quiver of your hands. (Some guys can pull it off, but 12× binoculars are nearly impossible to freehand; they almost have to be mounted on a tripod. A good choice for small game is 7× binos, though they are not as widely available as 8×.)

The second number in binocular descriptions, the one coming after the ×, refers to the diameter (in millimeters) of the objective lens.

All other things being equal, a pair of binoculars will produce increasingly brighter, sharper, and wider images as the objective diameter increases. The trade-off is an increase in weight. A pair of 50 mm binoculars can give you a big, beautiful image, but it can also feel like a brick around your neck. Really, the decision for a small game hunter comes down to 30 mm vs. 40 mm. If you live out West and hunt big game as well, go with 40 mm. If you live in the East and/or primarily stick to small game, go with 30 mm.

Another important consideration is the prism style. This refers to the inner workings of binoculars, particularly the way the image is "righted" after passing through the objective lens. Most binoculars are either roof prism or Porro prism. You can usually tell them apart because roof prism binoculars have two straight barrels, while Porro prism binoculars have barrels that bulge out beyond the eyepiece. (Porro prism binoculars look more old-school; that's what your granddaddy had.) Porro prism binoculars will produce a brighter image than roof prism binoculars of the same magnification, objective size, and optical quality. However, roof prism binoculars are generally lighter, narrower, easier to hold, and better able to withstand abuse and water intrusion. Most manufacturers of quality hunting binoculars use the roof prism design, and for good reason.

Finally, consider the warranty. Spend the money and buy binoculars with a lifetime warranty. Manufacturers that back their products with such force are usually building a product of value. Some of the companies will charge you for parts to repair a broken piece, while others, like Vortex Optics, have an unconditional no-charge warranty and will repair or replace a damaged product at no charge to you no matter how it happened.

BLADE TOOLS

SOG PowerLock multi-tool; Outdoor Edge game shears.

MULTI-TOOLS: When it comes to blade tools, a small game hunter can get by in the field quite nicely with nothing but a quality multi-tool. A folding or sheath knife might be nice for cutting a block of cheese during your lunch break, but in a pinch your multi-tool's blade will do the job just as effectively. Both Leatherman and SOG make high-quality multi-tools, each with their own upsides. Leatherman tools have great locking mechanisms, high-quality files, and excellent corrosion resistance. SOG tools have the best needle-nose pliers on the market. They can also be customized so that you're carrying only the blades and tools that you actually use; if it's been decades since you actually opened a tin can in the field, you can easily remove the can opener and replace it with a tool that better suits your needs—say, an extra saw blade, or SOG's V-notch cutter. Another benefit of SOG tools is that their bit driver will accept standard $\frac{1}{4}$-inch sockets. With a simple adapter, available at any hardware store, you can run all of the bits that you need to service your firearms, outboard engines, and so on. Leatherman also has an integrated bit system, but it's based on a proprietary fitting that's not widely available.

GAME SHEARS: Not many hunters think to use them, but a good set of poultry shears can make quick work of small game butchering jobs. Nothing is better for breaking down squirrels and rabbits, and the tools are also valuable for severing wings and feet on upland birds and waterfowl. But don't even bother messing around with low-quality shears. They only lead to heartbreak. Buy good, or don't buy at all.

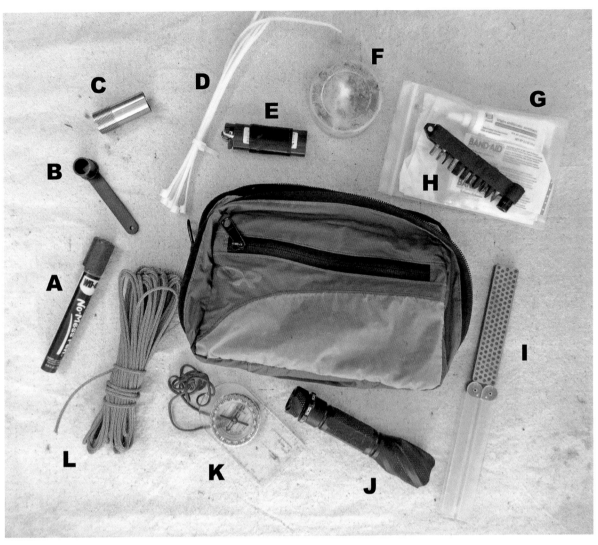

A: WD-40. **B:** Choke wrench. **C:** Extra choke. **D:** Cable ties. **E:** Lighter with duct tape wrapped around body. **F:** Fire-starting paste. **G:** First-aid kit. **H:** Various bits for SOG multi-tool. **I:** DMT knife sharpener. **J:** SOG Dark Energy flashlight. **K:** Compass. **L:** 50 feet of utility cord.

SMALL GAME UTILITY KIT

You can avoid the annoyance of forgetting any of your essential odds and ends by building a small utility kit that always stays in your game vest or pack. A properly packed kit will not only keep you hunting when conditions turn bad but also might end up keeping you alive when conditions turn *really* bad. Every hunter's kit will look different, because we all hunt different locations with their own peculiar demands. But no matter the scenario, each hunter's kit should include at least a minimal amount of survival and first-aid supplies, plus some basic repair materials. Take a look at the kit that's pictured at left and use it as a basic guideline for building a kit that works for your own particular location and style of hunting.

DAYPACKS, FANNY PACKS, AND VESTS

I once met a guy who bragged that he's been hunting small game for twenty-five years without ever needing to wear a backpack, as though being chronically ill-prepared was something to be proud of. I like to carry with me everything that I need to stay comfortable in the woods for as long as possible—at least up to the point that the weight becomes too much of a hindrance. Depending on the scenario, that might include extra clothes, rainwear, water, food, and even a pair of chest waders if I'm hunting a location where I might indulge the whim to cross a river or enter a cattail marsh.

Here I'm using the term *backpack*, but it should be understood that a small game

On left, a turkey hunter with an Outdoorsman's Muley Fanny Pack.

Grouse hunters wearing a Badlands hunting vest and an Outdoorsman's backpack. Notice the built-in scabbard on the Outdoorsman's backpack, handy for long walks into your hunting area.

hunter's backpack can easily be replaced by a game vest or a fanny pack. (Some guys loathe the term *fanny pack*, thinking it's effete and cutesy. Most of these fellas opt for the name *lumbar pack*. In my opinion, though, *lumbar pack* adds an unnecessary layer of confusion. It's a fanny pack, and there's nothing you can do about it.) Below are a few considerations, in the form of pros and cons, that I kick around when deciding how I'm going to carry around my gear on a small game hunt.

BACKPACKS

Pros: Due to their larger size, backpacks allow you the freedom of carrying more stuff. You can find ones in varying sizes and styles with adjustable shoulder and lumbar straps that easily accommodate different body shapes and provide back support. Most modern outdoor packs allow for easy storage and access of hydration systems, whether it's a water bottle or hydration bladder. In addition, they offer other storage areas for smaller items. Overall, backpacks are extremely versatile.

Cons: Carrying a larger pack allows for overpacking. Sometimes extra space is filled with excess equipment simply because the room is there. The larger size also may make getting through thick brush or maneuvering in tight spaces difficult. They can be heavy and may make a simple day hunt more difficult due to unnecessary weight.

VESTS

Pros: Hunting vests provide space to store extra shells, radios, whistles, water, and harvested quarry, all on your person. They have multiple pockets to organize small but vital pieces of gear. Available in varying types, they can help keep you warm or cool, concealed or visible, all while providing an additional cushion for your shoulder while shooting. Vests provide adequate storage for most items you will need while in the field, with limited reductions to your mobility.

Cons: When overloaded, vests can become cumbersome and make shooting awkward. They take some getting accustomed to, especially when they're being used to store the majority of your day's hunting gear. On the other hand, they may not be able to carry all of what you need for your trip, and therefore may be needed only for specific hunts or limited uses while in the field. Due to their limited capacity for holding heavy or bulky items, vests are less versatile than backpacks.

FANNY PACKS

Pros: Fanny packs are small, light, and easy to carry. They allow increased mobility while providing storage for your essential hunting gear. They give you quick access to shells, hunting licenses, keys, calls, or whatever you need to have on your person. They are great for low-intensity hunts and can be adjusted, opened, or removed with great ease. Modern fanny packs now come in a range of sizes and styles for intended uses, so you may find that this simple but effective storage unit is all you need. They also pair well with a backpack or vest for additional storage and access to high-priority items.

Cons: Fanny packs are far more limited than both backpacks and vests. Because they do not have as much space available, the wearer must know exactly what should go inside. There are fanny packs that allow for storage of a water bottle and other large items, but those may become uncomfortable due to lack of support and additional weight around the lumbar. These are usually not primary pieces of equipment, so relying solely on the capabilities of a fanny pack may create some difficulties when deciding what gear goes with you and what stays behind.

FOOTWEAR AND APPAREL

BOOTS

Feet ruin hunts. Cold feet, blistered feet, wet feet, tired feet—I've seen dozens of hunts either compromised or cut short because someone had a foot problem. Luckily, most of these issues can be avoided if you choose your footwear carefully. A versatile small game hunter should have a number of high-quality boots at his or her disposal, so that it's easy to keep your feet happy in the field. If I had to limit myself to just three pairs of footwear for small game hunting, here's what I'd choose:

From left: Xtratuf neoprene knee boots (wear these when things get wet and muddy; they are the most comfortable rubber knee boots that I've ever worn); Schnees Wilderness 6-inch hiking boots (for general wear; these work well in dry or semi-dry conditions ranging from hot to near freezing); Schnees Hunter II pack boots (the best boots for active, cold-weather hunting).

For some small game hunting, pretty much anything goes with regard to apparel. These hunters had a great day chasing cottontail rabbits in Wisconsin with very little technical hunting apparel.

The apparel for a small game hunter can be as simple or as complicated as you choose. When I was a kid, my brothers and I would often head out squirrel or rabbit hunting in the same clothes we wore to school. We'd just throw on our game vests and hit the woods, with no thought to technical fabrics or camouflage.

This casual approach isn't perfect for everything, though. Trying to hunt midwinter waterfowl in a marsh would be disastrously cold if you were wearing nothing but school clothes, and trying to bust quail out of a thorny briar patch while wearing your school duds would leave you looking like you'd lost a prolonged and nasty battle with a family of bobcats. When thinking about apparel, it's wise to consider the basic concept of layering before getting into specialized apparel that you might need for certain types of hunting.

BASIC LAYERING

The opposite of layering would be to head out on a winter day wearing nothing but an insulated one-piece snowmobile suit. The moment you start to get a little warmed up from exertion, you'd have to make the choice between being drenched with sweat or naked and cold. That's an extreme example, to be sure, but you get the point. Layering allows you to add or subtract layers of clothes in order to make subtle adjustments according to your needs at a given moment.

A pair of upland bird hunters, Chip Parkins (left) and Ronny Boehme (right). Notice a few important things about their apparel: blaze orange brimmed hats, for safety and blocking the sun; protective and durable long-sleeved shirts (with more blaze orange) for busting through brush; game vests for carrying shells, basic equipment, and downed game; brush pants for wading through thick and thorny vegetation; and leather gloves (on Chip) for hand protection. You can't see it here, but they are both wearing merino-blend socks and lightweight leather hiking boots with plenty of support.

A pair of waterfowl hunters, Steven Rinella (left) and Brandt Meixell (right). Notice the heavy-duty camouflage chest waders on each, imperative for hunting near the water. Also notice the billed camouflage hats; neck gaiters that double as face masks; waterproof, in-sulated jackets with lots of pockets for shells; call lanyards for duck and goose calls; insulated camouflage gloves (on Steve) for hunt-ing in the blind, and waterproof wrist-length neoprene gloves (on Brandt) for handling wet decoys and birds.

A turkey hunter, Jerod Fink. Notice that he has camouflage everything. First Lite brimmed beanie; mesh face mask; very quiet First Lite merino wool shirt; camo Outdoorsman's Muley fanny pack; Muck waterproof knee boots.

CAR CAMPING FOR SMALL GAME

For whatever reason, it seems as though big game hunters are far more likely than small game hunters to hit the road and spend a few nights camping out in the field. That's too bad, because road trips can be extremely productive for small game hunting—especially when you travel to areas that receive very little hunting pressure. At various points in our lives, my brothers and I have done annual road trips for cottontail rabbits, quail, ducks, geese, and turkeys, and I count these forays as some of the most memorable small game hunts that I've been involved with. Unlike the kind of big game hunts that I enjoy, where I usually end up camping in backcountry locales far away from my vehicle, the best small game hunts are typically located in places where you camp right at your truck or car.

If you've got a pickup, you can rig it up with a sheet of reinforced plywood that rests on top of the wheel wells. This gives you plenty of room to sleep (the plywood makes a better bed than the steel floor of the pickup) and it gives you a ton of gear storage underneath. If you really want to trick out your camping rig, glue a layer of indoor/outdoor carpet to the top side of the plywood surface. You'll be sleeping in style.

As for packing, keep a simple pre-packed car camping setup in your garage or closet so that hitting the road is as simple as loading a box into the back of your rig. You can think of your car camping setup as being divided into four categories: sleeping gear, eating gear, field care gear, and odds and ends. Here's a packing list that can form the basis for building your own small game road trip kit.

SLEEPING GEAR

1. Sleeping bag. A high-quality 15° synthetic sleeping bag is a great all-around bag that will meet 90 percent of your hunting needs.
2. Sleeping pad. The Nemo Astro Insulated Lite 20 R is a great sleeping pad.
3. Lightweight backpacking tent, unless you have a vehicle such as a pickup, SUV, or a wagon that allows you to stretch out in the back. Definitely avoid the temptation to spend a night slouched in the front seat of your car. The time you save by not pitching a tent will not make up for the horrible night of sleep and the cramped legs that you'll wake up with.

EATING GEAR

1. Five-gallon jerrycan of water, or 2 gallons per person per day
2. Camp stove (Jetboil or Coleman-style two-burner camp stove)
3. Stove fuel
4. Pot for heating water
5. Small frying pan
6. Quality cooking tongs
7. Backpacker's cup, bowl, spoon, and spork (Snow Peak makes an excellent line of titanium products)
8. Coffee-making apparatus (though you should forgo brewed coffee in exchange for Starbucks Via, which gives you more time in the woods and less time monkeying around in camp)
9. Plenty of nonperishable foods to get you through a few days of hard hunting. Think about one or two Mountain House freeze-dried meals per day, a few bags of jerky, cans of nuts, energy bars, instant oatmeal, dried salami, a bottle of cooking oil, and prepackaged seasoning blend for frying grouse breasts and rabbit thighs.

FIELD CARE GEAR

1. Poultry shears

2. Zip-top bags

3. Ice for the cooler

ODDS AND ENDS

1. Medium-sized cooler for carrying beverages and perishable food items to the hunting location, and for carrying game meat back home.

2. Small shovel (for digging catholes; don't litter the woods or trailheads with exposed human waste)

3. Toilet paper (burn used toilet paper whenever possible; when that's not possible, bury it deep)

4. Basic toiletries kit: toothbrush, toothpaste, etc.

5. Headlamp and handheld flashlight

6. Lighter and waterproof matches

7. Heavy down jacket and insulated bibs for hanging around camp on cold nights

HUNTING DOGS

Two different dogs doing their thing. A pointer shows his master the location of a grouse, and a beagle brings in the fixings for hasenpfeffer.

Hunting dogs are unlike any other kind of hunting gear, for the obvious reason that they are alive. Unlike a good shotgun, they cannot be abused and neglected and still be expected to function. The decision to get a hunting dog is a huge one and should be taken very seriously. While there is plenty of dog information distributed throughout this book, it's way beyond the scope of this project to detail everything that you need to know to properly train a dog. If you're committed to doing that, you need to invest in a library of books about training hunting dogs, including *The Care and Training of Versatile Hunting Dogs* by Bodo Winterhelt and Edward Dailey, *Bird Dog* by Ben O. Williams, *Game Dog* and *Water Dog* by Richard A. Wolters, *Pointing Dogs Made Easy* by Steven Mulak, and *Wing and Shot: Gun Dog Training* by Robert G. Wehle.

Now that I've made that disclaimer, I'm going to let a close friend and superb dog handler explain his take on the subject. I defer to Ronny Boehme on all things related to dogs. He's a font of information on the subject and has that peculiar trait common among serious gun dog owners. He loves dogs as much as or more than he loves hunting, which is something that I cannot say about myself.

RON BOEHME WEIGHS IN ON VERSATILE HUNTING DOGS

"I've got fifteen years' experience as a field judge for hunting dogs, and here I'd like to offer up some of my opinions on the subject of versatile hunting dogs. **Versatile** is the word given to the twenty-eight distinct breeds of Continental European pointing dogs that are recognized by the North American Versatile Hunting Dog Association. All of these breeds have the ability to search for and point game, and to track and retrieve wounded or downed game on both land and water. Thus, these breeds show their usefulness both before and after the shot. While all of the twenty-eight breeds can do the required jobs of a versatile hunting dog, they each have their own particular pros and cons. You'll notice that I've lumped some of these breeds together, as many breeds have significant overlap in their talents and shortcomings. And I've omitted others, as some breeds are too rare to warrant much attention here. Also bear in mind that these assessments are generalizations. Each individual dog within a species has its own personality and style."

(continued)

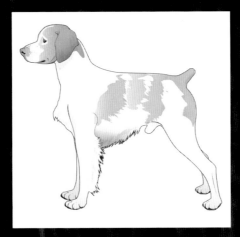

BRITTANY

Pros: Medium-sized dog that's easy to care for.

Cons: Soft, silky hair that never dries and holds the stink of whatever they've been rolling in—and they'll roll in anything they can find, the worse the better.

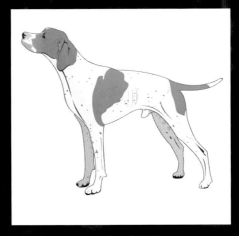

ENGLISH POINTER

Pros: Great nose, staunch point.

Cons: Their acute sensory perception allows them to point birds that are very far away—often too far away for the hunter to make a shot once the bird flushes.

ENGLISH SETTER

Pros: Good nose, with an ability to move through the woods with grace and balance.

Cons: Poor retrievers. If you shoot a bird over a setter, be sure to mark where it falls; most setters believe their owner should do the retrieving.

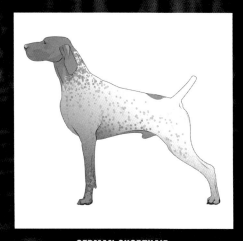

GERMAN SHORTHAIR

Pros: Dependable and strong; will retrieve almost anything you shoot.

Cons: Will retrieve almost anything you didn't shoot, including dead skunks. They also have a poor attention span and memory. I once saw a German shorthair (my own) get sliced up by running through a barbed-wire fence. He got stitched up in the morning and then sliced himself open on the same fence before dinner.

(continued)

GERMAN WIREHAIR

Pros: Powerful, tireless trackers that'll trail anything. They'll recover crippled game after all other dogs have given up the chase.

Cons: Ruthless. A male wirehair will fight his own reflection if you let him. They will hunt anything, in season or out, including goats, chickens, and your neighbor's cats.

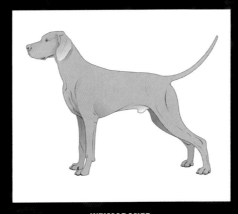

WEIMARANER

Pros: Tenacious and loyal to owners.

Cons: Ugly dogs. And it can be hard to get them to remember anything you trained them to do when they're not wearing a shock collar.

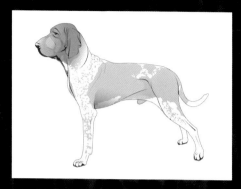

BRACCO ITALIANO, SPINONE ITALIANO

Pros: My personal favorites. Excellent connectivity to owner. Great noses, solid retrieving, good swimmers.

Cons: Horrible shedding, plus their drool will travel great distances when shaken from their lips and it'll stick to any surface. They also have a tendency to think that their owners are highly fallible.

CAMERON MITCHELL, A TENNESSEE HUNTER AND DOG OWNER, WEIGHS IN ON HIS LOVE OF LABRADOR RETRIEVERS

"Labs are working dogs with an instinct for retrieving game. With the right kind of attention and training, they can also be a loving and loyal companion. Labs sometimes get a bad rap because they are one of the breeds that are often produced by puppy mills and sold to ill-prepared owners who don't tend to the animal's need for exercise, mental stimulation, and companionship. But I love Labs exactly because they are a diverse breed. I have had several Labs, some short and stocky with long hair, others tall and slim with short hair, and they have proven to be the perfect all-around dog for both an intensive bird hunting life and a happy family life.

"It is no coincidence that Labs are chosen for everything from search-and-rescue operations to customs and immigration work to assisting the disabled. They are intelligent dogs who are eager to please, which makes them highly effective at many tasks if trained properly at an early stage of development. Labs require basic obedience from the beginning to establish a relationship with their owner and to control their exuberant love for running and retrieving. Simple consistency of commands and agreement about discipline and behaviors toward the dog within a family can avoid all the pitfalls of intense retrievers (digging, chewing, running off, jumping up, etc.). Quite frankly, the breed's intensity is what makes them such great hunting dogs and so much fun.

"I have seen a Lab sit on a dog platform attached to the side of a tree in flooded timber for hours, shivering not from the cold but from the desire to jump in the water. They patiently wait because they have been trained and because they simply love the routine of the retrieve: the blow of the whistle, the special 'go' command, a big splash or jump, grabbing the bird, and bringing it home. When they get back to the house, they are just as happy to curl up on the rug with small children crawling all over them.

"I was once told this story about a Lab: The dog grew up hunting many different kinds of birds. He was a seasoned waterfowl dog as well as the owner's best friend in the world. For some reason, there came a day when the gentleman had to leave his retriever at home when he left to hunt. As he was leaving, the dog sat behind the closed screen. He cried and moaned as the hunter drove away. When the hunter returned, for the first time in the dog's life, he chose to not greet him at the door. Instead he remained in his bed with his head hung low. These dogs not only love the hunt, but they love their people. Needless to say, that Lab was never left home again."

THE BASICS

WHERE TO HUNT

Relative to big game hunters, small game hunters have an easy time finding hunting locations. That's not to say that hunting locations will simply fall into your lap—they won't—but a lack of a hunting spot is hardly an excuse for missing out on the excitement and great food that can be had by hunting small game.

As I stressed in Volume 1 of this guidebook series, the best hunters spend more time thinking about where they'll hunt than about any other aspect of the hunting process. Identifying and gaining access to good hunting spots is more than simply a hobby for them—they treat it like a job. Year round, they study maps, scout locations, swap information with their fellow hunters, and make phone calls to landowners and government agencies responsible for the management of public lands. All this effort goes into solving the primary question that should be on every hunter's mind: *Come hunting season, where will I be?*

Most hunters mentally divide hunting lands into two categories: private land and public land. Private lands are those places where you need permission from a landowner to hunt. Public lands are owned by the people and are open to all hunters. (Note that these are simplified definitions. There are many private lands made open to public-access hunting through various state-sponsored programs; likewise, some public lands are managed by various branches of government as restricted-access hunting grounds, which are meant to provide high-quality hunting experiences to a limited number of hunters who are randomly selected through raffles and drawings.)

Public and private lands each have their advantages and drawbacks. Public lands are beautiful simply because they are public; we have the best game management system in the world, a system based on the belief that wildlife should be held in the public trust. Public lands give hunters of all backgrounds and economic statuses a chance to utilize the renewable wild game resources we all hold title to. The drawback to public land, especially in the eastern United States, is that it tends to get a lot more hunting pressure than private land. At times, it can seem as though your local public lands are devoid of game, while birds and animals abound on nearby private lands. One of the marks of a truly talented hunter is that he or she can hunt public land and still do as well as the hunters with access to private land.

In general, hunters on private land are better able to plan their hunts according to the movements and whereabouts of animals rather than the movements and whereabouts of competing hunters. For instance, a duck hunter on public land might know that opening day is his best chance to hit a pond that holds a flock of mallards, since his competitors are almost certainly going to be targeting the same birds. Meanwhile, someone hunting private land with a limited-access location might know that it's best to wait before hitting his pond because the birds that are already there will attract flocks of ducks that are getting bumped off public lands by the sudden influx of opening-day hunters.

Yet private lands do have drawbacks, especially for independent-minded hunters who want to operate with autonomy. Private land-owners often exercise a lot of control over hunters on their land. They can tell hunters where to hunt, when to hunt, and what to hunt. I used to hunt squirrels and woodcock on a property in Michigan that was loaded with cottontails, but the landowner forbade me from shooting them because his nephew liked to hunt rabbits in the winter with his beagles. Sometimes I'd hunt that place and see nothing but cottontails, which always frustrated me. I had another property I hunted that didn't allow Sunday hunting. Another landowner forbade me from being on his land outside of regular daylight hours, which made it impossible to get an early start setting out duck decoys. Yet another landowner allowed me to hunt his squirrels but not his Canada geese, even though the geese outnumbered the squirrels by about a hundred to one. Obviously these people had every right to make such decisions, and they did so for valid reasons. I always respected their wishes. But hunting on those properties made me acutely aware of the inevitable trade-offs that happen when you give up high-pressure public land in exchange for low-pressure private land.

Certainly, private lands and public lands each have their advantages and disadvantages. A well-rounded hunter should maintain a stable of hunting spots that include each. Here's how to begin doing just that.

PUBLIC LAND

A welcome sign for small game hunters. Limited-access lands can offer prime hunting opportunities away from the crowds.

All states have at least some public lands that are available to hunting, though exact amounts vary wildly. Less than 6 percent of Texas is publicly owned, and a significant portion of that state's public land is administered by the National Park Service and therefore closed to hunting. Nevada, on the other hand, is about 77 percent public land, and the vast majority of that is open to hunting.

Public lands come in many forms, depending on the region and state. Some of the more common land designations are state parks, state game areas, state forests, state wildlife refuges, national parks, national forests, national wildlife preserves, national wildlife refuges, and Bureau of Land Management lands. Typically, but not always, the terms *park*, *preserve*, and *sanctuary* designate lands that are *not* open to hunting. (Don't confuse this with being unfriendly to hunting. Park and preserve lands serve a valuable role for fish and game by providing sanctuaries that help prevent overharvest; often these areas serve as source locations that continually produce game that is harvested on neighboring lands.) The terms *forest*, *game management area*, *refuge*, and *BLM* typically indicate lands that are open to hunting—but again, there are many notable exceptions.

Due to the nuanced nature of land designations, questions about hunting on public lands—both state and federal—should always be put to representatives of your state's fish and game agency. These agencies are responsible for the management of game within their state's boundaries, and they have a vested interest in helping you decipher the landscape of where you want to hunt. Since they rely largely on hunting license sales as a funding source, they want you to get out there and have a good time as much as possible; and since they are also tasked with the enforcement of game laws, it's in their own best interest to arm you with reliable information now rather than having to punish you later. In fact, many states actively promote awareness about public land hunting opportunities with website pages devoted specifically to the subject.

But don't let your search end with published

STATE	WEBSITE	STATE	WEBSITE
Alabama	www.outdooralabama.com	Montana	www.fwp.mt.gov
Alaska	www.adfg.alaska.gov	Nebraska	www.outdoornebraska.ne.gov
Arizona	www.azgfd.gov	Nevada	www.ndow.org
Arkansas	www.agfc.com	New Hampshire	www.wildlife.state.nh.us
California	www.dfg.ca.gov	New Jersey	www.nj.gov/dep/fgw
Colorado	www.wildlife.state.co.us	New Mexico	www.wildlife.state.nm.us
Connecticut	www.ct.gov	New York	www.dec.ny.gov
Delaware	www.dnrec.delaware.gov	North Carolina	www.ncwildlife.org
Florida	www.myfwc.com	North Dakota	www.gf.nd.gov
Georgia	www.georgiawildlife.org	Ohio	www.dnr.state.oh.us
Hawaii	www.dlnr.hawaii.gov	Oklahoma	www.wildlifedepartment.com
Idaho	www.fishandgame.idaho.gov	Oregon	www.dfw.state.or.us
Illinois	www.dnr.illinois.gov	Pennsylvania	www.pgc.state.pa.us
Indiana	www.in.gov/dnr/fishwild	Rhode Island	www.dem.ri.gov
Iowa	www.iowadnr.gov	South Carolina	www.dnr.sc.gov
Kansas	www.kdwpt.state.ks.us	South Dakota	www.gfp.sd.gov
Kentucky	www.fw.ky.gov	Tennessee	www.state.tn.us/twra
Louisiana	www.wlf.louisiana.gov	Texas	www.tpwd.state.tx.us
Maine	www.maine.gov/ifw	Utah	www.wildlife.utah.gov
Maryland	www.dnr.state.md.us	Vermont	www.vtfishandwildlife.com
Massachusetts	www.mass.gov/eea/agencies/dfg	Virginia	www.dgif.virginia.gov
Michigan	www.michigan.gov/dnr	Washington	www.wdfw.wa.gov
Minnesota	www.dnr.state.mn.us/fishwildlife	West Virginia	www.wvdnr.gov
Mississippi	www.mdwfp.com	Wisconsin	dnr.wi.gov
Missouri	www.mdc.mo.gov	Wyoming	wgfd.wyo.gov

lists of public land hunting areas. Some of my best public hunting spots are under-the-radar locations that are not listed on any compilation. Growing up, we hunted squirrels, grouse, and waterfowl on a lot of property that was owned by the township, a type of governmental body in the Northeast and Midwest that holds varying powers over parcels of land. We identified township land by looking at plat maps, which show legal property boundaries of land parcels as well as ownership. In this case, the plat maps showed the parcels as individual quarter-acre lots that were owned by the township, but together these lots formed a large contiguous tract of undeveloped land that bordered some very productive lakes and marshes.

We also used plat maps to find a favorite late-season duck hunting slough in Montana. Every December, we'd watch as a small roadside slough filled up with hundreds of mallards. At first glance you'd assume that the slough belonged to an adjacent farm that was plastered with No Trespassing signs—and I'm sure this assumption is what kept other hunters away. But on closer inspection you could see that the triangular slough was bordered on one side by a public road, on another side by a navigable river, and on the third side by the right-of-way for an underground gas line. Following a hunch, my buddy investigated the plat books and saw that the land was actually owned by the public. We killed some fine greenheads out of that slough.

More recently, my older brother has been hunting turkeys on some large islands in a major river in western Montana. For years he would see turkeys on the islands while fishing, but he could find no information about who owned the land. The islands were not demarcated as public land on his maps that showed public land holdings, and a search of plat maps with landowner names didn't help solve the mystery. Finally, he inquired with a state agency and learned that no one was paying taxes on the islands. Despite the fact that these islands had mature stands of cottonwoods and plenty of land that was well above the high-water mark, they did not exist in any official way and were therefore just part of the public river corridor. He's been hunting them ever since.

I've already mentioned maps a number of times. These are imperative for both identifying and hunting new territory. Maps come in many forms, and they contain a wide array of information that is helpful to the hunter. Here they are broken into three categories, with explanations of what you need and how to use them.

1. Satellite imagery. Pictures taken from high above the landscape offer a detailed view of the vegetation that cannot be deciphered from topographical maps alone. This is important to hunters, as finding huntable populations of small game often comes down to locating small

Montana hunter Matt Rinella has identified a number of prime public hunting locations that no one else knows about. He does a lot of scouting and map reading and isn't afraid to make a few phone calls.

patches of cover, water sources, and feeding locations that would be impossible to identify on a conventional map. Use resources such as Google to pre-scout areas and get a feel for the land. Mark the coordinates of good-looking spots in your GPS, and then check them out on scouting trips. Also bring along a laminated printout of satellite imagery. During the hunt, you can take a moment to peer over a satellite image and identify valuable details that perhaps didn't jump out at you before you had firsthand experience of the area.

2. Topographical maps. The problem with satellite imagery is that it's very hard to discern the vertical aspect—the ups and downs, if you will—of a landscape. These are covered in detail on topographical maps. For hunting purposes, USGS quad maps in 1:24,000 scale are the best. Use these in conjunction with satellite imagery and you'll develop an intimate understanding of your hunting area before you even set foot on it. You can also get overlay maps, which combine satellite imagery with topographical lines and even land ownership details. The downside of these overlay maps is that details sometimes get lost when a map becomes overcrowded with information. (There are multiple sources for such maps; do an Internet search for "custom hunting maps.") Of course, you can get all of the above information from a GPS unit, but it's hard to beat the "big screen" of a paper map. And paper maps don't need batteries.

3. GPS. While all of us should know how to find our position on a map, it is faster and way more convenient and accurate to do it with a GPS. Today's GPS units can be loaded with detailed topographical maps and land ownership information as well. Armed with this info, the hunter never has to wonder if he or she is trespassing or if a patch of pheasant cover on the other side of the fence is fair game.

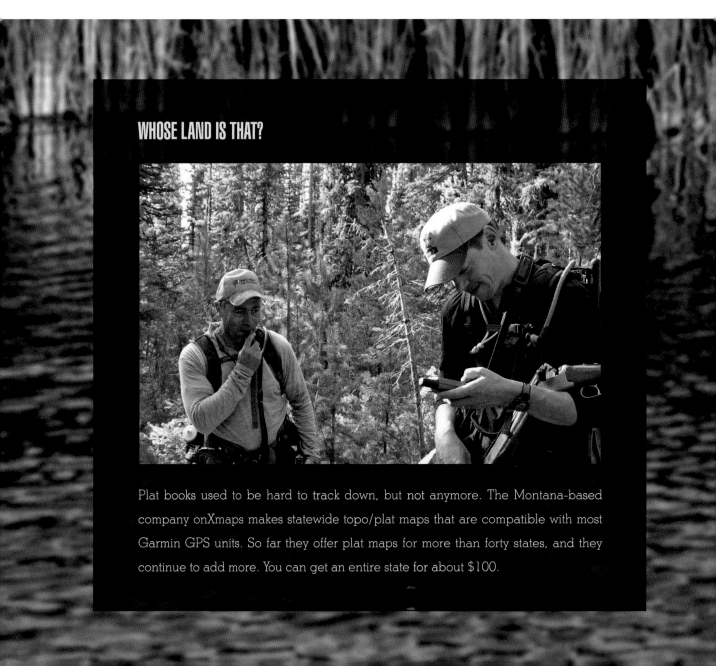

WHOSE LAND IS THAT?

Plat books used to be hard to track down, but not anymore. The Montana-based company onXmaps makes statewide topo/plat maps that are compatible with most Garmin GPS units. So far they offer plat maps for more than forty states, and they continue to add more. You can get an entire state for about $100.

Once you identify lands where you *can* hunt, you need to narrow those down to lands where you *want* to hunt. This is the hard part, and doing it well mandates that you spend hour upon hour in the woods, on the phone, and in front of the computer. The first and most obvious question that needs to be addressed is what lands have the animals or birds you're interested in hunting. Sure, you might have identified thousands of acres of prime grasslands and pine forest that is full of turkey, but that won't do you much good if you're dreaming about hunting wood ducks. The most obvious way to accomplish this is by taking the time to put your boots on the ground and scout the land. I've done this many times in many places, just by taking a drive out to some potential hunting ground in order to walk around and have a look. As much as possible, I time my scouting trips for optimal benefit in terms of both season and time of day. If you're looking for a snow goose location in North Dakota, it doesn't do any good to scout in July, when the birds are all up in the Arctic. If you're looking for wild turkeys, a great idea is to scout by ear in the predawn darkness of early spring mornings, when you're most likely to hear the far-traveling gobbles of males, or toms, that are getting ready for the breeding season.

While scouting a new location, it's wise to bring along a GPS and notebook as well as any paper maps you have. Make note of the weather conditions and date of your visit. Record all of the sign you see, as well as interesting features and notable discoveries. Make a note of any animals you see, plus animal tracks, droppings, trails, and bird calls. Record evidence of other hunters, such as spent shell casings or the remnants of waterfowl blinds built from native materials. Mark trails, patches of mature nut-producing trees, potential campsites, creeks, ponds, and so on. Don't just limit your observations to the specific species you happen to be looking for. If you find a beaver pond while scouting for spring turkeys, make a note to visit that spot in the fall to see if any ducks are using it. Be sure that your notes are clearly written, and store them in such a way that you'll be able to find them in the future. I can't tell you how many times I've had to call my friends or brothers to ask something like, "Hey, what road were we on that one time when we were hunting rabbits and ran that covey of quail across the road?" And when it comes to GPS, name your waypoints so that they will still make sense in a couple of months or even years. It's frustrating to look at your GPS and see numerically assigned waypoints that you never bothered to label and that now make no sense whatsoever.

Remember, good record keeping can make all the difference. Last spring, one of my brothers was driving home from a successful turkey hunt in one of his standard locations when he decided to take a new route. He ended up getting lost in a maze of winding dirt roads that added an hour to his drive time. While he was lost, a pair of jakes crossed the road in front of him. He happened to have his GPS turned on in an effort to find his way out of there, and he noticed that he was driving through a section of state land. He logged a waypoint named "jakes." A year later, he returned to his tried-and-true hunting spot and found that the turkeys he'd been hunting for eight years were gone. Three days of hard hunting turned up nothing but one set of tracks. He hiked back to his van and returned to the "jakes" waypoint. Over the next couple of days we killed a pair of gobblers.

Scouting isn't the only way to get up-to-date information about public land hunting areas. State fish and game agencies can be a great resource for this kind of material. They have waterfowl and small game biologists with extensive information about population trends and productive hunting locations. Get these folks on the phone and start peppering them with questions. They get a lot of such inquiries in the weeks leading up to hunting season, so be novel and hit them up during the hunting off-season. Call in March to talk about upland game birds and you'll probably be the only inquisitive hunter who's contacted them about the subject in months.

State wildlife biologists are somewhat limited in what they can say. Most won't give specific coordinates to every hunter who calls, because that would certainly diminish the quality of the area and make it so that none of the hunters who went there had a quality experience. They will, however, give you a good head start on your scouting. And if you are persistent and lucky (plus kind and polite), they just might throw some concrete, actionable tips your way.

While competition is certainly a downside to public land hunting, a smart hunter puts that competition to use by collecting firsthand information from other hunters who have been there. Call small, privately owned sporting goods stores in the area you're thinking about hunting and throw yourself at their mercy. (Large chain sporting goods stores have plenty of employees who hunt, but it's harder to get these folks on the phone for any appreciable amount of time.) Tell them that you've never hunted such-and-such area but you're looking for some insights. Sure, you might get some bum information from guys who are trying to protect their locations from outsider intrusion. But by placing five or six such phone calls to different locations, and by checking this against information from your state fish and game agency, you'll be able to tell which information is good and which is bogus. You might also be talking to a big game hunter who doesn't care about small game, and this fella might be pretty free with information that he doesn't personally use. Another great trick is to track down hunters (usually friends of friends) who used to hit a certain spot but then moved away. A guy who lived in Montana for ten years but then moved to Alaska is going to be a gold mine of information about Montana. He's no longer worried about protecting his spots, and often he'll divulge locations just because he's curious to hear about what you turn up. Rural bars are another great spot. Buy a couple of drinks for an old barfly near Patagonia, Arizona, and you might be pleasantly surprised to hear him divulge information about his buddy's quail hunting locations that his buddy would never in a million years want divulged. Online forums are another great resource. Let's say you're interested in hunting Canada geese along the Powder River in eastern Montana. It's smart to sit down and do an online search with the following keywords: "hunting Canada geese, Powder River, Montana." Once you start sifting through the hits (and bypassing the offers for guided hunts), you'll eventually find folks talking very specifically about locations and methods and strategies that can be used on do-it-yourself hunts.

A final thing that warrants mention here is that the public land hunter needs to plan around his competition. Of course, this isn't always necessary. Oftentimes, even in the East, the public land hunter can enjoy perfect solitude. But he needs to be aware that his solitude can be broken at any moment, and he needs to be ready to adapt to changing circumstances. And he also needs to be realistic in his expectations. If you've been watching a flock of turkeys feeding every morning in a meadow next to the parking lot of a state game management area, you can bet your ass that you're not the only person who's planning on working those birds. At daybreak on opening day, they'll be spooked into hiding.

The best public land hunters have a knack for anticipating what the other guys are going to do, which in turn enables them to anticipate what their quarry will do. When I was growing up in western Michigan, my family always hunted the Muskegon State Game Area in the Muskegon River marshes on the opener of the state's waterfowl season—right along with every other duck hunter within a 50-mile radius. You could consistently kill a limit of ducks within a few hours, but after that first day the marsh would become almost completely devoid of ducks. They simply packed up and flew away. Instead of sticking around there lamenting the lack of birds, my brothers and I would spend the next few days jump-shooting ducks off the surrounding potholes and marshes. These places we hit would have been empty of birds on the opener, but we knew from all of our wanderings in the woods that they filled up after the ducks got bumped off the Muskegon River marshes. Often, we had better hunts on the small surrounding ponds than we ever had in the marsh, thanks in large part to the hordes of competition that we cursed on opening day.

PRIVATE LAND

The easiest private land hunting permissions come through first- or second-degree personal connections. The familiarity helps ease the tension of the interaction. You know each other, or at least you know *of* each other, and so it's not such a leap for them to let you wander around on their land with a gun. Of the dozen or so active hunting permissions that I maintained as a kid around my home in Twin Lake, Michigan, 90 percent were on lands owned by acquaintances of my parents—or friends of those acquaintances. When you're thinking about finding permissions of your own, scour your mind for any and all connections you might have through immediate family, in-laws, neighbors, coworkers, and friends of friends, plus fellow members of clubs, churches, fraternal organizations, or sports teams. These connections are your best chance to get access to low-pressure hunting lands.

Securing a hunting permission from a complete stranger is ten times harder and twenty times less comfortable, but that doesn't mean it's impossible. In fact, I've done this many times, and have enjoyed some great hunting because of it. My friends and I refer to this method of gaining permission as "banging doors." To make it work, you need to know when to ask, how to ask, and what to ask.

The "when" portion of the equation refers to timing, both in terms of time of day and time of year. Obviously, you don't want to be that guy who scares the farmer's wife by banging on the door at 11:00 p.m. Rather than earning you a permission, that's likely to earn you an ass chewing. Instead, you should limit your landowner visits to business hours only. Some guys suggest that you try to fine-tune your visits to avoid a farmer's dinnertimes and his peak periods of work activity, but it's nearly impossible to anticipate such things and it can be like trying to hit a moving target. Instead, use common sense. Don't make a farmer shut down his combine in order to talk to you, but then don't make him uncomfortable by staring at him from the window of your truck for an hour while he repairs a section of fence.

As for the time of year, keep in mind that farmers and ranchers sometimes get so bombarded by hunters during hunting seasons that they begin to dread the sound of their own doorbell. A wise hunter pays visits to landowners during midsummer. This way, hunting season is close enough that the landowner doesn't feel as though you're talking about some abstract event in the distant future, but it's far enough away that he doesn't feel pressured to make an immediate decision. Under these circumstances a landowner might opt to defer his final answer until later, but that's fine. A month or two later, when you're a little closer to the season, you can remind the landowner about your previous visit and he's likely to treat you more charitably as a known person who had the courtesy to ask for hunting permission well in advance of the actual season.

When it comes to how you ask, think brevity and conciseness. The moment you walk up to a landowner's home and bang on the door, he's going to be wondering whether you're selling religion or fertilizer. Don't keep him guessing. Many articles on this subject suggest that you start out by complimenting the landowner on how beautiful the property is, but you just end up looking like a phony. Instead, say something simple like this: "Excuse me, ma'am. I'm sorry to bother you, but I wanted to ask about the possibility of doing some small game hunting on your property. I'm sure you get asked often, but I want you to know that I'm more than willing to return the favor by helping out with any chores or errands that might come up between now and hunting season." By coming right out and stating your purpose, you do risk getting shut down immediately. But I'd venture to say that any landowner who says no right away would have still said no if you'd started out by saying how beautiful the grain silo looks in the light of the setting sun.

The "what" portion of the equation refers to what kind of birds or animals you'd like to hunt. Small game hunting permissions are far easier to get on private land than are big game hunting permissions. Many landowners reserve the big game opportunities on their land for family and friends, and there is little or no room for outsiders. Typically, the more coveted the species, the less likely it is that a private landowner will give you permission to hunt it. Besides big game, these highly coveted species include pheasants, quail, and turkeys. Consider this when asking hunting permissions, and start by trying to get your foot in the door with a permission to hunt less universally admired critters, such as squirrels and rabbits.

I recently hunted sandhill cranes in the Texas Panhandle with a biology graduate student named Michael Panasci who'd been living in a nearby town for just a handful of years. Already he had lined up literally dozens of hunting permissions, and he estimated that he ran about a 90 percent success rate when asking permissions from complete strangers. The secret to his success was twofold. First, he had a very brief pitch that was clear and concise and that he could deliver even in situations when he was nervous. The pitch established his professional link to a nearby school, explained that he was a biologist, and clarified that he had plenty of references—all

The author with Michael Panasci. Michael has fantastic luck securing hunting permissions on private land. His strategy: be courteous and concise. He focuses on hunting for sandhill cranes, probably the best-tasting bird to ever fly. Notice Mike's decoys behind us and to the right. He makes his own decoys, or "stuffers," by curing the skins of birds that he's killed and stuffing them with wood and sprayable foam.

things that he chose because they helped to portray him as a trustworthy person.

Second, he started out by asking permission to hunt sandhill cranes, which group on the Panhandle by the tens of thousands in the winter. It's an intensely agricultural area, with lots of cotton, sorghum, and winter wheat, and the enormous flocks of cranes can have a devastating effect on the output of a field. Thus, by asking for the favor of a hunting permission, he was also offering the favor of pressuring the crane flocks off their crop fields. The approach helped to get him onto some prime hunting ground, and he was able to leverage those relationships into chances to hunt for everything from ducks to wild hogs.

By gaining an understanding of the ecology of your own hunting area, you can identify similar situations that might help in your own search for permissions. Feral pigeons can cause trouble for farmers who store grain, squirrels can cause trouble for corn farmers, Canada geese are troublesome to winter wheat farmers, and the list goes on and on. The key is to be creative and adaptive when approaching landowners. Don't just think that they are doing you a favor; instead, find ways to make it a symbiotic relationship.

Here, in one big handy list, are the absolute most important things to keep in mind when seeking hunting permission on private land. Some of this advice is applicable to situations where you're dealing with personal connec-

tions; all of it is applicable to dealing with strangers. Read it carefully and take it seriously.

- Vow to abide by all regulations, and then stay true to your word. Even if it's a seemingly silly law, like those stating that rifles and shotguns be cased at all times when inside a vehicle, adhere to it. Save the civil disobedience for your own land.

- Be specific about what you want to hunt. Don't say you're going to hunt squirrels and then come walking out of the woods with a dead rabbit—unless of course you were granted permission to hunt rabbits as well. Each landowner has idiosyncrasies about wildlife on his or her land, and it's your responsibility to find out what these are and then adhere to them.

- Tell the landowners when you want to hunt. If you say that you'll be hunting on Monday, then don't show up on Tuesday without checking in first. Maybe the landowner has given someone else hunting permission for that day, or maybe there will be a group of contract crop harvesters coming in and a hunter won't be welcome on the land that day. Eventually, most landowners will tell you to come and go as you please. But until then, don't make any assumptions.

- Tell the landowner who will be hunting, and then stick to what you said. This is the most common mistake that hunters make, and it infuriates landowners. If you ask permission for yourself, then don't bring along a buddy without checking to see if it's okay. One time my brother secured a great goose hunting permission from a wheat farmer whose crop was getting devastated by the birds. At the last minute, though, my brother decided to take me along. Our intention was to clear this with the landowner before we started hunting, but we never got a chance. When we pulled up with two guys in the truck, the landowner angrily kicked us off his property before we could open our mouths to explain.

- Go alone when you ask permission, even if you're hoping to get permission for more than one person. No one wants to be outnumbered by strangers on their own property.

- Ignore the above rule if you plan on hunting with your kids. In that case, absolutely bring them along. Families make people feel comfortable (at least in small doses), and many landowners would be pleased to know that they are facilitating positive, out-of-doors interactions between parents and children.

- If you're a man and your wife will be hunting with you, have her ask permission. If nothing else, the landowner will appreciate the novelty. And let's admit it—female strangers are typically less threatening than male strangers.

- Dress nicely, but not too nicely. If you just got done working and you're covered in paint or you smell like a deep fryer, get cleaned up first. But don't dress too nicely. Remember, you don't want to look like a salesman or like you're gonna start passing out religious pamphlets.

- Always look the landowner in the eye. Stand tall. Don't mumble, but speak firmly and confidently. Exercise politeness, but don't be an ass-kisser. If the answer is no, say thanks anyway. Finally, when the interaction is over, it's time to comment on how beautiful the property is. At this point the landowner might actually believe you.

I don't like to pay for hunting access, but sometimes a personal quest inspires me to bend my own rules. Such was the case when I decided to complete what's known as a Turkey Super Slam, which involves harvesting all five subspecies of the American turkey. After killing Merriam's, Eastern, and Rio Grande, I still had the Osceola and the Gould's turkey to go. Opportunities for Gould's turkey hunts are very limited in the United States, existing solely in New Mexico and Arizona. Instead, I turned my attention to Mexico, where the birds are abundant and hunts are widely available to those willing to pay. I hooked up with Jay Scott, from Colburn and Scott Outfitters, who leases some of the most beautiful Gould's country in all of Mexico. I have only hunted with guides a few times in my life, and this experience was the best by far. I harvested two Gould's turkeys, something I never would have done if I hadn't been willing to part with a little money.

THE HOWS AND WHYS OF HUNTING LICENSES AND REGULATIONS

Hunting is a highly regulated activity in the United States. Wildlife is managed at the state level, with state game agencies, supported by license sales, deciding who gets to hunt what, where, and how. These rules and regulations can and do change annually and are published in a booklet and online. Each state's regs are different, and it is the hunter's responsibility to get hold of a copy and study and know the laws inside and out. The information below is meant just as a primer, in order to introduce you to some of the lingo in your hunting regulations and to explain some of the thinking behind it.

LICENSES AND TAGS

One of the major differences in licenses is whether you are a resident or nonresident of the state you'll be hunting in. All states charge more for nonresident licenses than they do for resident licenses. In New York, for example, the cost of a resident small game license is $22, while a nonresident license is $100. Residents typically enjoy greater legal access to a state's population of big game than do nonresidents, but with small game things are fairly equal. Residents and nonresidents typically have the same seasons and bag limits.

No two states have the same licensing systems, but in general all you need is a small game license in order to hunt furred small game and upland birds. For turkey hunting, you typically need a small game license or a habitat improvement stamp of some sort in addition to a turkey tag or turkey permit, which is physically attached to the bird upon harvest. These tags usually have an additional fee, and one is required for each bird that you kill. (You need to get the tag or permit *before* you kill the bird.) Some states have an over-the-counter system of turkey tag allocation, where you can just go online or walk into a license vendor and buy a license and turkey tag. Other states have what's generally known as a draw. This is when tags are allocated to the public through a randomized drawing, or lottery.

Draws are necessary when the interest in a resource outweighs its ability to produce; that is, there are more guys who want to hunt turkeys than the population of turkeys can support. Often, though, turkey draws go undersubscribed. A state game agency may be awarding a hundred turkey tags for a specific portion of a state, yet only ninety guys apply for the drawing. Everyone gets a tag. In such cases, the lottery system serves to guarantee that only the most dedicated hunters who are willing to plan ahead and fill out their application on time will get turkey tags. Such hunts usually produce a quality experience with less hunting pressure, fewer people, and a greater chance at multiple mature gobblers.

Some turkey tags are pretty hard to draw, and you won't get lucky every year. Thankfully, many states use a bonus point or preference point system that rewards hunters who apply

every year. Basically, your name will go into the hat once for each year that you applied unsuccessfully. With this system, there aren't many areas in the country where you need to go more than a year or two without drawing a turkey tag. But again, lottery draws are an exception for turkey hunting. Typically, you can just buy a tag and go hunting.

Waterfowl hunting doesn't involve lottery draws, except in the rare instances where a state issues tags for tundra swans and/or sandhill cranes. But you do need your state's equivalent of a small game hunting license along with a state and federal duck stamp. Federal duck stamps have been $15 since 1991, though in 2014 they finally increased the cost to $25. This is a positive development, as the money all goes to wetlands conservation. State duck stamps are generally much cheaper. (You can find a more complete breakdown of waterfowl regulations and license requirements in the waterfowl portion of Section 3.)

SEASONS: This is an easy one. Basically, the season dates tell you when you can hunt. Most small game species have a single window when the season is open. For instance, the Michigan squirrel season runs from September 15 to March 1. Other critters have a more complex system, with multiple windows. Some states have an early Canada goose season, a regular goose season that is open for Canada and snow geese, and then a late winter and early spring season just for snow geese. It's common for states to run two separate turkey seasons, one in the spring and one in the fall. States will also further divide the spring turkey season into a handful of short seasons. Wisconsin runs a total of seven turkey seasons through the spring. There's a youth-only hunt during the second week of April, followed by six roughly week-long seasons that run all the way into late May. Each hunter's turkey tag will specify which season it is valid for; take this into account when applying for turkey tags, so that you get a season that meshes with your schedule.

BAG LIMITS AND POSSESSION LIMITS: With the exception of turkeys, a bag limit refers to how many of something you can harvest in a single day. Most bag limits are very straightforward: five squirrels, two sharp-tailed grouse, six rabbits. Others are a tad more complicated, as they might specify gender. Bag limits on pheasants are almost always for males only; it is generally illegal to kill a female pheasant. Waterfowl

A pair of hunters with their legal daily bag limit of turkeys. Notice the Gatorade bottle packed full of turkey giblets to be simmered in salted water for a camp meal.

bag limits are extremely complex. In Texas, for instance, you're allowed a total of six ducks in aggregate per day, though your six birds may not include more than two hen mallards or five mallards total, three wood ducks, three scaup, two redheads, two pintails, one canvasback, and one "dusky" duck, which includes mottled ducks, black ducks, and various hybrids.

A possession limit is the number of birds or animals you're allowed to have in your possession while in the field or in transit. It's usually two or three times the daily bag limit. Possession limits restrict how many game animals you can have in your possession until the animals are processed and reach their final destination—usually defined as the hunter's home. A hunting camp does not count as a final destination, unless of course you eat the animals there. At that point, they no longer count against your possession limit.

METHODS OF TAKE: This refers to how you're allowed to kill something. Methods of take are broken down according to weapon types: shotgun, archery, muzzle-loader, rimfire, centerfire, long gun, handgun, air gun, you name it. Some small game species, such as cottontail rabbits, might be open to any of the above methods of take. Others, such as turkeys or waterfowl, might be open to only archery or shotgun. Sometimes there will be additional restrictions that further specify shotgun gauges or centerfire caliber sizes.

OTHER LEGAL WILDLIFE SPECIES	Centerfire Rifle	Centerfire Handgun	Muzzleloading Rifle	Other Rifle Shooting Black Powder or Synthetic Black Powder	Black Powder Handgun	Crossbow	Archery	Handgun Shooting Shot	Shotgun Shooting Slugs	5 millimeter or .22 Magnum Rimfire	.17 Magnum and .22 Rimfire	Shotgun Shooting Shot	Falconry	Pneumatic Weapons	Slingshots	Pursuit with Dogs	Trapping
BADGER	✔	✔	✔	✔	✔	✔	✔	✔	✔	✔	✔	✔		✔		✔	✔
BLUE GROUSE						✔	✔	✔				✔	✔	✔		✔	
BOBCAT	✔	✔	✔	✔	✔	✔	✔	✔	✔	✔	✔	✔		✔		✔	✔
CHUKAR PARTRIDGE						✔	✔	✔				✔	✔	✔		✔	
COATI	✔	✔	✔	✔	✔	✔	✔	✔	✔	✔	✔	✔	✔	✔	✔	✔	✔
COTTONTAIL RABBIT	✔	✔	✔	✔	✔	✔	✔	✔	✔	✔	✔	✔	✔	✔	✔	✔	
COYOTE	✔	✔	✔	✔	✔	✔	✔	✔	✔	✔	✔	✔		✔		✔	✔
CROW	✔	✔	✔	✔	✔	✔	✔	✔	✔	✔	✔	✔	✔	✔	✔	✔	✔
EUROPEAN STARLING	✔	✔	✔	✔	✔	✔	✔	✔	✔	✔	✔	✔	✔	✔	✔	✔	✔
FOXES	✔	✔	✔	✔	✔	✔	✔	✔	✔	✔	✔	✔		✔		✔	✔
HOUSE SPARROW	✔	✔	✔	✔	✔	✔	✔	✔	✔	✔	✔	✔	✔	✔	✔	✔	✔
JACKRABBITS	✔	✔	✔	✔	✔	✔	✔	✔	✔	✔	✔	✔	✔	✔	✔	✔	✔
PHEASANT						✔	✔	✔				✔	✔	✔		✔	
QUAIL						✔	✔	✔				✔	✔	✔		✔	
RACCOON	✔	✔	✔	✔	✔	✔	✔	✔	✔	✔	✔	✔		✔		✔	✔
RINGTAIL	✔	✔	✔	✔	✔	✔	✔	✔	✔	✔	✔	✔		✔		✔	✔
RODENTS (excluding beaver, muskrats, tree squirrels & porcupines)	✔	✔	✔	✔	✔	✔	✔	✔	✔	✔	✔	✔	✔	✔	✔	✔	✔
SKUNKS	✔	✔	✔	✔	✔	✔	✔	✔	✔	✔	✔	✔		✔		✔	✔
SQUIRREL General	✔	✔	✔	✔	✔	✔	✔	✔	✔	✔	✔	✔	✔	✔	✔	✔	
Archery Only							✔									✔	

LEGAL METHODS OF TAKE

Each state's hunting regulations will include rules about methods of take. Above is Arizona's published breakdown of legal methods of take for small game. (Source: Arizona Game and Fish Department)

BASICS OF MARKSMANSHIP AND SHOOTING

BASICS OF WINGSHOOTING

Knocking a fast-flying bird out of the sky with a shotgun is one of the greatest challenges in hunting. Doing it once or twice a season is tough enough; doing it consistently from one year to the next, with a variety of species, can seem damn near impossible. In fact, achieving a base level of proficiency with a shotgun is much more difficult than with a rifle. That's because wingshooting—the art of hitting flying targets with a shotgun—occurs on a much more instinctive level. When shooting a rifle, there's usually time to adjust your form and to correct mistakes before they happen. With a shotgun, there isn't. Once your quarry flushes into the air, you have seconds at most to shoulder your piece and fire. Lots can go wrong, and it usually does. You grip your shotgun too tight and it twists off target as you pull the trigger. Or you don't get a proper lead by swinging the shotgun through the fast-moving target and your load passes through the vacated airspace in the bird's wake. Or you simply miscalculate the speed, angle, and distance of the bird and your shot is wildly off. The only way to get really good with a shotgun is to spend a lot of time shooting clay targets at the range. It takes dozens of hours of practice and hundreds of rounds of ammunition just to get good enough that you don't totally suck. Or as my bird hunting buddy Ronny Boehme puts it, "If you can't hit a clay target, you're never gonna hit a bird." Here's a quick checklist to keep in mind the next time you have a nanosecond or two to drop a ruffed grouse that's about to fly into a thick patch of . . . oops. He's already gone.

GRIP: Not too tight, not too loose. With the trigger hand, think of a comfortable

handshake. You want your thumb rolled over the top of the grip, not resting on top of it. When it's time to fire, use the fleshy part of your fingertip, just above the last joint, to pull the trigger. Your forearm hand should cradle the forearm of the shotgun comfortably, with a gentle grip.

SHOULDERING THE GUN: When raising the shotgun to fire, the forearm hand pushes the gun out and up toward the target. The trigger hand simply raises the stock up to your face. All the while, remain focused on the target. Let the bead of the shotgun enter your sight picture without moving your eyes to find it. Unless you're shooting directly overhead, your weight should shift to your front foot as you "lean into" the gun. For overhead shots, keep your weight on the rear foot and move the forearm hand toward the body and the stock of the shotgun for a more comfortable position.

FOOT AND BODY POSITION: Physically, positioning is tough to master. At a shooting range, you're typically on flat ground with plenty of time to assume the proper stance. In the field, game has a way of flushing at the worst times: while you're making your way over rocks, crawling under downed trees, or trying to extricate your hat from a grabby patch of briars. The trick is determining how long you have to prepare for the shot, and then doing as much as you can to assume the proper position before it's too late. Ideally, you'll end up with your front knee slightly bent and rear leg straight. For foot

placement (for a right-handed shooter), imagine that you're standing on the face of a clock with your target out beyond the twelve o'clock position. Your left foot should be pointing to about eleven o'clock, your right foot to about two o'clock. Heavyset shooters tend to find their most comfortable position by squaring off to the target even more, lessening the angle.

THE SWING-THROUGH METHOD

MAKING THE SHOT: Here, of course, is where things get tricky. You're trying to connect pellets that will be flying at about 800 miles an hour with a target that might be going 40 or more miles per hour. Causing the two things to collide in midair (or on the ground, in the case of rabbits) requires significant skill. Most hunters use a shooting method called swing-through or pass-through. The gun is inserted into the hunter's sight picture behind the traveling target. The hunter then swings the shotgun through the target's flight path in a smooth arc. The swing continues through the target in a contin-

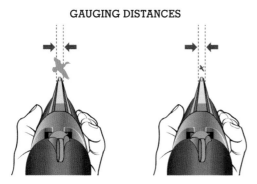

Learn to use your shotgun's muzzle as a rangefinder. A duck whose body appears to be bigger than the muzzle of a 12-gauge might be in range; a duck whose body is smaller than the muzzle may be out of range

uous motion, with the muzzle of the barrel acting like a brush that is going to sweep the target out of the sky. For close-range shooting, the trigger is pulled just as the muzzle passes the bird's head. For longer shoots, the trigger pull comes after the muzzle has passed the bird by a distance that is one, two, or three times the length of the bird's body. Sometimes fast-flying ducks and geese at distances of 50 or 60 yards are killed with leads the length of a car. One time, after my buddy Ronny Boehme dropped a high-flying Canada goose, he jokingly estimated his lead as "about a Greyhound bus." Unfortunately, there is no formula or rule that can help you calculate lead distances. These

By looking at a shot pattern on a paper target, it's easy to imagine that a shotgun shoots out a one-dimensional disc of shot that resembles a Frisbee composed of pellets. In truth, a shotgun puts out a "string" of shot that brings to mind a cartoonist's rendition of a swarm of bees. All of the pellets do not arrive at the target at the same time. When shooting at a flying bird, imagine that you want the bird to fly into the middle of that string.

are decisions that are made instinctively, in the heat of the moment. Again, the key to successful wingshooting is practice, practice, practice.

MARKSMANSHIP WITH A RIFLE (OR AIR GUN)

Practice makes perfect. This saying holds very true concerning our ability to make a good, lethal shot on an animal with a rifle. Our hunting ethics dictate that we respect the animal enough to know our limits and capabilities when considering a shot. There is no substitute for trigger time. This can be as easy as dry-firing your rifle at home. This allows you to

On left, offhand position; top right, prone position; bottom right, sitting position

practice your body positioning, the trigger pull, breathing, and follow-through. Live rounds are even better, so spending time at your local range is imperative. At the range, make sure to practice shooting from all positions, not just from the rest on the bench. Bench shooting is great for properly zeroing your rifle, but it has little resemblance to real-world small game hunting situations. To practice for the real thing, you want to work on prone, seated, kneeling, and standing shots without the use of a rest. But the really important thing is to learn to shoot well with improvised rests such as walking sticks, tree limbs, fence posts, and downed logs. I have killed many squirrels and rabbits with a .22, and I'd bet that I used an improvised rest on over 75 percent of the shots I've taken.

When you are shooting, your focus must be on the shot alone. I like to run through a brief checklist in my mind just before taking the shot.

- Do I have a good rest?
- Is my breathing under control?
- Is my grip on my rifle secure, but not so strong that it torques the rifle?
- What is my point of impact? Have I picked the exact spot where I want my bullet to go?

Improvised rest

AFTER THE SHOT: HOW TO RECOVER DOWNED GAME

You made the shot, and the bird crumpled and fell toward the ground. If you're lucky, recovery will be as simple as walking over there and picking it up. Often, though, things are much more tricky than that. Recovery can be hard, time-consuming work when hunting in brushy or swampy areas where downed small game can be hidden from sight. Here are some tips to help you recover more game and bring more meat to the table.

1. If you connect on a shot, carefully mark the location of your downed quarry before taking a second shot at another bird or animal. Getting doubles is great, but don't do it at the expense of losing an animal.

2. Before moving from your shooting position, make sure you've memorized the location where you think your quarry fell. Also mark the place where you were standing when you shot.

3. If you've got a buddy with you, have him stand in the place where you shot so that he can guide you to your mark. Or else stay in your shooting position and guide your buddy to the mark. Being off in your search by just 10 feet can make a huge difference, so precision really matters here. If by chance you don't recover your game immediately, go back to your original shooting location and replay the shot in your head. This often helps to adjust your area searching to come up with the animal.

4. Keep the concept of inertia in your head. If you saw a speeding mallard crumple from a shot as he flew past a snag on an old cottonwood tree, remember that his body probably didn't hit the ground until he was 10 or 20 yards past that point.

5. Look for blood. Small animals bleed just like big ones, and following a micro blood trail can lead to meat.

6. Look for feathers. A cluster of feathers that appear to have drifted to the ground can tell you where a bird was hit in the air. Feathers that are matted and plastered to the forest floor can tell you where a bird hit the ground. Lots of feathers and no bird might mean that the bird walked away. If so, keep searching.

7. When hunting furred game, a tuft of fur usually pinpoints the location where the animal was when it was hit. Look for more tufts of fur on nearby brush to show which direction it traveled.

8. Use ever-widening circles to search. If the bird or rabbit isn't exactly where you thought it would be, mark that spot with your hat, and walk circles until you find it. The central location of your hat keeps you focused on the right area and you're less likely to wander off course.

9. Be ready for follow-up shots. Especially with waterfowl, whose feathers deflect much of the energy from shotgun pellets. Keep your gun loaded until you have your hands on the quarry. Many wounded ducks have escaped in the time that it takes a hunter to walk to his blind to retrieve more shells.

10. Dead animals don't always fall from the sky directly to the ground. Many birds and especially squirrels often get hung up in the notches and forks of tree limbs. When the search for a downed animal is getting tough, remember to look up; what you're looking for might be dangling right above your head.

11. Get a dog. Even a poorly trained dog has better sensory perception than you. If you take the time to train your dog right, nearly all your game will be recovered.

A Basic Glossary of Small Game Hunting Methods

It's been speculated by anthropologists that human language came as a result of our need to organize hunting activities. As hunters, we rely on a commonality of terms in order to share information, swap stories, and ask questions. When one of us says something, it's helpful if the rest of us know what he or she is talking about. To that end, here's a basic rundown of methods and strategies used by small game hunters: still-hunting, spot-and-stalk hunting, jump-shooting (or flushing), drive hunting, ambush hunting, and calling/decoying.

If there's a problem with such a rundown, it's that it attempts to categorize all hunts under this small handful of terms. Rarely do things happen so cleanly. You and a buddy might head out to decoy some mallards and then notice a few ducks landing in a small backwater off the river. On the way home, you make a detour to kick up those ducks and try to get a shot at them as they fly off. Thus, your decoy hunt has suddenly turned into a jump-shoot.

Of course, most hunters would never think of things in this way. When you're hunting, they'd say, you do what makes the most sense in the moment. That's very true. Still, it's good to know the lingo. If you're going to break the rules, you at least ought to know what they are. Below are the basic hunting methods, explained through in-the-field scenarios.

STILL-HUNTING

Still-hunting is the most basic hunting method, because that's pretty much what you're doing when you take a quiet and slow walk through the woods in search of game. In the situation on the next page, a hunter in a northern state is doing some late winter still-hunting for snowshoe hares with a .22 rifle. There's more than three feet of snow on the ground, and he's wearing snowshoes to keep afloat on the surface. His hunting location is a network of

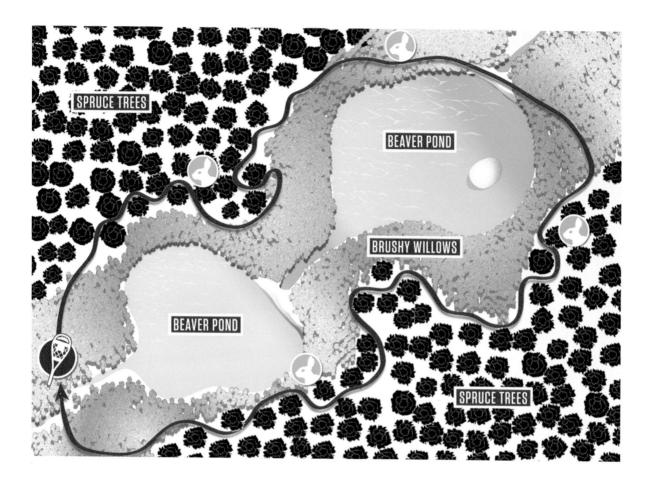

SPRUCE TREES

BEAVER POND

BRUSHY WILLOWS

BEAVER POND

SPRUCE TREES

beaver ponds where hares often congregate in good numbers to feed on willow shoots when other food sources are buried under snow. A few more inches of powder came down the day before—perfect conditions—and he's surprised by the abundance of fresh tracks that were laid down in the last twelve hours. The bulk of the tracks seem to be congregated along the seam between the surrounding spruce forest and the willow stands along the creek and beaver ponds. There are too many tracks to simply follow a single animal, as every set of tracks gets confused and lost beneath the others. Instead, the hunter moves very slowly along the seam. He's not trying to flush a hare—it'd be gone without him getting a shot if it took off in a hurry. Instead, it's his intent to spot the hares before they take off and then make head shots on them with his .22. He takes just a step or two between stops, studying the undergrowth and peering beneath every overhanging limb. It takes him several hours to cover just a mile of terrain as he works downstream, crosses on a beaver dam, and then hunts his way back upstream.

JUMP-SHOOTING/FLUSHING

Jump-shooting and flushing have slightly different connotations. Jump-shooting generally refers to kicking ducks and geese up off the water and then taking flying-away shots at the birds. Flushing implies upland game, flushed out of heavy cover. But despite these casual differences, the concepts are very similar in practice.

In the scenario at right, a hunter and her Lab are working some old clear-cuts and abandoned farmstead properties for ruffed grouse and woodcock in late September. The hunter has yet to hit this location this year. She has no idea where the birds might be hanging around. So, rather than working just one type of cover, she's going to sample around and hit as many different microhabitats as possible in hopes of kicking up a couple of birds. If she gets one, she can examine the crop to see what it's been eating. This will help her better narrow down the search for more birds, because all she has to do is find more sources of the chosen food—something that's easier than searching for birds from scratch.

There are still some leaves on the trees, which makes it difficult to see any appreciable distance. She tries to stay out in the open as much as possible, where it's more likely that she'll actually catch a glimpse of a flushing bird. Meanwhile, her dog works the thick edges of cover that she's paralleling. If the dog flushes a grouse or woodcock, the bird will likely escape by flying out through more open cover rather than trying to blast deeper into the thickets where it's been feeding. The hunter's route takes her along the cut edge of a power line, along a brushy creek channel, along the edges of an old apple orchard, and around a Christmas tree plantation. All are likely places for a game bird to hide and, she hopes, flush.

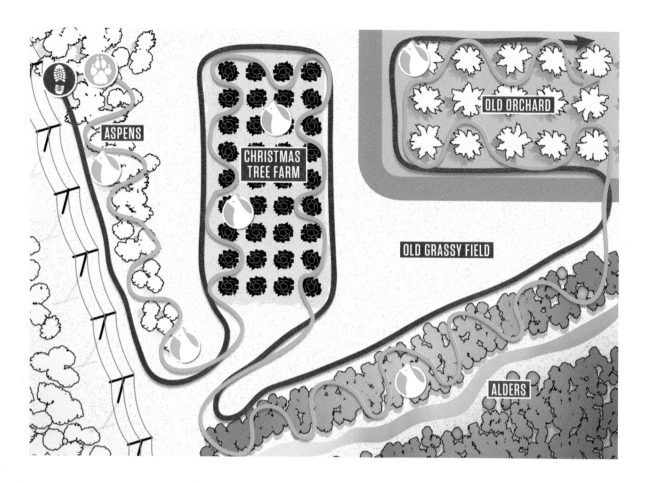

ASPENS

CHRISTMAS TREE FARM

OLD ORCHARD

OLD GRASSY FIELD

ALDERS

SPOT AND STALK

With an hour to go before this hunter needs to be at school, he starts to walk back from where he was trying to call a stubborn tom that he's been working for the last two weeks. It's the last day of the season, and on his way back to the truck he's surprised to see the gobbler with a small flock of hens at the back end of a crop field near its border with a woodlot. There's no time to try to set up and call the bird, so he plans a stalk instead. Using a brushy ditchrow for cover, he gets as close as he can. From here, he'll have to belly-crawl through the water in

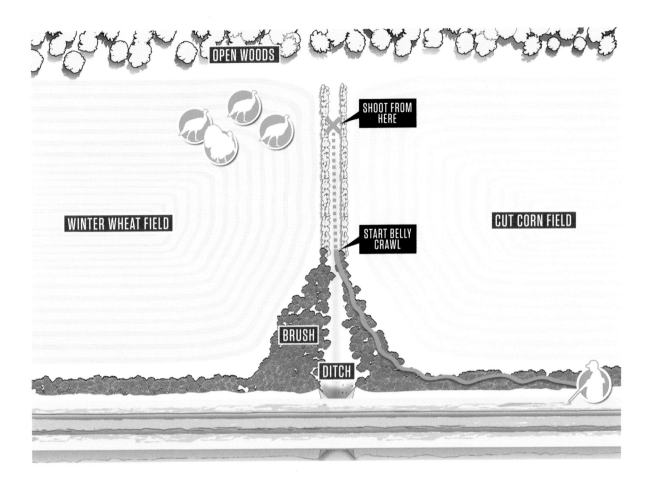

OPEN WOODS

SHOOT FROM HERE

WINTER WHEAT FIELD

CUT CORN FIELD

START BELLY CRAWL

BRUSH

DITCH

the bottom of the ditch or risk getting busted by the wary bird. With a range finder, he takes a distance reading on both the woodlot and the turkeys. He calculates that the tom is about 75 yards shy of the woods. As he crawls his way up the ditch, he keeps checking his distance from the woodlot. When he's 75 yards away, he knows that he's just about even with where he last spotted the tom. Now he can pop up out of the ditch and make a quick shot.

A group of three hunters has watched at least a half dozen male pheasants, or roosters, fly into a brushy windrow between two fields. From past experience, they know that this windrow is a very difficult place to hunt. When they try to flush the pheasants, the birds are almost impossible to get into the air. Instead, the birds simply run ahead and make it into the next patch of cover without ever offering a shot. A dog might be able to catch up to the birds and force them into the

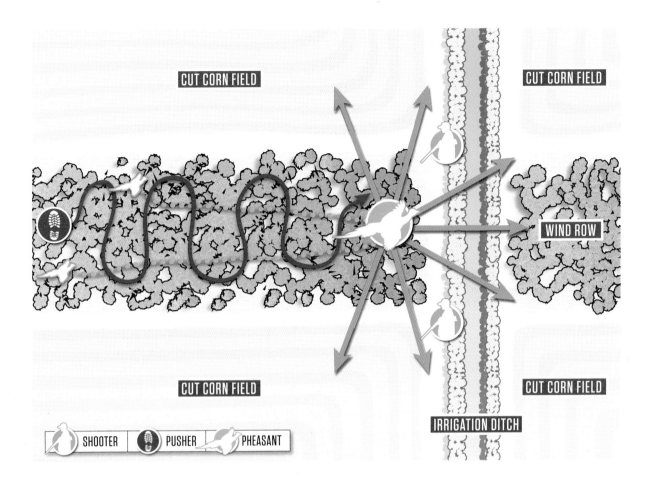

CUT CORN FIELD · CUT CORN FIELD · WIND ROW · CUT CORN FIELD · IRRIGATION DITCH · CUT CORN FIELD

SHOOTER · PUSHER · PHEASANT

air, but they don't have a dog. Instead they hatch another plan. Two of the hunters will sneak around to the end of the windrow and position themselves on either side of it. The third hunter will then start pushing, or driving, the pheasants toward his waiting partners. The roosters will try to do their usual trick, which is to run ahead, but this time they'll bump into the standing hunters and be forced into the air. The standers will most likely get the shooting, but there's a good chance that the birds will fly back in the other direction and give the driver a chance at them as well.

AMBUSH HUNTING

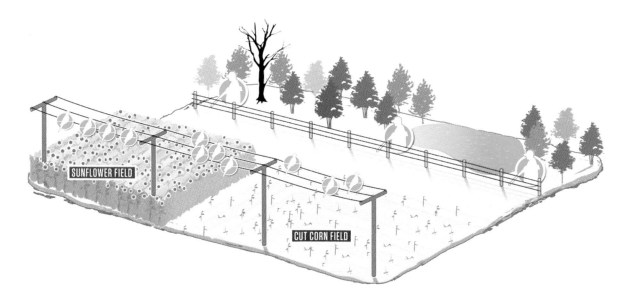

SUNFLOWER FIELD

CUT CORN FIELD

To ambush something is to lie in wait and let it come to you. That's just what these dove hunters intend to do. They've selected a hiding position where they can have their back to the dove roosting areas provided by the mesquite thickets behind them. Mixed in with the mesquite are a few stock tanks, perfect for attracting birds who will come to water in the afternoon before roosting. In front of them is plenty of dove feed; farther out, a power line provides daytime perches. With evening coming on, the hunters don't need to do anything but wait patiently and let the birds come to them.

CALLING AND DECOYING

Unlike the dove hunters mentioned above, this duck hunter isn't nearly so cocky as to think that the birds he's after will be coming into his selected pond. There are dozens of similar ponds in the area, and this one isn't particularly special. In order to draw birds in, he's going to have to sweeten the deal for them and provide both visual and audio stimulation. The visual stimulation comes from the spread of decoys that he's got in the pond. Ducks flying overhead will see the birds and be soothed into thinking it's a safe place to land. The additional audio enticement comes from a mouth-blown duck call.

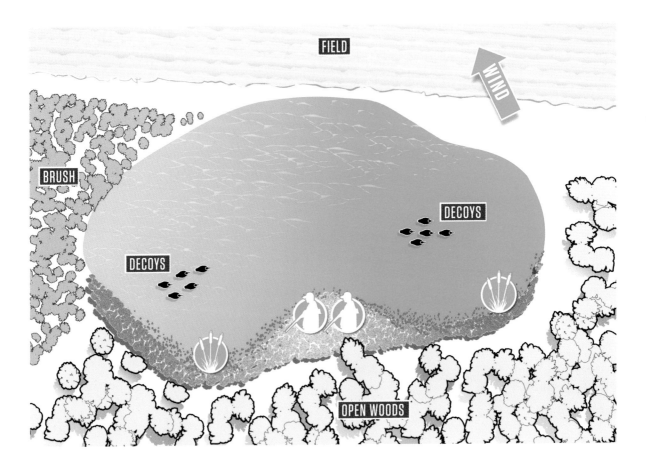

SPECIES

THE WILD TURKEY

WILD TURKEY
Meleagris gallopavo
A.K.A.: Gobblers

Wild turkeys are the big game of the small game world. Weighing upward of 25 pounds, a mature bird is capable of supplying multiple meals for even a large family. While many states have fall turkey hunting seasons, hunting for these birds is generally regarded as a spring activity. April or May brings on their breeding season. This is the time of year when males fill the woods with the sounds of their raucous and unmistakable gobbles, which serve to both attract females and challenge rival gobblers, or toms. If there's a mistake that beginner turkey hunters make, it's thinking that these boisterous birds are easy prey.

Sure, the turkeys running around the enforced no-hunting zone of your suburb or golf course might seem half tame. But the gobblers that make their living out in the wild, where hunters pursue them on a regular basis, become the smartest and wariest creatures in the woods. Becoming a successful turkey hunter requires a mastery of turkey language and also a solid understanding of stealth and camouflage. But the effort is well worth it. Handled properly, the flesh of wild turkeys is well flavored, tender, and versatile.

BARROOM BANTER: At the time of European contact, wild turkeys occupied a land area that today covers thirty-nine states; by the early 1900s they had been extirpated from over half of that. Now, thanks to the efforts of organizations such as the National Wild Turkey Federation, the turkey has completely recovered—and then some. Forty-nine states—all but Alaska—have regulated turkey seasons. (There are substantiated rumors that wild turkeys can now be found on Alaska's Kenai Peninsula, so someday we may have turkey seasons in all fifty states.) Considering the great abundance of turkeys in the United States, it's hard to believe that about 50 percent of all turkey nests are destroyed by predators. And of the polts that do hatch, well below 50 percent will live long enough to turn one year old. From there, things don't get any easier for turkeys. A study in Kentucky showed that 70 percent of the male turkeys that reach two years of age are killed by hunters every spring. Despite the high attrition, turkey populations remain strong across the United States, and the long-term viability of turkeys and turkey hunting looks great.

Another interesting thing about turkeys is the breast sponge, a spongy layer of fat that sits above the bird's breast. An adult gobbler's breast sponge is most fully developed right before breeding season, when it might account for 10 percent of the bird's total weight. (It is not nearly so prevalent in a one-year-old tom, called a jake.) The reserves in the breast sponge allow a gobbler to devote all his ener-

gies to breeding without needing to worry about eating. That is why you so rarely kill a spring gobbler with a full crop. They just do not eat all that much in the spring.

PHYSICAL CHARACTERISTICS: Largest game bird in North America. Males stand 46 inches tall and average around 20 pounds. Females stand 37 inches tall and average around 10 pounds. Both sexes appear generally dark in color, but on closer inspection they have an array of iridescent colors including bronze, green, and copper. Wings have bold barring of white or cream; rump and tail feathers are tipped with white or cream. The necks and heads of turkeys are slender, generally featherless, and reddish in color; the heads of males can change colors from blue to red, depending on their mood. Males have spurred legs and a feather tuft, or beard, protruding from their chest. Beards on mature males can be 10 inches or longer. Perhaps as many as 15 percent of hens will have a beard as well, though they are generally much thinner and less conspicuous than the beards of males.

Traditionally there are a number of turkey subspecies that are recognized by hunters and biologists: the Eastern turkey of the eastern United States, the Osceola turkey of Florida, and the Merriam's, Rio Grande, and Gould's turkeys of the West and Southwest. Each variant has its own subtle differences in appearance, though it usually requires a trained eye to tell them apart.

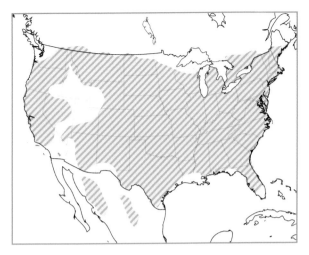

HABITAT: Turkeys occur in a wide variety of habitat types, from desert riparian zones to the Florida savanna. They generally require open ground for feeding and mating, and denser forested areas for evading predators and roosting. The species does particularly well in areas of mixed agriculture, particularly with brushy or timbered riparian zones.

TELLTALE SIGN: Look for tracks, feathers, salad-bowl-sized dusting bowls, scratch marks from feeding on the forest floor, and wing-tip drag marks on dusty roads or field edges where gobblers strut during breeding season.

DIET: Widely varied. Acorns, beechnuts, and other hard mast; fruits and seeds; a wide variety of grasses, forbs, and shrubs; agricultural crops such as wheat, corn, sorghum, and rye; insects, small reptiles, snails, and even rodents.

LIFE AND DEATH: Life span is typically three to five years, though some turkeys live much longer. Nest raiders such as snakes, foxes, skunks, crows, ravens, raccoons, black bears, and coyotes prey on the unhatched. In addition to those predators, hawks, owls, bobcats, and mountain lions will snatch young birds and sometimes adults.

BREEDING AND REPRODUCTION: Mating season can be as early as February in some southern areas, though April and May are the most common breeding months. Hens lay an average of twelve eggs, usually laying one per day. Incubation begins when all eggs are laid, in order to synchronize hatching. The incubation period is twenty-eight days.

EDIBILITY: Breast is tender white meat. Thighs, legs, and wings are tougher dark meat. Turkeys can be roasted or smoked whole, but many careful wild game cooks handle the light and dark meat differently. Turkey giblets—the gizzard, liver, and heart—are excellent.

HUNTING OPPORTUNITIES: Hunting is available in forty-nine states. Sometimes there is a lottery, but in most cases tags are sold over-the-counter or included with the purchase of an upland game license. There is wide availability, with separate spring and fall seasons. Spring hunts are usually only for male turkeys, while fall hunts typically allow for both sexes to be harvested.

HUNTING METHODS: During spring turkey seasons, hunters are limited to gobblers. For that reason we'll be dealing solely with the pursuit of male turkeys in this discussion of spring methods. While it's possible to kill gobblers in a variety of ways, including ambush-

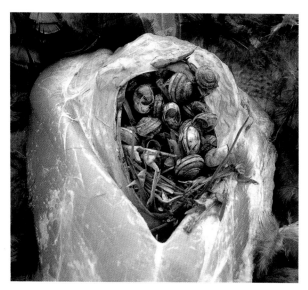

Turkeys are omnivorous; you never know what they might be eating. Colorado hunter Brody Henderson was surprised to find this turkey's crop packed full of snails.

Turkeys are big and they have big hearts; simmer these in lightly salted water for a nice camp snack.

ing them along travel corridors and in feeding areas, turkey hunters who want to consistently kill turkeys from one year to the next should learn to target gobblers by calling and decoying the birds into range of either a bow or shotgun.

Below I'll break the process of hunting turkeys into five steps: (1) locating a gobbler, (2) approaching a gobbler, (3) setting up on a gobbler, (4) calling a gobbler, and (5) shooting a gobbler.

LOCATING A GOBBLER: This step should begin with preseason scouting. The first day of your hunt is no time to wonder if a particular woodlot or valley has a population of resident turkeys. Scout prospective locations for evidence of turkeys or the actual turkeys themselves. Make careful note of roost trees, feeding areas, and travel routes. Scouting trips can

be as easy as driving around on forest service access roads or as involved as multi-day backpack trips through likely turkey country. When scouting, don't worry if you're only seeing hens. As long as you find the females, or hens, you can be fairly certain that some toms are already in the immediate area or will be in the area once the spring breeding season approaches.

On an actual hunt, plan on spending a lot of time using your ears to find gobblers. Toms can be vocal at any time during the day, but they make the most noise in the early morning darkness. If you're in the woods two hours before daylight, you are not wasting your time. Focus your listening efforts near the roosting areas that you identified while scouting, and try to position yourself in places where you're most likely to pick up distant sounds. Avoid listening near busy roads or noisy streams. Instead, seek out quiet locations on hilltops, ridgelines, or timber edges where you can maximize the amount of area that you're "covering" with your ears.

If you're not hearing any birds, you can try "shock-gobbling" a tom. In the spring, male turkeys will often gobble at any loud noise they hear. It's not entirely clear why they do this; the game call maker Will Primos has suggested that it's simply a turkey's way of announcing that it's his time of year. Most often, hunters will shock-gobble toms by using calls that mimic the natural sounds of coyotes, crows, red-tailed hawks, or barred owls. However, the slamming of a car door or a loud yell is just as likely to elicit a gobble—though such unnatural sounds might also notify the turkey that a hunter is lurking nearby. When using shock-gobble calls, make sure that the sounds you're making are short. If a call is too long, you risk drowning out an immediate reply from a gobbler. Personally, I like to use a crow call. Crows are quite common throughout most of the turkey's range, so it's not a foreign sound to the birds. And since crows don't kill turkeys, it's probably not as alarming to the birds as the yip of a coyote. (Coyotes are avid turkey hunters; in coyote country, you're just as likely to call in a coyote as a turkey when you're mimicking the sounds of a hen turkey.) A crow call makes a quick, crisp noise with a clean finish; you can hit two notes in rapid succes-

sion and then listen for a reply. Avoid blowing your call too much. Once every five minutes as you move through turkey country is plenty enough. And once you get a reply from a bird with a shock call, resist the temptation to keep hitting the bird with a call over and over again. Excessive calling, no matter the form, will turn a bird off. Also remember to listen carefully after loud noises that you didn't make. There have been many times when I haven't been able to get any responses from my crow and owl calls, and then suddenly I'll hear a bird gobble to the sound of thunder or the distant bark of a dog.

Once you hear a gobble, whether it comes naturally or at the behest of a crow call, try to determine the bird's exact location. Move around a bit and listen to the bird from different angles in order to fix its position. In the open country of the West, a turkey's gobble can carry a long way, but in the denser cover of the East, a gobbling turkey is often much closer than you think it is. Move with caution as you try to fix a bird's location. You don't want to spook it before you ever get a chance to try calling it in. If it's in the evening and the bird has roosted, it will remain in that location until daybreak. Plan on returning well before dawn in order to get set up for an early morning hunt. If you hear a gobbler in the pre-morning darkness, keep in mind that the bird will probably be pitching out of his roost as soon as there's enough light to see. The exact

In the dry, open country of the West, a turkey's gobble can sometimes be heard from a mile or more away. These Montana hunters are working their way toward a distant though highly vocal tom; with luck, they will sneak in within 100 or so yards before they start calling.

time that a gobbler will leave his roost is hard to pin down. Wind, temperature, and fog all seem to affect a turkey's schedule. A frigid and windy day might keep a gobbler in his roost quite a bit longer than he'd stay up there on a warm, calm day.

Use your eyes as much as your ears when trying to locate a gobbler. For whatever reason, a lot of toms are reluctant to make noise— perhaps they learned their lesson over past hunting seasons, when trouble seemed to materialize in the form of a hunter every time they opened their beak to gobble. It's quite common to locate gobblers using a set of bin-oculars, particularly if you spend time on high overlooks or where you can watch field edges or multiple travel routes from a single observation point. Glassing for birds generally works better in the open country of the West than it does in the East, but it's a reliable tactic either way. Carefully study field edges and other turkey hangouts from a distance before you go traipsing through. If you visually pinpoint a gobbler, you can try working the bird using the same methods that you'd use if you heard it gobble.

APPROACHING A GOBBLER: Sometimes you'll hear a gobble that's so close—say, 100 yards or less in wooded cover, even farther away in open country—that you can't risk moving out of fear that you'll spook the bird. In these cases, it's best to immediately take a position against a tree or other backdrop and hold tight. The bird could be headed your way, and you don't want to let your movements scare it off. At other times, you might hear a gobbler that's pretty far away. Such situations present you with a conundrum. Some turkey hunters take an aggressive approach and try to close as much distance as possible between themselves and the gobbler. Other hunters are more cautious, preferring to hold tight and start calling even if the bird is several hundred yards away. Personally, I like to move toward gobblers whenever possible. Not only do I enjoy sneaking in on turkeys just for the fun of it, I also find that toms are much more receptive to calling once you violate their personal space and get so close that they simply cannot ignore your calling.

There's an art to approaching a turkey that you intend to call in. First off, you need to practice utmost stealth. Under no circumstances should you give the bird a chance to see or hear you. If it does, the game is over. Use brush, timber, or topography to shield your movements from the bird. Second, it's difficult to guess exactly where the bird is. Humidity, denseness of cover, and what direction the tom happens to be facing when it gobbles can all create a lot of confusion about where the

bird happens to be. And keep in mind that the turkey is likely to move around a bit. Even if your original guess about his whereabouts is correct, the reality on the ground will be shifting all the time as the bird feeds or pursues mates. There have been several times when I was putting a slip on a turkey that seemed to be gobbling from a fixed position a couple hundred yards away when I happened to run smack into the bird. In these situations, when you and a turkey surprise each other, killing the bird is out of the question. It'll be gone before you're able to throw the safety switch on your shotgun.

Knowing how close you can get to a gobbler takes time and practice. Only the birds themselves can teach you what you can and can't get away with. Plus, each situation is different with regard to ground cover, topography, and the wariness of the birds. I have slipped within shooting distance of many turkeys without the birds knowing I was there, but admittedly it's usually happened in remote Western locations where the turkeys receive little hunting pressure. In high-pressure areas typical of the eastern United States, you need to be a lot more conservative. If you can get within 100 yards of a turkey without spooking it, consider yourself lucky. In many situations, even getting within 300 or 400 yards is out of the question due to open, flat terrain that provides no plausible routes for a stalk. In thick cover it's often possible to get closer than 100 yards, but I rarely find myself getting closer than 75 yards to where I suspect a bird to be hanging around. At that distance, there's just too much that can go wrong. Rather than risk getting closer, you should find a place to get set up.

SETTING UP ON A GOBBLER: You need to put a lot of thought into your setup before you start calling to a turkey. You'll hear from plenty of hunters who will claim to have done things like killing a turkey while wearing a white T-shirt, but those guys are no different from the jackasses who brag about someone's grandpa living to be ninety years old despite smoking three packs of cigarettes a day. They are in love with the exceptions and blind to the norms. When picking your calling location, you should consider approachability, visibility, and concealment. By approachability, I mean the gobbler's ability to approach you. The way things typically work in the turkey world is that a hen will travel to a gobbler when she is ready to be fertilized. By attempting to lure a gobbler to you, you're subverting that arrangement. So you need to make sure that the gobbler has a fairly easy avenue of approach to reach you. You don't want to set up deep inside a thicket where the turkey can't see what he's getting into. And you shouldn't expect the turkey to cross marshes, creeks, or multiple fence-rows. The bird is perfectly capable of doing any of these things if he wants to, but it should be your priority to make things as simple as possible for him. Offer him an easy, safe way to reach you and your job as a hunter will be easier. Remember, gobblers are paranoid. Give them a reason to ignore your call and they'll happily take it.

Not only does the gobbler need to be able to reach you, you need to be able to see it coming. As I mentioned above, turkeys usually prefer to travel the route of least resistance. You want to be able to cover the obvious travel routes that a bird might use to reach you. But also keep in mind that turkeys will surprise you. For every ten that walk the trail, there's one who'd rather bushwhack through a hell-hole of multiflora rose than walk down a road. It's out of the question that you'll always be able to cover 360° of your surroundings, particularly because you'll usually want to sit against a backdrop such as a tree or bush for enhanced concealment. That backdrop is going to impair your vision, and so are the myriad other stationary objects—trees, fence posts, ditches, windrows, thickets—that tend to surround you in turkey country. Rather than seeking unimpaired visibility in a 360° circle, you should seek a location without any large, un-interrupted blind spots. If a turkey should pass behind you as it approaches, are there at least a couple of open gaps that would allow you to clearly identify your target and take a shot? How about off to the sides? Trust me, it's agonizing to work a turkey into range and then miss the opportunity only because you didn't have a clear shooting lane.

Not only does your setup need to provide good visibility, it needs to conceal you from approaching turkeys. Unlike most forms of hunting, you don't need to worry about wind direction. Turkeys do have a sense of smell, but it's not acute enough (or they don't use it in such a way) that you need to factor in the dispersal of human odor when selecting a calling location. But you do need to factor in a turkey's eyesight and hearing. The birds can see color, and they will pick up on anything that looks out of place. The single best thing you can do to hide from a turkey is to lean against a backdrop such as a tree, stump, or shrub. This blurs your outline and helps to absorb any slow movements that you need to make as you work your turkey calls and aim your weapon. While actual camouflage patterns are not essential, there's no good reason not to use them. Ghillie suits are uncomfortable and bulky, but nothing hides you quite as well. If you do forgo camo, make sure to wear a collection of mixed earth tones such as green and brown. (Don't wear any red, blue, or white, because these colors can be mistaken for a turkey's head by any careless hunters who happen to be working the same area as you.) Absolutely cover your face and hands. Your face mask should allow you to insert calls into your mouth without having to raise it or lower it. If need be, you can cut a small hole in your mask for this purpose. Your gloves should be lightweight and flexible so that you can manipulate your turkey calls and work your bow and shotgun without hassle. Practice shooting with your mask and gloves before you actually hunt. Countless hunters have screwed themselves over by hunting with untested gear that, for whatever reason, prevents them from shooting properly.

All of the camouflage clothing in the world won't do any good if you can't hold still. Turkeys have an uncanny ability to detect movement. And since an approaching gobbler is looking for a hen that isn't actually there, you can bet he's going to investigate any movement that he sees in order to determine the source of the calling. When a gobbler is drawing near, and especially when he's within eyesight, you need to hold absolutely still unless the bird's head is turned away or he's passing behind a tree or other obstruction. Even then, move with extreme care.

POP-UP BLINDS FOR TURKEYS

A pop-up blind makes camouflage so **simple** that it almost feels like cheating. Blinds are a hassle to carry **around** and they take time to set up, but they make it almost impossible for the **turkey** to see **you** or your movements. Most bowhunters regard pop-up blinds **as** necessities. An archer **needs** to rise up to **his** knees to shoot, a movement that can be hard to pull off without being detected by a turkey standing just yards away. And even if you do get to your knees without spooking the bird, you've still got to draw your bow. That's a lot of movement. Pop-up blinds are almost equally advantageous to shotgun hunters, though for many, the extra barrier between the birds and themselves is an unwanted intrusion. The experience of a turkey hunt is much purer and rawer when nothing but air separates you from the thunder of a turkey's gobble.

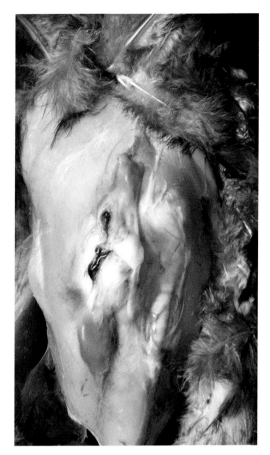

Two interesting turkey images. On left: This Oregon gobbler came in to a hen call despite the huge wound on its breast, which was apparently caused by a midair collision with a sharp tree limb. On right: A pair of turkey spur earrings that the author had made for his wife. She even wears them now and then!

CALLING A GOBBLER: Gobblers are called in by mimicking the vocalizations and other sounds made by hen turkeys. I hesitate to write even a single word on this subject. To master the skill of calling turkeys, you need to be able to hear the sounds produced by real turkeys, and you need to be able to see and hear expert callers as they make turkey sounds. For this, it's really hard to beat YouTube. On YouTube you can watch turkey-calling champions who are willing to share their secrets. You can also find footage of Will Primos and his crew of turkey-calling experts, including Brad Farris, all of whom are articulate, skilled, and passionate about talking turkey. Also spend some time on the website of the National Wild Turkey Federation (www.nwtf.org). They have a great rundown of basic turkey sounds as well as audio recordings of real birds making real sounds in the wild. If you don't use the Internet, find the instructional DVDs and CDs of Will Primos and study those.

Having said that, I'll give a handful of opinions that have been developed over the years through experience and then fine-tuned through the input of many friends and colleagues. First off, keep it simple. Avoid having a ton of calling gadgets in your arsenal that you don't know how to properly use. If you're going to get really serious about turkey hunting, learn how to use both a diaphragm-style mouth call and either a slate or glass pot call. It's more difficult to gain a basic level of proficiency with a mouth call, but the expanded range of sounds and cadences that come with a mouth call make it well worth the extra effort. But if you don't have the time or inclination to dive so deeply into turkey calling, then spend some time familiarizing yourself with a pot call. Whether you opt for glass or slate is largely a matter of personal preference. Mess around with each style and see what works best for you—or simply carry both and use each for the particular sounds that it does best. And if you want to add a third call on top of mouth calls and pot calls, add an old-fashioned

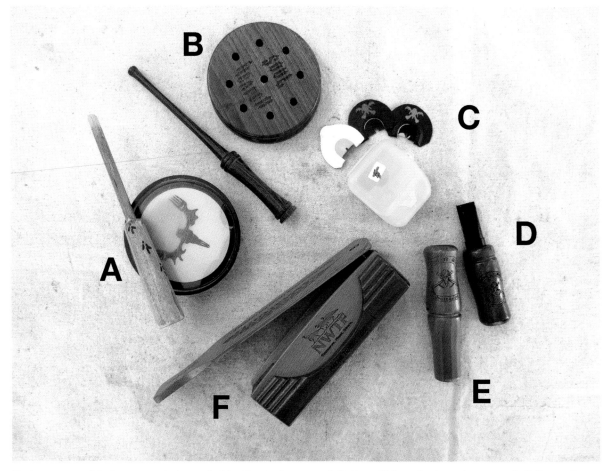

Starting at nine o'clock, moving clockwise: A. Silas Creek glass pot call. B. Down-N-Dirty Outdoors slate pot call. C. Various Primos diaphragm mouth calls. D. Down-N-Dirty Outdoors crow locator call. E. Down-N-Dirty Outdoors owl hooter locator. F. National Wild Turkey Federation box call.

wooden box call. You can get a lot of volume out of a box call (as well as very realistic yelps), which can be helpful when hunting in windy conditions or wide-open country where you're really trying to reach distant birds with hen calls.

Your arsenal of sounds doesn't need to be any more complicated than your arsenal of turkey calls. You can use the cluck and the yelp to call in turkeys just about anywhere that you can find the birds. The cluck seems to signify contentment. If done loudly enough for gobblers to hear, it works well to get their attention. Yelps seem to have a lot of meanings, depending on the delivery. In simplest terms, though, it seems to say something like, "Hey, I'm a turkey and I'm over here." Most gobblers who are receptive to calling will respond just as well to this call as they will to any other. As you study turkey calling, the cluck and the yelp should be your starting points.

From there, learn how to purr and cut. A purr is a quiet call that, like the cluck, seems to signify contentment; this call will drive gobblers nuts, though they need to be fairly close to hear it. It's especially effective on gobblers that are reluctant to come in close enough for a shot. Cuts are loud, sharp clucks that carry a long way. This sound can get a distant gobbler's attention, but it is an excited, aggressive sound and should be used sparingly. There are other sounds in the turkey

vocabulary, but by the time you feel the need to add those sounds to your repertoire you'll be advanced enough to disregard the suggestions presented in this book. (The kee-kee run, used for turkey hunting in the fall, is a possible exception.)

Learning how to make turkey calls is much harder than learning when to use them. Most novice turkey hunters make the mistake of calling too much, which really seems to turn gobblers off. You want to call just often enough—and just loudly enough—to get a gobbler's attention and move him ever so slowly in your direction; anything more than that is superfluous or downright detrimental. With a gobbler who's ready to breed, it sometimes takes little more than a couple of soft clucks to start him in your direction. If that sound is working and it moves the bird, stick with it. There's no need to try to impress the turkey with a loud series of cuts that might just send him in the other direction. Conversely, if the gobbler pays no attention to your soft clucks despite several attempts over the course of five or ten minutes, then by all means switch it up. But whatever you try, keep it sparse at first and only let the excitement increase if you find that the gobbler simply refuses to heed your calling. Also be mindful of the cadence of your calls. You can learn all of the right words, but if you don't have the proper tone and rhythm, you'll never be an effective caller. This can only be learned by listening to recordings of real turkeys or learning from a master caller who has an ingrained sense of how turkeys talk.

Here are some other rules and suggestions for calling turkeys:

1. It's easy to get overly excited when calling to a highly vocal gobbler who's still in his roost. With the bird answering every one of your calls with a thunderous gobble, you can't help but want to hit him again and again with yelps. Resist this temptation. One call is all the gobbler needs to hear in order to pinpoint your exact location. Once you've got his attention, wait to see what happens when he comes down from the roost. And be ready—he might be in your lap within seconds of flying down.

2. If the tom doesn't approach right away after he flies down from his roost, remain patient. Often a gobbler will take care of more urgent business—breeding the hens that he roosted with, feeding, checking out some favorite hen hangouts—before he pays you a visit. You don't want to waste an entire day waiting for a gobbler that will never show up, but you don't want to leave prematurely either. It's a delicate balance, best learned through experience.

3. There are some excellent turkey hunters who don't walk into the woods until 9:00 a.m. No aspect of turkey hunting is more exciting than calling to a gobbler in the moments before he flies down from his roost, but the effectiveness of that strategy isn't nearly as good as some guys would have you believe. The reason is that it's very hard to call a tom away from an actual group of hens, and unfortunately that's usually what you're trying to do in the early morning. But after a few hours, once the gobbler has bred the sexually available hens and/or harassed the sexually unavailable hens, he'll often become much more receptive to calling. In all honesty, if I had to pick one hour to hunt turkeys, it would start at 10:00 a.m.

4. There's still hope if the woods are silent and you simply cannot locate a gobbler. Cold-calling, which amounts to calling without being prompted by the gobble of a tom, can sometimes work very well. Rather than heading back to your truck or car on quiet days, find a likely location with good visibility and concealment and spend an hour or two calling. Start slow and soft at first, in case a bird is nearby, and then steadily increase in loudness as time goes by. Wait at least ten minutes between calls. Sometimes gobblers will come sneaking right in without ever making a peep. If you sit an hour or so without any action, move to a new location and try again. Your chances of success are way better when you're doing a little cold-calling than they are when you're sitting in front of your TV.

5. A gobbler who refuses to be drawn away from his hens is referred to as "henned up." When working a henned-up gobbler, try mimicking whatever sounds come from the loudest, raspiest hen in the group. This is usually the boss hen, the bird who calls the shots for her flock. If you can start a conversation with her, or begin to piss her off with loud calling, you might pull her to your position. The trailing gobbler will follow. These situations require good camouflage and absolute stillness on the hunter's part. Not only does he have to visually deceive the gobbler, he has to deceive one or more hens as well.

DECOYS FOR TURKEYS

The bird on the left is a real feather decoy made with a hot-glue gun by the son of South Carolina hunter Robert Abernethy. The bird on the right is the thirty-third gobbler to have ever laid its eyes on the decoy. Like the rest, he came to stand within 12 inches of the decoy.

Decoys work extremely well for turkeys. This is especially true for birds that have never encountered them before. A single hen decoy can be effective, though it seems to work much better if you pair a hen or two with a decoy of a young tom, or jake, in strutting mode. The sight of a jake strutting for females seems to outrage mature males, and they will often run up to attack the decoy. Place your decoys on level ground in an open or semi-open location where they are visible to approaching birds. For bowhunting, place the bird facing you at 20 or so yards. When a gobbler approaches the decoy head-on, you might get a great shot at the base of its fan. Put the decoy out at 30 or so yards when hunting with a shotgun. There are many decoys on the market, and you can find one to match almost any budget. But the best decoys can be made yourself. Start out by plucking a turkey and separating all the feathers according to where they came from—tail, wings, breast, and so on. Then use a hot-glue gun to affix the feathers onto a cheap foam decoy of a jake. Even if your decoy looks like something made by Dr. Frankenstein, the iridescent shimmer of those real feathers will draw in every tom that lays eyes on it.

SHOOTING A GOBBLER: Get ready to shoot before you start calling. This means having a shell chambered and the gun partially raised to a shooting position. When you're leaning against a tree, the best place to rest your shotgun is over your knee. Have the stock close to your shoulder so that you don't need to move the gun a lot in order to make a shot. You'll have your muzzle (and your body) aiming toward the most likely line of approach for the gobbler, but take a moment to make a plan about how you'll shoot in other directions as well. Map out the necessary movements so you can do it quietly and smoothly.

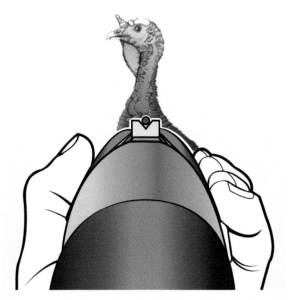

When aiming at a turkey, keep the bird's head above the bead. A common practice is to aim for the turkey's wattle.

Before you start calling, take a moment to consider shooting distances. If you carry a laser range finder, take some readings on surrounding trees. There are endless debates about how far away you can effectively kill a turkey with a shotgun or a bow, but for our purposes here let's say we're limiting our shots to the very safe distance of 40 yards with a shotgun and 30 yards with a bow. Mark those distances, or whatever distances you've deemed appropriate for your own skill level, so that you can tell when a turkey is in range. Over time, you'll develop the ability to know when a turkey is in range just by looking at it.

If you need to move in order to adjust the position of your shotgun before shooting, wait until the turkey's head passes behind a tree or other obstruction. A gobbler's own tail fan will periodically block his vision when he's strutting. Take advantage of the moment by readying your shotgun. When the bird turns back in your direction, you can break him out of his strut by giving an alarm putt with your mouth call. The tom will instantly extend his neck, giving you an excellent shot opportunity with a low likelihood of peppering the meat with shotgun pellets.

When shooting a shotgun, you want to hit the turkey in the head and neck. It's a small target that moves a lot, and plenty of hunters miss turkeys every year. Most birds are missed by shooting too high, right over the tom's head. To avoid this mistake, always keep the bird's head above the bead on your shotgun—that is, never blot out the bird's head with your muzzle. A great trick is to aim for the turkey's wattles. And by aim, I mean *aim carefully*. Don't just assume that, since you're using a shotgun, you're guaranteed to hit. That sort of thinking is a sure way to miss.

Many states have fall turkey seasons that allow hunters to kill birds with rifles. If you encounter a turkey while deer hunting and decide to take the shot, aim for the base of the neck. Hitting a turkey square in the body with a deer rifle is a good way to destroy your Thanksgiving dinner.

Killing a turkey with a bow is much more difficult than killing one with a shotgun. Even expert archers will routinely lose wounded turkeys due to improper shot placement or failure of their broadheads. A strutting tom looks like a huge target, but there's a lot of non-vital space beneath all those feathers. On broadside shots, aim for the butt or base of the wing. This will usually bust the wing bones, preventing the bird from flying off, and often results in destroyed lungs as well. Shot placement is very difficult on a turkey that is facing away from you unless the bird is in full strut. If so, hit him right at the base of the fan. On a strutting tom that is facing toward you, hit him right at the top of the beard. If the bird is standing erect, with his neck up, hit him in the top third of his breast. Some bowhunters like to aim for a turkey's neck or head. For many, the goal is to decapitate the bird. There is a lot of room for error with this approach. In the wrong hands, it can border on stunting rather than hunting. Leave it to the true experts with a ton of turkey hunting experience. Until you get to that place yourself, stick with body shots.

When bowhunting for turkeys, shot placement changes according to the bird's position. On broadside turkeys, aim for the base of the wing. Head on, aim for the base of the beard. Facing away from you, shoot for the base of the tail fan.

WISCONSIN HUNTER JEROD FINK WEIGHS IN ON BOWHUNTING FOR TURKEYS

"The use of a commercial ground blind when bow-hunting for turkeys is not essential for success, but it sure stacks the odds in your favor! Today, you can't just set a pop-up blind out in a field and assume that the turkeys won't spook. Too many birds have seen that trick too many times over the past decade; the fear is ingrained in them. To up your chances, be selective where you set your blind, and make sure you have plenty of background cover or else brush it in. Yes, that's right. You need to camouflage your camouflage-colored blind.

"Decoying turkeys (especially highly pressured eastern gobblers) can be a blessing and a curse. Sometimes it works, and sometimes birds will run the other way at the sight of a fake bird. However, I still feel that decoys are basically essential when bowhunting turkeys—even if it means scaring off a bird or two in the process. Shot placement is crucial to success for archery turkeys, and a decoy helps you to position a bird for a clean kill. There are many theories about decoy placement out there, but what works for me is to simply place my decoys in the best possible location for a shot. That might be 20 yards, it might be 10 yards, it could even be 5 yards.

"One of the best ways to put a turkey on your dinner table with a bow is to study a flock of turkeys and figure out their travel routes and also what time of day the birds are passing through particular areas. (Turkey patterns change quickly, so scouting more than a week in advance is usually a waste of time.) Then take your pop-up blind and set up almost directly in their line of travel in order to intercept the birds. Put out either a single hen or a hen and a jake decoy (I prefer extremely realistic decoys, such as those by Dave Smith), and do some soft calling. A few purrs and clucks from a slate will usually do it for me, since I'm set up where they want to go anyway.

"Your killing equipment shouldn't be much different from what you use for deer. Really, the only difference is in your choice of broadheads. Make sure to use the

(continued)

largest-cutting mechanical broadhead you are comfortable with. My suggestion is something with at least a 2-inch cut. Turkeys have small vitals and a big will to live; you need as much help as you can get.

"In the past, a lot of guys recommended turning down the poundage of your bow to hunt turkeys in order to prevent the arrow from passing through and supposedly to limit the bird's ability to travel. I absolutely do not recommend this. I want that arrow blowing right through. Too many times I have had to chase birds down and finish them off by hand. The last thing I want is a razor-sharp broadhead flailing around my arms and wrists while I'm trying to grab my bird."

BUSHWHACKS, AMBUSHES, AND FALL HUNTS

Calling gobblers during the spring breeding season is the most educational, rewarding, and thrilling way to hunt turkeys. Honestly, nothing else comes even close in terms of excitement. But there are other ways to kill turkeys. I have taken many of the birds using spot-and-stalk strategies. This is easy to explain but hard to pull off. You simply locate turkeys and then try to put the sneak on them. There's no need to worry about wind direction, but you do need to keep low and move slowly. The best turkey sneaks are those when you can use a ditch or creek bottom for concealment while you close the distance. It also works well to wait for the turkeys to drop into a nat-ural depression such as a creek bed or water-hole before you try to advance in their direction. One problem with sneaking up on turkeys is that flocks of birds will bunch together when they are nervous. If you pop up and see a mixed cluster of male and female turkey heads close together, don't take the shot. The risk of hitting the wrong turkey, or more than one turkey, is high.

Ambush hunting is also quite simple in theory but can be difficult in execution. By watching flocks or studying the ground for tracks, you can pattern their movements and select likely pinch points or high-activity areas where you can set up an ambush. Dust bowls, where birds dust themselves to clear away parasites, are great spots for a midday ambush. So are water sources when hunting dry country, or dry areas when hunting wet country. (Turkeys don't seem to like getting their feet wet; they'll go out of their way to walk on dry ground rather than wade through water or fly over it.) In the afternoon, ambushing food sources or travel corridors near roosting areas can be productive. The birds will often go for one last bite of feed before heading into their preferred roost tree for the evening. Be in these places an hour before dark and wait it out.

Many states have fall turkey hunting seasons. These hunts are increasingly controversial because they allow for the harvest of female turkeys, something that is frowned upon by many turkey conservationists and biologists, who fear that wildlife managers are taking for granted the wild turkey's current state of abundance. By accidentally overharvesting hens, they fear, we could send turkey populations into a sudden downward spiral.

Most fall turkey hunters kill their birds opportunistically; they simply run into turkeys while hunting deer or other game and then make an attempt on the birds with whatever weapon they happen to have in hand.

Michigan hunter Tracy Breen with a favorite turkey dog and a fall-killed bird.

(Several states allow hunters to harvest turkeys in the fall with rifles, something that is generally illegal in the spring.) Hunters who actually target the birds in the fall use a strategy referred to as "flock busting." They'll locate a flock of turkeys and then rush the birds on foot or with the use of a specially trained dog. The goal is to startle and disorient the flock so that it breaks up into several small groups. The hunter then selects a suitable location and begins calling to the turkeys with several varieties of regrouping calls. These include the assembly call, kee-kee, and kee-kee run.

JOHN HAFNER, A LIFELONG HUNTER AND WILDLIFE PHOTOGRAPHER, WEIGHS IN ON HIS FAVORITE QUARRY—THE AMERICAN TURKEY

"Scout early and often. Figure out where birds like to be at different times of the day throughout the season, and get there before they do. To you, your hunting grounds might just be a jumbled mix of fields, woodlots, and croplands, but to a turkey, they're his back-yard, bedroom, living room, and kitchen. He knows every inch of his kingdom, and so should you. Using the terrain to your advantage—and to slip in close whenever possible—can mean the difference between eating tag soup and turkey schnitzel.

"In general, call less and listen more. It took years of chronic impatience and mistakes to teach me a very valuable lesson: In the turkey woods, patience is truly an invaluable virtue. Unless a gobbler responds ravenously to aggressive calling, a good move is to sit tight, call softly, and keep your eyes peeled. Sometimes a few seductive come-hither purrs, soft clucks, or a little leaf scratching are all you need to fool a longbeard. After you make a call or two, a gobbler has you pinpointed. If he doesn't run right in off the roost, odds are good he'll head your way after he's visited his morning strut zone and serviced his hens.

"Even if you do everything else right, things will still fall apart at the moment of truth if you can't sit still. You might consider yourself a camo-clad ninja, but odds are you're not. A turkey's eyesight and survival instincts are much keener than yours. If you make even the slightest movement at the wrong time, you're busted. When a bird commits and closes the distance, anticipate his line of travel, find your shooting lane, get your gun up, and get ready. If there's enough cover, or if the bird is in full strut with his tail facing you, you can usually get away with last-second movement.

"The movement patterns of a turkey change throughout the season. While their behavior may seem random, there's usually a biological basis for their actions. A basic understanding of what makes turkeys tick, like breeding and nesting cycles and the pecking order within the flocks you're pursuing, will no doubt help you consistently draw a bead on gobblers."

ROBERT ABERNETHY, A SOUTH CAROLINA HUNTER, WEIGHS IN ON TURKEY HUNTING SAFETY

1. "Hunt defensively. Expect other hunters to be in the woods. If you hear a hen call, expect it to be another hunter.

2. "Never stalk a calling hen. It could be another hunter.

3. "Always set up with a tree behind your back that is wider than your shoulders and taller than your head.

4. "Never wear red, white, or blue in the woods. These are the colors of a gobbler's head. Turkeys are black. Avoid black. Wear full camo, including gloves and face net.

5. "When hunting with a buddy, never separate. Hunt together. If you do decide to break this rule and separate, have hard boundaries on your hunt area and your buddy's hunt area. Hard boundaries might be a road or stream or field. Do not move in on a bird in your buddy's area.

6. "If you get to your hunting spot and someone is already there, move on and find another spot. Never crowd another hunter who got there first. You should have gotten up an hour earlier. Don't make that mistake twice.

7. "Learn to use a map and compass. GPS batteries die. Compasses do not.

8. "Be sure of your target before you pull the trigger. It has been said before and it bears repeating: once the trigger is pulled, you cannot take back the shot.

9. "Treat every gun as if it were loaded—all the time. Check the safety incessantly. Every few minutes is not too often.

10. "Make safety a habit."

FURRED SMALL GAME

COTTONTAIL RABBIT
Sylvilagus floridanus

The beauty of the cottontail rabbit lies in its near ubiquity. The vast majority of hunters in America are within an easy drive of prime cottontail country. Chasing these rabbits allows you to master the art of the carefully planned drive as well as the ability to connect on moving targets with a shotgun or rifle. What's more, cottontails make for excellent eating. You can braise them, grill them, bake them—really, just about anything that can be done with chicken. Their seasons are plenty long. In many states, you can legally hunt for cottontails more days a year than you cannot.

BARROOM BANTER: For many folks, the biological difference between rabbits and hares is not well understood. Both belong to the family *Leporidae*, of which there are eighteen species in North America. Even the names of these species leads to some confusion, as jackrabbits are not actually rabbits—they are hares. One of the primary differences between rabbits and hares is that hares are precocial, meaning they give birth to well-developed and fully furred young that have open eyes. Rabbits are altricial, meaning they give birth to poorly developed young that are bald and with closed eyes. If you know what to look for, you can distinguish between adult rabbits and hares based on appearance alone. Hares are usually larger than rabbits and have longer ears and longer, more powerful hind legs. Hares are generally fast and outrun their predators. Rabbits are slower and evade predators by hiding in thick cover. You can taste the difference, too. The flesh of hares is darker and strong-flavored, while rabbit flesh is lighter and often as mild as chicken. This perhaps explains why there are domesticated rabbits but no domesticated hares.

PHYSICAL CHARACTERISTICS: The eastern cottontail, which is the most common of the cottontail rabbits, has grayish-brown fur on its back and sides that is often grizzled with black hairs. The neck is rust-colored. The underside of the tail and the lower belly are white. The other cottontails are very similar in appearance. The largest of the cottontails is the swamp rabbit, which weighs up to 6 pounds. The mountain cottontail is less than half that size, at around 2½ pounds.

Of the cottontail rabbits, there are many species: swamp rabbit (*Sylvilagus aquaticus*), desert cottontail (*Sylvilagus audubonii*), Eastern cottontail (*Sylvilagus floridanus*), mountain cottontail (*Sylvilagus nuttallii*), Allegheny cottontail (*Sylvilagus obscurus*), marsh rabbit (*Sylvilagus palustris*), and New England cottontail (*Sylvilagus transitionalis*). The distributions of these various species often overlap.

DIET: Most cottontails feed primarily on herbaceous plants but will eat bark from a variety of trees in the winter. Different cottontail species have their own food preferences according to their range. Swamp rabbits will feed on aquatic plants; mountain cottontails will eat juniper berries; marsh rabbits will feed on cane; New England cottontails have been known to reingest their own droppings.

LIFE AND DEATH: Even if a cottontail survives to leave its nest, it will most likely be dead before it's a year old. A four-year-old cottontail is an old-timer. A list of their predators runs very long, but to name a few: foxes, coyotes, bobcats, minks, weasels, feral housecats, hawks, owls, and snakes.

BREEDING AND REPRODUCTION: Varies among species, ranging from two to five litters per year, with two to nine offspring per litter.

HABITAT: Typically thick, brushy areas. Western species often hang around areas with rocky outcroppings where they can bask and seek protection from predators.

TELLTALE SIGN: In snow, look for tracks and droppings. Without snow, look for droppings and mazelike networks of trails and tunnels coursing through thick brush and grass. When feeding on woody plants, rabbits sever the twigs and stems at sharp angles. The cuts will show teeth marks, similar to those left by beavers but much smaller. Cottontails will also girdle small trees, leaving them barkless for the first couple of feet. Keep in mind that cottontails seem to leave a disproportion-

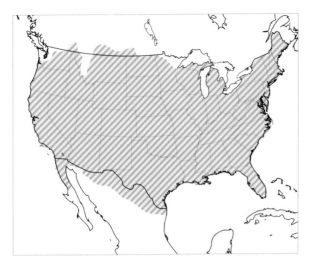

ate number of tracks in a small area. What seems like the tracks of ten rabbits in a briar patch might just be two.

EDIBILITY: Truly excellent, one of the finest of all wild game meats. Can be used for many chicken applications.

HUNTING OPPORTUNITIES: There are several species of cottontail throughout North America with wide availability. Seasons tend to run from fall through winter with varying bag limits due to regional availability. Some states do not regard cottontails as a game animal; there seasons are open year-round with no limit.

HUNTING METHODS: Below is an explanation of the deadliest and most versatile rabbit hunting strategy, but first we'll touch on a couple of other methods. The first of these is running them with beagles. When pursued by dogs, a rabbit will travel in a looped pattern that eventually brings it back around to the place where it was originally hiding. Once the dogs start to chase a rabbit, the hunter tries to posi-

tion himself where he has a clear shooting lane in the proximity of where the animal was flushed. He then waits for the rabbit to come back around. The rabbit usually keeps a strong lead on the dogs, so they aren't always running at full blast when they pass by. A hunter who is good with a .22 can often connect on these slower-moving passes. However, a shotgun allows you to hit a much higher percentage of rabbits, especially in thick cover, where it's often necessary to shoot through a veil of brush.

Still-hunting is another way to hunt cottontails. This method works extremely well in the arid regions of the West, as the mountain and desert varieties of cottontails do not hide themselves as well as eastern varieties and do not flush as readily. On cold and sunny days, they can be found basking on south-facing slopes near outcroppings of rock that give them some protection from avian predators overhead. They are also fond of abandoned prairie dog and ground squirrel burrows, where they can bask in the sun while being just a split second away from shelter. It's best to still-hunt rabbits with the aid of binoculars. Use them to study outcrops and other likely basking areas in order to find the rabbits before they're aware of you. A .22 is a great option when still-hunting cottontails in the West. Shots are often long, and the stationary targets allow for head shots, which minimizes meat wastage.

For true versatility and reliable action, a cottontail rabbit hunter should learn how to

Most hunters associate cottontail rabbits with farmland in the eastern United States, though some of the best cottontail hunting in the nation can be found in the Rockies. This area here is a proven producer of prime-tasting rabbits.

drive rabbits. This method works virtually everywhere that cottontails can be found. All it takes are a few hunters who can work together and follow a plan. Ideally you'll have five or six guys, though as few as two or three hunters can have good success in an area with plentiful rabbits. Basically, the method comes down to having pushers flush rabbits in a controlled fashion that more or less forces the animals to pass the locations of carefully positioned standers. The best way to understand this strategy is to study a few scenarios. The

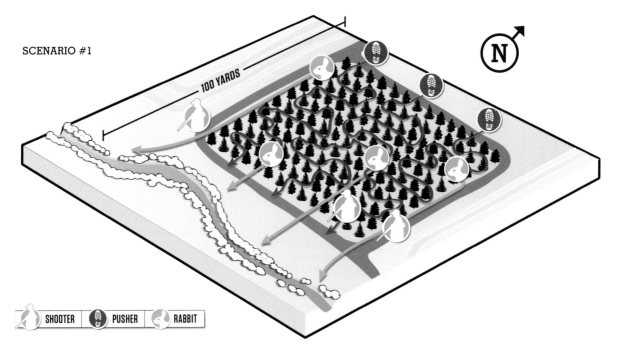

100 YARDS

N

| SHOOTER | PUSHER | RABBIT |

thinking behind these scenarios can then be applied to pretty much any cottontail hunting location.

Scenario #1: Here's a situation where the cottontails are utilizing cover provided by a planting of Christmas trees. When flushed from hiding, the cottontails are going to head toward the nearest cover—in this case, it's most likely going to be the brushy creek bed to the south of the trees. And since there are open fields to the east and west, they're most likely going to travel through the Christmas trees in order to get there. Rather than trying to get the rabbits to go somewhere they don't want to go, the hunters should take advantage of the animals' natural tendencies and position themselves where they can exploit them. The pushers (either two or three hunters) are going to come in from the north and begin zigzagging

their way toward the south. They need to kick around the bases of any tree with limbs that come down to the ground, as rabbits will lie beneath these limbs and just watch you pass by unless you pretty much step on them. The sitters are positioned where they can intercept the rabbits as the animals bust free of the plantation and head toward the creek bed. In this situation, as in all rabbit drives, it's important that the standers maintain absolute silence except for shooting. If the rabbits detect their presence before the drive begins, they are likely to double back and escape to the north, or else risk crossing the open fields.

Scenario #2: Here's a situation where a low and marshy area has caused an incongruity in a farmer's field, forming a sort of brushy peninsula that juts out into his crop of corn. Over the years, the point of the peninsula has

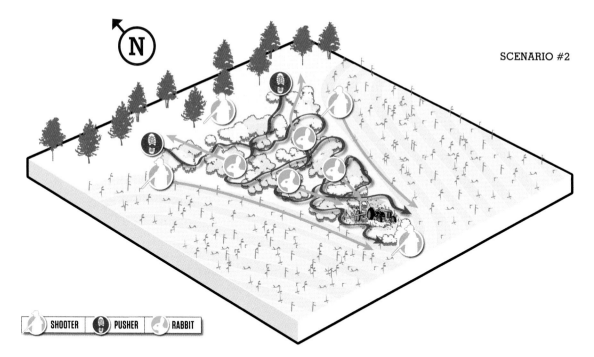

SHOOTER · PUSHER · RABBIT

turned into a garbage dump of sorts. Rusted fencing materials, a few junked implements, an old wood stove, and dozens of old buckets and drums have joined the briars and high grass. Because the peninsula melds seamlessly into the open woods, it doesn't seem wise to push the rabbits in that direction. Visibility is just too low in there. Instead, the two pushers will come in from the north and thoroughly kick out the briar patches as they move south. Stander #1 has positioned himself overlooking the trash heap, knowing that the flushed rabbits will likely be headed in that direction to take shelter amid the impenetrable junk. Due to the strong possibility that the rabbits might double back and head toward the open woods, standers #2 and #3 will parallel the pushers in order to cover the ground both ahead of them and behind them. By the time the pushers reach the dump pile, all three standers will be surrounding the pile and ready to cover it as the pushers climb in there to start kicking around. Notice also the placement of a fourth stander in the open woods to the north, which is an optional position. He might get a lucky crack at any rabbits that head that way, especially if the pushers shout a heads-up when they see a rabbit that's attempting to double back.

Scenario #3: Cottontails love to utilize the cover provided by brushy creek beds. In a situation where the creek is wide enough to prevent the rabbits from jumping across, it's possible to hunt each side of the creek independently. In this situation, there are two areas that the rabbits are going to head for: the dense thicket of willows to the south of the bend in the creek, or the cattail marsh to the west of

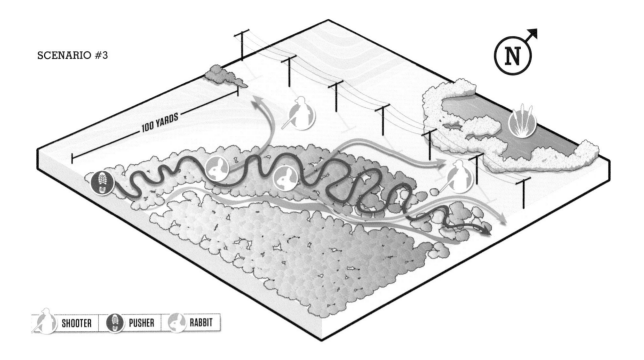

100 YARDS

N

SHOOTER | PUSHER | RABBIT

the creek. The single pusher is entering the creek bed about 100 or so yards down from stander #1, and he'll follow the creek to the east and north. Stander #1 is able to watch the approaches to the willow thicket as well as a small portion of the creek bed itself. Stander #2 is positioned along the power line, where he can get shots at any rabbits that leave the creek bed in order to cross over toward the cattail marsh. He's also able to cover the entire creek bed itself, as he's looking over a section where the streamside brush forms only a very narrow strip between the power line and the water. By positioning himself in order to utilize small breaks in the brush, he can pick off any rabbits that follow the creek.

Cottontail rabbits are often taken incidentally by hunters pursuing other prey. Here, a spring turkey hunter grills a rabbit that he killed while hunting turkeys in a state where rabbit hunting is open year-round.

BRODY HENDERSON, A COLORADO BIG GAME HUNTER, WEIGHS IN ON HIS FAVORITE OFF-SEASON QUARRY

"The mountain cottontail subspecies of the cottontail rabbit is an overlooked and underutilized small game animal in my part of central Colorado. These small, mild-tasting rabbits are a welcome change from my venison-heavy diet.

"I first started chasing them here a few years ago, after taking notice of numerous cottontails while hunting deer in sage, pinyon, and juniper country. I enjoy still-hunting a great deal, and while quietly sneaking up on mule deer I would sometimes notice a cottontail sitting motionless under a juniper only a few feet away. I reasoned that with a scoped .22, I might reliably bag a few of these rabbits after the close of the big game seasons.

"The first thing I learned was that sage flats and grassy meadows are rarely worth hunting even if they are littered with rabbit tracks. Because cottontails are targeted by a range of predators, including raptors, they are primarily nocturnal and shy away from open country during daylight hours. I found that significant overhead tree cover was the key to stalking rabbits during the day. The best hunting areas are in pinyon and juniper groves with a little ground cover such as sage, serviceberry, or oak brush. Rock piles are also attractive habitats. Mornings and late afternoons are the best times to find the rabbits, as they often lounge aboveground near their holes. It's best if you can wait until there's an accumulation of snow. Fresh tracks make locating productive areas much easier. Additionally, seeing rabbits is much simpler because they are

(continued)

silhouetted against a white background. Sunny days after a snowfall are the absolute best, because cottontails will bask on the warm, sunny sides of trees and rocks.

"Killing a few rabbits for the pot with a rimfire might seem simple, but in fact it requires patience and good woodsmanship. You need to learn to hunt at a snail's pace, using your eyes more than your feet. I believe that running is actually a last resort for rabbits, and these mountain cottontails seem less likely to bolt when approached slowly. Look for dark, compact, ball-shaped objects on the ground beneath trees and rock ledges, and also for the pinkish ears and black eyes. Once you get the hang of it, you'll start to see the bunnies in plenty of time to place a careful shot with your .22.

"Keep in mind, though, that it isn't always over if the rabbit runs. Sometimes, following an initial sprint, it will stop near some cover to assess the danger. Rather than shooting at a running bunny, I prefer to wait to see if it gives me a stationary target. I keep my scope adjusted to its lowest power for quick shots that average 10 to 30 yards.

"Give spot-and-stalk rabbit hunting a try. Because the season runs through late winter, it keeps me in hiking and hunting shape long after big game seasons end, and my shooting skills stay sharp. Since the habitat mountain cottontails live in overlaps with the winter range of deer and elk, I get to see a lot of animals. That and some tasty rabbit stew help to take the sting out of waiting until the following September to once again hunt my beloved big game in the mountains."

SNOWSHOE HARE
Lepus americanus
A.K.A.: Varying hare

Snowshoe hares provide a great way to beat the winter doldrums. Where the animals are abundant, they can be hunted from the early fall through the late winter. As with cottontail rabbits, snowshoe hare seasons are often open for more days of the year than they are closed. It's easy to take advantage of these long seasons as often as you'd like because hunting for snowshoe hares is a simple endeavor. Beagles work well on snowshoe hares and that's a popular way to hunt them, but the animals can be pursued on your own, with no more equipment than a .22 rifle. Deep snow can be a complicating factor, but it is easily overcome with a pair of snowshoes or skis. For many northern hunters, the perfect way to spend a late winter day is to silently stalk through fresh snow in a cedar swamp or spruce forest while searching the underbrush for this well-camouflaged quarry. In addition to securing some fine table fare, you can polish your stalking and shooting skills at a time of year when they might otherwise atrophy. Snowshoe hare populations are cyclical, with each cycle running around seven years. At the apex of a cycle, with abundant hares, hunting can be ridiculously easy. At low points, it can be challenging just to find a single animal.

BARROOM BANTER: Snowshoe hares have many predators. One of the more surprising of these is the red squirrel, sometimes known as a pine squirrel. Working in the Yukon Territory, researchers conducting a snowshoe hare mortality study fixed radio tracking devices on 254 newly born hares, called leverets. Within the first month, 170 of the leverets were dead. Of these, 47 percent were found in red squirrel middens or up in spruce trees—almost certainly the victims of red squirrel predation.

PHYSICAL CHARACTERISTICS: Snowshoe hares weigh up to 3 pounds, a bit larger than Eastern cottontails. They typically change color (known as molting) from brown to white during the fall-winter transition, and then back to brown in the spring. In areas that are predominantly snow free, such as western Washington and western Oregon, snowshoe hares stay brown year-round. Ears have black tips. Feet are long and fully furred.

DIET: In the summer, snowshoe hares eat grasses, forbs, and the buds and twigs of willow, aspen, and alder. In the winter, they feed on twigs and bark of willow, aspen, and alder, as well as conifer buds. Snowshoe hares have also been known to scavenge animal carcasses and dead fish.

BREEDING AND REPRODUCTION: Females will have two or three litters per year, numbering up to six offspring per litter.

LIFE AND DEATH: The vast majority of snowshoe hares die within their first year of life. A three-year-old snowshoe hare is an old-timer. Predators include foxes, coyotes, lynxes, bobcats, weasels, wolverines, red squirrels, and a variety of hawks and owls.

HABITAT: Boreal forests and mountains with abundant conifers. Often found in transitional zones where conifers abut growths of young willow and aspen.

TELLTALE SIGN: Look for tracks in the snow, particularly those forming networks of well-used trails. The trails are often deeper than they are wide, measuring just 4 or 5 inches across but perhaps a foot deep when there's significant snow cover. Also look for droppings, which are slightly compressed spheres a little larger than those of an eastern cottontail. Feeding areas can be identified by an abundance of tracks as well as saplings that have been girdled of bark just above the snowline.

EDIBILITY: Snowshoe hares are the best-tasting hares by far, and are generally much better than jackrabbits. The flesh is darker and stronger-flavored than cottontail meat and should be slow-cooked with moist heat for best results. Suitable for many chicken applications.

HUNTING OPPORTUNITIES: Snowshoe hares are found throughout Canada and northern portions of the United States and are available for harvest in over twenty states. The season usually starts close to that of cottontails but tends to run longer into the winter. Limits vary from state to state, with some having no closed season and no limit.

HUNTING METHODS: A single hunter, working alone and without dogs, can consistently take snowshoe hares by using still-hunting tactics. Timing is crucial, as hunting is best within a day or two of a fresh snowfall. This helps you determine active travel routes and bedding areas, which might otherwise be lost

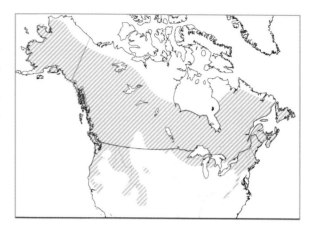

amid the great abundance of tracks and droppings that accumulate on older surfaces of snow. Concentrate your hunting efforts on bedding areas, where the hares can hide from predators during the day. These are located in and around the thickest patches of vegetation that an area has to offer—think spruce bogs, cedar swamps, willow-covered gravel bars, early-succession clear-cuts, the edges of beaver ponds, brushy south-facing slopes, and so forth. Tracks and sign found in more open and sparsely vegetated areas are probably getting laid down at night, as snowshoe

On left: Early-season snowshoe hares killed before their winter molt in Michigan's eastern Upper Peninsula. On right: A collection of winter-phase snowshoe hares from northeastern Vermont taken by Jason Carey and friends. As you can see, beagles can be a great asset when hunting hares..

hares are nocturnal and do most of their feeding under the cover of darkness.

The key to still-hunting a bedding area is to move slowly and quietly, just a few steps at a time. Follow established hare trails as much as possible. Carefully study the ground ahead of you. Examine any patch of cover capable of hiding a hare, whether it's a few yards away or 40 yards. Pay special attention to the protected areas beneath low-hanging evergreens, under or near downed timber, or in dense stands of saplings and underbrush. Binoculars work great for this purpose, as they force you to concentrate on specific places and details instead of just sweeping your eyes casually across the ground. Sometimes the hares are fairly easy to see—you might happen to catch them when their molting phase is out of step with the weather conditions (brown hare against a white backdrop of snow, or white hare against a brown backdrop of dead leaves). Also try sunny weather, which lures the hares from their shaded hiding places and into basking positions. But even in cloudy weather it's still possible to find them if you pause for several minutes at a time in prime areas and concentrate on looking for just pieces of hares rather than the whole animals. You might see just the black shiny marble of a hare's eye, or the curvature of its back hip, or the black-tipped ends of its peninsula-shaped ears.

No matter how careful you are, though, it's almost inevitable that you'll flush some hares before you see them. Keep your shotgun or rifle ready at all times, and be prepared to make snap shots. Another advantage of hunting on fresh snow is that you can more easily track a flushed hare that you didn't get a shot at. Follow slowly in the hare's path, watching ahead of you for the animal as it pauses to assess the danger. A spooked hare will sit upright and is therefore much easier to detect, though they'll be quicker to take off at a run as well. If you get a shot, take it as quickly as possible. The opportunity will not last long.

Snowshoe hares can be driven, though usually not as easily or effectively as cottontail rabbits. The scale and uniformity of snowshoe hare habitat makes it a bit more difficult, as it lacks the hard edges and borders that are common in aggressively manipulated ecosystems such as farms. In other words, it's harder to divide the larger tracts of snowshoe hare habitat into easily managed chunks that can be pushed toward standers who are positioned along open shooting lanes or "hard" edges such as farm lanes and open fields. Instead, consider dividing the available habitat along less conspicuous borders such as game trails or transitional zones between different types of vegetation. Pushers might move through a spruce bog, scaring hares toward standers who are positioned in a grove of paper birch, or they might push the thick vegetation of a streamside willow flat toward standers who are positioned along a moose trail that bisects the valley floor.

HANK SHAW, A CALIFORNIA HUNTER AND CHEF, WEIGHS IN ON HIS LOVE FOR THE LOATHSOME JACKRABBIT

"There may be no more maligned game animal in North America than the humble jackrabbit. In fact, Mister Jack isn't even classified as a game animal in many states. Shoot all you want, whenever you want. This is a sad state of affairs, as our jackrabbits are just hares by another name.

"We have four main species here in North America. The black-tailed and the white-tailed jackrabbits are the main residents of the United States, with the antelope jack-rabbit (yes, the 'real' jackalope!) living in the Sonoran Desert and the snowshoe hare living in the alpine and coldest places of the country. Go farther north and you will find the giant Arctic hare, which can weigh up to 15 pounds. All are good eating.

"Here in the lower forty-eight, I've seen eager cooks spend close to $100 to have a wild Scottish hare shipped to them. Madness, considering that there's virtually no difference between that animal and the jacks probably living in the scrub or forest near their house. Somehow the thought that the local jack is similar never occurs to most people.

(continued)

"Hare is an admired ingredient in European cooking, so how did it get such a bad rap here? Blame westward expansion and the Depression. In both times, many homesteaders in the Great Plains subsisted on jackrabbits as their only protein, not knowing that for some odd biological reason, jackrabbit meat is not a complete protein—so if that's the only meat you eat, you will become deficient in several key amino acids. 'Rabbit starvation' was a problem during these times, and so the meat got a reputation as being fit only for the poorest of the poor.

"That stigma has persisted. Couple that with the distressing habit of botfly larvae—horrible *Alien*-like nasties!—embedding themselves in the skin of jacks during warmer months, and you have the makings of a pariah.

"But I am here to tell you that a jackrabbit is, for all intents and purposes, a tiny mule deer. The meat is similar, the bone structure's not all that different, and the flavor is very close, although jackrabbit meat is lighter in color and often milder than a muley's. Wait, you say: how can a rabbit be like venison? Because true hares are dark-meat animals.

"Hares also tend to be older and rangier animals than their cousins the cottontail. It's a rare hare that can be fried. Slow and low is the way to go. The exception is the snowshoe hare, which has a lighter-colored meat and, interestingly, does not share the same stigma as the jackrabbit. I've fried snowshoes many times and they weren't tough at all.

"Look to Europe for recipes. Italy and Germany are nations especially fond of hare, and the French, Belgians, British, and Scandinavians also feature the animal in their cuisine. Remember hasenpfeffer, from Bugs Bunny fame? Well, a true hasenpfeffer must have hare, not rabbit. After all, *hase* is 'hare' in German.

"Oh, and for the record: Bugs was a hare, not a rabbit."

Hank Shaw runs the wild foods website Hunter Angler Gardener Cook (honest-food.net) and is the author of the cookbooks **Hunt Gather Cook** and **Duck, Duck, Goose**.

Eastern fox squirrel *(Sciurus niger)*

Eastern gray squirrel *(Sciurus carolinensis)*
Western gray squirrel *(Sciurus griseus)*

Squirrels should be regarded as a worthy quarry for beginner hunters and seasoned veterans alike. Hunting squirrels can help you learn and maintain stalking skills, and it can hone your abilities as a precision shooter. Squirrel seasons are long and bag limits are generous. In most states, hunters can legally chase squirrels for several months or more per year and can typically harvest between four and six squirrels (combined species) per day. They provide continuous action through the fall and much of the winter, often when nothing else is open.

BARROOM BANTER: There's a long-running debate about whether or not squirrels can actually remember the locations of their cached nuts. Some studies support the view that they can't, and suggest that squirrels recover nuts cached by other squirrels at the same rate as nuts they themselves cached. Other studies support the view that they can. For "Grey Squirrels Remember the Location of Buried Nuts," a paper published in the journal *Animal Behavior*, researchers released multiple squirrels in an outdoor arena and allowed them to cache ten hazelnuts each. When the squirrels were put back into the arena after periods of time ranging from two to twelve days, they retrieved significantly more nuts from their own caches than from the caches of the other squirrels. The great squirrel debate rages on!

Some folks refer to the eastern fox squirrel as a red squirrel, which is erroneous and misleading. The actual red squirrel, sometimes known as a pine squirrel, is a very abundant tree squirrel in northerly latitudes that is typically ignored by hunters due to its small size (about ½ pound) and the piney flavor of its flesh.

PHYSICAL CHARACTERISTICS: The eastern gray squirrel is gray above with paler gray underparts. Black-phase gray squirrels are common in the northern portions of the species's range, sometimes outnumbering gray-phase specimens. A big eastern gray squirrel might weigh 1½ pounds. The western gray squirrel has grizzled grayish fur above and whitish underparts. They are heavier than easterns, weighing up to 2 pounds. The eastern fox squirrel is the largest tree squirrel in North America, weighing upward of 2½ pounds. They occur in three color phases, the most common being rust-colored.

DIET: Tree nuts from hickory, beech, and oak are squirrel staples, though they will readily consume tree buds, seeds, fungi, pinecones, berries, and agricultural crops such as corn and apples.

LIFE AND DEATH: Avian predators such as hawks and owls are the primary killers of squirrels. Their life expectancy is usually just a few years, though there are documented cases of squirrels living to be twelve years old.

BREEDING AND REPRODUCTION: Fox squirrels and eastern gray squirrels usually have one or two litters of two to four young every year, born during spring and summer. Western gray squirrels usually have only a single litter, born in the spring. Gestation for all species is around forty-five days.

HABITAT: Mixed forests, usually with an abundance of nut-bearing trees.

TELLTALE SIGN: Look for bushel-sized and smaller nests of leaves and twigs in the high crotches of treetops. These resemble the nests of crows but are more leafy and disheveled. Evidence of feeding includes divots in earth or snow where squirrels are caching or retrieving nuts; also, gnawed husks of tree nuts on or near stumps or horizontal logs that serve as feeding platforms. When feeding on corn, fox squirrels will devour entire kernels; gray squirrels will often eat just the germ end and discard the rest. In the snow, squirrel tracks are typically "paired"; unlike the tracks of a rabbit, the front prints fall side by side.

EDIBILITY: Good. Reminiscent of chicken, though usually tougher, darker, and more full-flavored. Suitable for many chicken applications.

HUNTING OPPORTUNITIES: Of all squirrels, the eastern gray and fox squirrels are the most common. Both have native ranges in the eastern states but are widely available in western portions of the United States as well. Most states have squirrel seasons that run from September

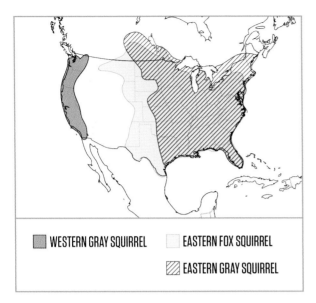

WESTERN GRAY SQUIRREL   EASTERN FOX SQUIRREL

EASTERN GRAY SQUIRREL

to January, with some states including a limited spring season. Most states have a limit of around six squirrels, but some western states have lower limits due to lower availability.

HUNTING METHODS: The best squirrel hunting method uses a combination of tactics taken from a variety of hunting styles, including spot-and-stalk, still-hunting, and ambush hunting. The exact approach differs somewhat according to whether or not the deciduous trees have shed their leaves.

When the leaves are on, you can't see squirrels at long distances—and, thankfully, they can't see you. Action tends to occur at close range. While a .22 rifle is suitable at all times for squirrel hunting (think head shots), many hunters prefer to use a shotgun loaded with #6 pellets at this time of year in order to capitalize on shot opportunities presented by squirrels that are moving in the treetops behind a thin veil of leaves.

Regardless of weapon choice, you should concentrate your hunting efforts on mornings and evenings as much as possible during the leaves-on period. (Squirrels become late risers when temperatures plunge in the early winter, preferring to let the air warm up before they leave their nests or tree cavities to begin foraging.) If you can, get into the woods about fifteen minutes before daybreak and sit against a large tree in an area that you know from past experience or preseason scouting to be frequented by squirrels. When daylight hits, spend the first half hour or so just looking and listening. You might shoot your first squirrel of the day like this, right from your seated position and possibly shooting into the same tree that you happen to be leaning against. When hunting in the evening (or even midday, if that's the only time you have), you still want to do the same thing: slip into a good area and then sit tight while the woods settle down around you and the animals go back to their business.

While sitting, listening is perhaps even more important than looking. Squirrels make a lot of racket as they bound through trees that are still holding their leaves, and it's especially easy to hear this during the period of early morning quiet. Also listen for the sound of tree nut husks raining to the ground as squirrels feed.

Eventually you'll want to move from your seated position, either because you've identified some distant squirrel activity or because nothing's happening in your area. If it's the former reason, keep some large trees between you and the squirrels you're stalking while you approach. This will help prevent them from seeing you and allow you to get into easy range. If it's the latter reason, head toward the greatest concentration of mature nut-bearing trees in your area, keeping in mind that field edges and ridgelines are generally good places to start looking. Either way, move very slowly and keep your eyes focused on the treetops. Watch and listen for fluttering leaves that might signify a feeding or traveling squirrel. Also watch and listen for close-range squirrels that are watching you in the hope that you'll simply pass by without noticing them. These are the easy squirrels, and they taste just as good as the hard ones. If you're toting a .22, aim for just behind the squirrel's ear in order to give yourself a little room for error. If you're toting a shotgun, hold your bead off the end of the squirrel's nose in order to limit the number of pellets that get into the meat. Ideally, you want to pepper his head but leave his body unscathed. (The exact hold-off needs to be estimated according to the distance of the squirrel and spread of the shotgun; it's wise to experiment with your shotgun ahead of time by shooting at paper targets from various ranges.)

When you do go after a distant squirrel, one of three things is going to happen.

1. You slip into range of the squirrel undetected, usually because it's distracted by its own feeding activities, and you make your shot at a stationary animal. That's ideal.

2. You get close and the squirrel goes streaking off through the treetops, bouncing from limb to limb. At this point the shotgunner simply does a pass-through swing on the squirrel—just like on a bird, only slower—and knocks the squirrel down to the ground. A hunter with a .22 rifle should follow directly beneath the squirrel as it travels, being very careful to not let the squirrel get out of eyesight—even though that's basically impossible because the squirrel is almost inevitably going to vanish. The goal, however, is to be able to pinpoint as closely as possible the place where it vanished. At this point, refer to #3, below.

3. The squirrel vanishes, seemingly into thin air. In this situation, the first thing you want to do is circle the suspected tree and check for holes, cavities, and nests in the vicinity of the squirrel's last known location. If you see a hole or cavity, especially one that shows evidence of squirrel use in the form of a gnawed and widened opening, you might as well give up and go look for another squirrel. Ditto if you see a nest. (No matter what, never succumb to the temptation to shoot up into the nest in the hope of knocking the squirrel out. It's reckless and imprecise, and it doesn't work.) Once you've ruled out the presence of cavities or nests to the best of your ability, it's time to start looking for the squirrel. You have to trust that it's up there hiding from you. Use your binoculars to study the crotches of limbs and the topsides of any large horizontal branches. You're not so much looking for a squirrel as

When the leaves are down, switch out your shotgun for a scoped .22 rifle. You need the extended shooting range when squirrels can see you from a long way off.

you're looking for a squirrel-colored lump or even a wind-tousled wisp of hair from the squirrel's tail. Study the tree from directly beneath, then circle the tree and study it at various distances and angles. As you move, the squirrel will move as well in order to keep portions of the tree between you and itself. Eventually, you hope, it'll screw up and expose a portion of its body. Often this portion happens to be the tail, as squirrels seem to be less aware of this part of their anatomy when it comes to concealment. Obviously you can't shoot the tail, so then your job becomes a waiting game. Without losing sight of the tail, get into the best position to make your shot when the squirrel inevitably changes position. The simple act of hunkering down against a tree may inspire the squirrel to move. Since it can no longer hear you walking about, it'll get curious about where you went and then it'll move to

get a better look. If it can still see you while you sit there, its patience will certainly outlast your own. But if the squirrel can see you, you should be able to see it. Keep your binoculars in hand and use them to do a detailed study of the tree. One of the more rewarding things in hunting is finally finding a squirrel that's befuddled you for the past twenty minutes.

When the leaves are down, things can be quite a bit different. First off, it's smart to leave your shotgun at home and bring along a scoped .22 rifle that you can comfortably shoot out to 50 or 60 yards. At this time of year, predators or hunters have picked off many of the less cautious and younger squirrels. Those that are left are naturally going to be a bit cagier; it's not nearly as easy to close the distance on them. You can spot the squirrels at much greater distances, but they can spot you at greater distances as well.

In the winter, it's common to see squirrels busting away from you across the forest floor 100 or more yards out and then disappearing without giving you a chance to pinpoint their location. Right off, it's clear that the easy pickings of autumn have come and gone.

The key here is to do a lot more sitting and a lot less moving. Think of it as setting up mini-ambushes. Picking your locations is easy when there's snow on the ground, because you can identify areas of strong activity by looking for tracks and burrowing marks in the snow. Once you find these spots, take a seat and hold tight. It might take an hour or more before the squirrels forget the disturbance and begin their activity again. In the absence of snow, you can do another form of "scouting" by just taking a walk through the woods on the day before your planned hunt. You're basically just strolling through the woods with the intention of spooking squirrels. Watch the ground as much as the treetops, because late-season squirrels spend a lot of time down there caching and retrieving nuts. Once you've bumped three or four squirrels (or seen them in the far distance), calculate the most central position to all the activity and then set up there against a tree the next morning. They'll have forgotten all about the previous disturbance by then and they'll likely be right in the same areas. When you see one, don't go heading off in that direction. You're too likely to spook it. Instead, just hold tight and wait. Let the squirrel go about its business and trust that it'll eventually come into range. If you're in a good area, you might even end up with several squirrels working around you as they come in and out of range. If so, wait until you have two within shooting distance. Shoot the farthest one first, then quickly ready your rifle for another shot. Quite often, the other squirrel will jump to the side of a tree and then freeze there while it sorts out what just happened. It's a great opportunity for a doubleheader.

Winter squirrel hunting is an entirely different game from early-season squirrel hunting; there are fewer squirrels and they are more cagey. However, the ability to find fresh tracks in snow makes locating active feeding areas very easy. The squirrel in the left image made the tracks in the right image.

KEVIN MURPHY, A FANATICAL KENTUCKY SQUIRREL HUNTER AND HOUNDSMAN, WEIGHS IN ON HIS FAVORITE QUARRY

"In most parts of the country gray **squirrels** like the big **hardwoods**, whereas fox squirrels like more open lands such as **river** bottoms. But both can be found in either habitat. Squirrels have two breeding periods, one in the late spring and early summer and another in the days leading up to the winter solstice. Nests are a sure sign that squirrels have been in the area. You may see a couple of different types of nests. A big round tight nest the size of a basketball will be used to raise young in or as a secure hiding place from avian predators. A smaller flat-type nest will be used for lounging. A shabby nest coming apart is most likely an abandoned

(continued)

nest and will not be used unless there is no other place to hide or escape. Fresh cuttings of nuts on stumps and logs tells you that squirrels are active and using the area.

"Hunting squirrels with a treeing dog happens mostly in the late fall when the trees have given up their leaves for the season and the squirrels are on the ground searching for food and mates. The best times of day to hunt are the first two hours of the morning and the last two of the evening, except when you have a foggy, misty day. Then squirrels tend to stir the entire day and will stay low in the tree on the main trunk or the lower limbs. This is my favorite time to hunt, because squirrels will tend to stay put when treed and they don't run into dens as much.

"As with all scenting dogs, squirrel dogs will cover more area and will find more game if you hunt your dog into the wind every chance you get. When a dog chases a fox squirrel, the squirrel might take the dog on a long run before it trees. You may think the squirrel dog is messing around and chasing off game, but it might just be doing its job. Know how your dog reacts to a treed squirrel. Most tree dogs have a standard bark that says, 'Hey, I got him over here; when you have an extra moment, come and shoot him.' But there are times when your dog will go berserk. This means the squirrel is on the move and potentially heading for a hole. If you want that squirrel to end up in your game vest, you better move fast.

"After a dog puts a squirrel up a tree and barks to tell you, 'Hey, he is over here,' he has pretty much earned his feed. Now it is up to you to find the squirrel. When approaching the tree, take a close quick look at the tree from top to bottom. Search for knotholes, splits, nests, grapevines, and any other hiding places, but most of all look for the squirrel itself. If you can't find it, look for a piece or part of a squirrel, such as a tuft of hair from the tail, the hump of a body, or the lemon shape of the head. If you've been gifted with good eyes, you can maybe see just a foot or claw.

"When there are two people hunting, you need to split up and take opposite sides of the tree to search for the squirrel. Squirrels can be very cagey and will try to keep some type of cover between them and their pursuer. It is best when the hunter with the best eyesight remains still while the other hunter shakes a bush or rattles a grapevine to try to scare the squirrel into giving up his location. If you are alone, it can be tough to locate a squirrel. I prefer not to wear any blaze orange unless it's required by law.

"During the first couple of weeks in December, in my part of western Kentucky, gray squirrels perform a mating ritual and may gather in numbers in the largest tree of the forest. The glands on boar squirrels swell, and the boars come into rut and will pursue any willing female gray squirrel. During this time, your dog may tree on a rut tree, and there may be several gray squirrels in the tree at the same time. This is the jackpot of squirrel hunting. In this situation you must abide by this rule: shoot the bottom squirrel first! If you choose to shoot a top squirrel, it will fall past the lower squirrels, spooking them and making them go into a frenzy of escape. A good friend of mine, who happens to be an excellent waterfowl shot, agrees that running squirrels are very hard to hit. An exception to the shoot-the-bottom-squirrel rule is when you see a squirrel with its head pointing down the tree. This means he is a runner! Shoot him first.

"When it comes to squirrel guns, I like to shoot a scoped .22 LR rifle that's zeroed for 35 yards, though I know where it shoots at 65 yards as well. My favorite is a Czech-made BRNO model 1 that I inherited from my dad. It has a 2×7 Redfield scope. My second favorite is a Ruger 10-22 with a Manlicher stock and a 3×9 scope. It's short and handy in the woods, and I have taken running squirrels with it. A shotgun is good to have as a backup to a rifle, but in my opinion it should only be used on running squirrels or in areas limited to shotgun use. I use #5 shot, which really puts the squirrels on the ground. I suppose if you really wanted to get serious about squirrels you'd get a Savage 24 DL, with the .22 WMR barrel that sits over a 20-gauge shotgun barrel. Top it with a 2×7 scope.

"For a hat, I like a short brim that does not cut down on my peripheral vision. I wear a Centerfire hunting vest that has all types of pockets for gear, water bottles, et cetera, and it lets you carry the bulk of the load on your hips instead of on your back and shoulders. I carry a sharp knife, a good pair of game shears, and a pair of catfish-skinning pliers for pulling hides on those old tough boars. A final good tidbit of squirrel information is that when you cook fox squirrel the bones will turn a pinkish color, whereas the bones of gray squirrels remain white."

BLUE GROUSE
Sooty grouse *(Dendragapus fuliginosis)*
Dusky grouse *(Dendragapus obscurus)*
A.K.A.: Hooters, Richardson's grouse,
mountain grouse, pine grouse

S ome folks refer to blue grouse as "fool's hen," a generically applied moniker meaning a game bird so lacking in caution that any fool could kill it. But rather than thinking of blue grouse as foolish, hunters should consider that this bird's "tameness" is actually evidence of the opposite: wildness. The blue grouse's behavior is a product of the high, rugged, and lonely country that it calls home. In the absence of pressure from humans, they haven't needed to adapt to our presence. Anyone who's fortunate enough to visit the spectacularly scenic habitats of the blue grouse should consider himself lucky. And if one of the birds happens to perch on a limb and give him an easy shot, he should consider himself even luckier still. After all, the blue grouse is one of the finest-tasting game birds on the continent.

BARROOM BANTER: Blue grouse are reverse migrators. They winter in the high country, largely confined to treetops by deep snow. They migrate to lower altitudes in the spring. The downslope migration is related to breeding, as the males seek out bare patches of ground where they can strut for females.

All of the blue grouse of North America were long considered to be a single species, but in 2006, the American Ornithologists Union announced their opinion that North America actually has two distinct species of blue grouse: the sooty grouse, *Dendragapus fuliginosis*, of the wetter Pacific coastal ranges; and the dusky grouse, *Dendragapus obscurus*, of the drier interior ranges.

PHYSICAL CHARACTERISTICS: Larger than other forest and mountain grouse, measuring up to 23 inches long with weights up to 2¾ pounds. Coloration is fairly uniform, being a mottled slate, gray, or grayish brown. Males have an eye comb that is colored yellow, orange, or red.

HABITAT: Ridges, saddles, and steep slopes in the high country. Common from 8,000 to 12,000 feet in the Rockies, but at lower elevations in the coastal ranges. Usually in close proximity to Douglas fir and aspen.

DIET: Needles, seeds, and twigs of conifers, especially Douglas fir. Also aspen buds, various berries, and insects.

BREEDING AND REPRODUCTION: Hens typically lay from six to nine eggs, with an incubation period of two to three weeks. Males are polygamous and highly territorial. They will physically attack intruding males.

LIFE AND DEATH: One of the longest-lived of all game birds. A specimen in captivity lived

to be over eleven years old. In the wild, they can live for five to ten years. Still, it's likely that the majority of hatchlings die within their first year of life. Predators include pine martens, weasels, foxes, bobcats, coyotes, hawks, and owls.

TELLTALE SIGN: The blue grouse leaves very little evidence of itself, even during snowy conditions. In the spring breeding season, they do leave audible "sign": the owl-like hoot of a male announcing his territory is unmistakable.

EDIBILITY: Truly excellent, one of the very best game birds.

HUNTING OPPORTUNITIES: Moderate to high availability in some portions of the western United States, Canada, and Alaska. Seasons run for varying lengths based on regional availability and usually start sometime in September. The limits are both separate or combined with other upland species, with an average daily bag limit of four.

HUNTING METHODS: For the uninitiated, blue grouse can be tough to find. They occupy huge chunks of country in relatively low densities. Generally, look for blue grouse in the vicinity of the tree line. Pay special attention to areas that have Douglas fir or aspen, or better yet both. The birds are commonly found in "islands" of conifers amid open high-country parklands. Also, you can find them near the crests of ridges and saddles, and amid fingers of conifers that parallel drainages in otherwise high and open country.

Chasing them can feel like the old needle-in-the-haystack routine, but things get a lot easier once you've found your first one. The birds tend to cluster up according to elevation and habitat. Find a bird at 8,000 feet above sea level on a ridge that's covered in whitebark pine and you're likely to find one or two more on the next ridge over so long as it fits the same description.

When trying to pinpoint the key habitats that the birds are using at a given time, move fast and cover a lot of ground. Some hunters have good luck scouting from a mountain bike. Ride trails and high roads until you see a bird,

On left: A blue grouse hunter heads into the hills after duskies. In this particular area, the best locations are the highest ridgelines. On right: Typical sooty grouse country. Notice the differences between dusky and sooty grouse habitat.

Brody Henderson's pointer with a couple of Colorado dusky grouse. For a dog to be useful on a blue grouse hunt, it needs to be well disciplined.

then get off and start hunting. If you're driving a high-country road in your truck and you see a bird, don't think of it as a fluke. Get out and start hunting. This is especially important in the early fall, when family groups are still bunched together. You might see one bird on the edge of a trail and then find four or five more within a 50-yard radius. It also pays to ask any elk or deer hunters that you happen to run into. They'll be the sorts of folks who'd take notice of a blue grouse, and they might not mind sharing the information with you.

Dogs can be helpful when hunting blue grouse, but they can also be a hindrance. Blue grouse hunting requires a lot of walking in steep country; dogs that are out of shape or that have soft feet can ruin a trip in a hurry. Remember, too, that blue grouse don't hide. Many pointers who can hold a point on a bird that they can merely smell do not have the discipline to hold a point on a bird that's standing right in front of them in plain sight. They'll often charge the bird and flush it. That's fine if it's a close-working dog, but it's trouble if the dog is ranging out ahead at 75 yards. If you do have access to a good, mellow pointer who understands the idiosyncrasies of the blue grouse, it's a definite asset. Likewise with a flushing dog who likes to work close to its handler.

Many blue grouse hunters use a .22, preferring to take head and neck shots on standing or perching birds. The birds can also be hunted with archery equipment. Flu-flu arrows are a good bet, as they allow you to take shots into the trees without losing every arrow you shoot. Tip the arrows with hard rubber blunts or any of the small game heads that are available from archery shops. If you flush a bird while hunting with a .22 or a bow, watch and listen for where it lands. You can often find them again and make another attempt at a standing shot. When using a shotgun, #7½ shot works very well. Go with modified or improved cylinder chokes. Do not aim directly at a standing bird; rather, aim high in order to minimize damage to the meat. If you prefer the challenge of a flushed bird, walk directly toward any standing birds that you see in order to get them to flush. If a bird is in a tree, try flinging a stick to get it to fly.

DIFFERENCES BETWEEN SOOTY AND DUSKY GROUSE

CHARACTERISTIC	SOOTY GROUSE	DUSKY GROUSE
General appearance	Darker	Lighter
Typical number of tail feathers	18	20
Appearance of tail, particularly in male	Gray, subterminal band	Solid dull black
Cervical apteria (air sacs visible during male display)	Yellow	Red
Volume of hooting sound made during display	Loud (1 mile)	Quiet (100 yards)
Typical display location	Trees	Ground

Source: Michael Schroeder, *Washington Birder,* Volume 14:3, Fall 2006, page 4.

BOBWHITE QUAIL
Colinus virginianus
A.K.A.: Northern bobwhite, Virginia quail

Bobwhite quail hunting is a great way to scare the hell out of yourself. These birds have a habit of busting up from cover so close by it seems as though they're emerging from your pant legs. You empty your shotgun at the rapidly dispersing birds, thinking there are so many that you'll at least hit a few as long as you point your barrel at the flock. You then watch the entire covey escape unscathed. After botching a few opportunities, most hunters learn to take it slow and pick a single bird before shooting, which helps tremendously. Fine eating is the reward for such discipline. The bobwhite quail is easily one of the finest-tasting wild game species in North America. Pluck them, brush them in butter seasoned with a touch of cayenne and salt, and throw them on the grill. It's one of the best things you'll ever eat.

BARROOM BANTER: Bobwhite quail roost on the ground. At night, a covey will form a tight "roosting ring," with their tails pointed toward the center of the ring and their heads facing outward. The configuration allows the birds to conserve body heat and to watch in all directions for approaching predators.

PHYSICAL DESCRIPTION: Both sexes have mottled brown back and wings. Males have whitish undersides and a white throat patch and a white bar that runs from their bill to the back of their neck on each side of the head. Females have a yellowish or buff-colored throat and forehead patch. Bobwhite quail weigh between 5 and 8 ounces.

HABITAT: Farmland, grasslands, open woods, and forest edges. Generally found in areas with a mixture of open country and thick protective cover.

DIET: Widely varied, including seeds, berries, agricultural crops, leaves, grasses, and small insects.

BREEDING AND REPRODUCTION: Supposedly monogamous. Males build the nests, and females lay twelve to sixteen eggs per brood.

LIFE AND DEATH: Bobwhite quail have very high annual mortality rates but also high reproductive rates. Nests are destroyed at a rate of up to 70 percent, but 75 percent of the mature hens produce young every year thanks to their habit of making multiple nesting attempts during a breeding season. Chick mortality is around 30 percent, with many young dying from wet and cold weather. Other predators include raccoons, skunks, foxes, snakes, and a wide variety of hawks and owls.

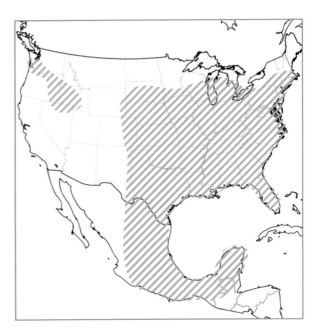

TELLTALE SIGN: Quail leave very little sign outside of tracks left in the snow.

EDIBILITY: Excellent table fare; can be grilled, roasted, poached, or fried. Very mild in flavor, but not bland.

HUNTING OPPORTUNITIES: Widely available in most states east of the Continental Divide, with some in the Pacific Northwest. Seasons tend to start sometime in November and run through February. The limits vary on a state-by-state basis, and range from eight to ten.

HUNTING METHODS: Bobwhite quail typically form coveys of around a dozen birds. While a covey is likely to diminish in size throughout the hunting season and to grow more wary, the birds can usually be found in the same general vicinity again and again. Even if an entire covey is destroyed by severe winter weather, it's likely that another covey

will take up the same piece of habitat the following year simply because the locality has
the proper mix of features that are attractive
to the species. They feed early in the morning
and again just before dark, spending the rest
of the daylight hours in thick cover. Unpressured birds will loaf around field edges, fence-
rows, and high grass close to their feeding
areas, but highly pressured birds will gravitate
toward thick creek bottoms and nearly impenetrable tangles of briars and thorns that can
keep out all but the most dedicated hunters.

The author's brother with a double on bobwhite quail in southern
Illinois. Quail are small but delicious. Cook them simply and not
too long.

Most serious bobwhite quail hunters use
dogs, particularly pointers. A dog is capable
of finding coveys of quail that you'd otherwise
pass by, and a good dog is capable of holding
them in place without spooking them until
you get within shotgun range. Great quail dogs
will range out to distances of a couple hundred
yards and then patiently hold coveys for several minutes while the hunters get into position. Quail will run along the ground ahead of
a dog, so it's generally assumed that the birds
are headed in whatever direction the dog is
pointing. Often they'll leave the area without
the dog realizing it, as he's pointing the resid-
ual scent that accumulated around the birds
as they loafed about. Approach from behind
the dog and walk in the direction of its point;
keep going even if you don't immediately flush
the birds. They might be out ahead of you.
When they do flush, they're likely to flush in
a direction that's directly away from you. This

is hugely advantageous, as quail are difficult
to hit. They're small, for one thing, so it's difficult to accurately range them; they seem to
be farther away than they are. The temptation
is to shoot right away, without giving them
time to achieve some distance. Hold off on the
birds and let them get far enough away so that
your shotgun pattern will have blossomed out
enough to actually connect on a bird—or, in
the case of direct hits, to not be so densely
packed that it destroys the edibility of your
target.

You can successfully hunt bobwhite quail
without dogs, especially if you've got a couple
of hunting partners. Line up to hunt strips of
cover and brushy field edges, with one hunter
placed out in the field when bordering croplands. Often, quail will run out to the edge of
a field and then run ahead or double back in
single file down the field edge without ever
flushing. Birds might also flush from thick
cover and fly toward the field, because they

A pair of quail hunters walk through some quality habitat.

When hunting patchy cover, try to surround the patches as well as you can before sending another hunter in to stomp the brush. This way, someone will get a shot regardless of which way the birds fly. And make sure that the brush stomper is a dedicated sort of person with the proper clothing and a high tolerance for discomfort. He or she needs to wade through nasty briars and thickets while doing a very thorough job of kicking every patch of cover. Quail will hold very tight, and in the absence of a bird dog you need to work doubly hard.

Because of their small size and camouflage color, bobwhite quail are easy to lose when hunting without retrieving dogs. When you do hit a quail that falls into thick brush, mark both the last known location of the bird and the position from where you took the shot. Then walk directly at the bird, even if it means trudging through some nasty cover. If a direct approach fails to turn up the bird, start walking in expanding circles as you continue the search. It also helps to go back to your shooting position and then try to direct a hunting partner to where you thought the bird landed. Keep at it, and don't give up until you retrieve the bird. For quail, use improved cylinder and modified chokes with #7½ or #8 shot.

don't like to fly through thickets. When possible, put someone ahead at the end of the strip of cover as well, in order to head off and flush any quail that try to escape that way.

CHUKAR
Alectoris chukar
A.K.A.: Red-legged partridge, Indian chukar, rock partridge, keklik

Chukars put the "up" into upland game bird. An introduced species native to the mountainous regions of Asia and the Middle East, chukars inhabit some of the highest and driest country of the western United States. Their preferred habitats bring to mind the landscapes occupied by bighorn sheep, and in many locations they share their ridges and canyons with this species. When escaping predators, chukars sometimes prefer to run before they fly. They'll often put 100 yards of ground—well beyond the range of even the best wingshooter—between themselves and their pursuers before lifting into the air. Successfully hunting these birds requires extreme tactics, accurate shooting, and a good set of lungs.

BARROOM BANTER: In the dry environs they call home, chukars will take advantage of any water source they can find. The birds have been observed drinking water in mine shafts 10 feet below ground level.

PHYSICAL DESCRIPTION: Overall gray-brown body. Wings are white with black bars. The face is buff-colored, with black markings. Tail feathers are chestnut-colored. The legs and bill are red. On average, chukars are about a foot long and weigh around 1½ pounds.

HABITAT: Rocky hillsides, craggy mountain slopes with grassy vegetation, open and flat desert with sparse grass and barren plateaus. Chukars will migrate to lower elevations to escape deep snow.

DIET: This non-native bird seems to prefer non-native foods; favorites include seeds from cheatgrass, Russian thistle, and downy chess. Also eats clover, alfalfa, fruits, berries, and grasshoppers.

BREEDING AND REPRODUCTION: During the breeding season of February through April, the males guard the females rather than a specific territory. Females lay seven to fourteen eggs and incubate them for about twenty-four days.

LIFE AND DEATH: Common predators of chukars include bobcats, foxes, skunks, raccoons, golden eagles, and many species of smaller raptors. Most chicks will die during their first year of life; adults can live up to five years, though that age is rarely achieved.

TELLTALE SIGN: When there's snow on the ground, look for concentrations of tracks.

EDIBILITY: Excellent. Considered by many to be a delicacy.

HUNTING OPPORTUNITIES: Available in some western and northwestern states, with a range that extends to some parts of southwestern Canada. Their availability in other states is increasing due to their continued introduction. Seasons vary greatly depending on the state but tend to start in early fall, some-

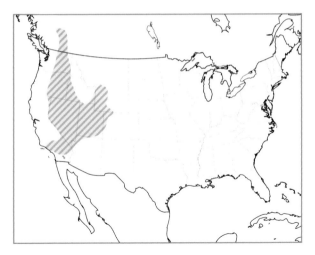

time around August or September. Limits typically range from three to six birds.

HUNTING METHODS: Chukars are popular at game preserves, where pen-raised birds are stocked in advance of the shooter's arrival so that he can pretend to hunt them. Hunting these half-tamed birds teaches you as much about real chukars as an obese zoo grizzly teaches you about wild bears. Real chukars—meaning wild-born birds—are extremely challenging to hunt. You need to be prepared to climb. Wear rigid boots meant for hunting big game in the mountains, and carry a daypack with plenty of food and water so that you can stray far and wide in search of birds without having to return to your vehicle.

Compared with other upland game birds, chukars are wanderers. A covey might move a mile or more per day, and dozens of miles over the course of a year. Look for them primarily in open, arid country with abundant brushy draws, coulees, and creek beds. Chukars roost on the ground, typically low on

Chukar country is rough; be prepared for some serious walking on difficult ground.

slopes, and then feed upward during the day. Look for them on south-facing slopes during cold weather, and in shaded or brushy areas during hot weather. During dry conditions, when water is scarce, they will concentrate in the vicinity of reliable water sources. During times of abundant water, expect the birds to be more widely dispersed. Deep snow will move them out of the high country and toward lower elevations. The birds are quite vocal, making a call that sounds like their name: *chucka-chucka-chucka*. It pays to stop often and listen for the birds when you're trying to locate a covey, especially on quiet, windless days when sound travels well.

Chukars become extremely wary when faced with hunting pressure. They tend to congregate into coveys ranging from ten to forty birds, which greatly increases the likelihood that at least one of them will see or hear you coming. One or more birds in a covey will sometimes post themselves atop rocks or other high points to act as sentries. When they sense danger in the form of an approaching hunter or his dogs, they typically run uphill. For this reason, it doesn't make sense to hunt them by working in an uphill direction. They will invariably outpace you. It's better to hunt them in a downhill direction, which will make them more likely to flush. It also pays to have multiple hunters spread out vertically on a slope and then push in a sidehill direction. When doing this, make sure to position a hunter or two higher than you expect to find birds; this way, when the chukars run uphill to escape lower hunters they will encounter an upslope hunter and be more likely to flush. If you see chukars running out ahead of you, run in an upward diagonal direction to head them off. It's not likely that you'll actually catch up to them, but you might make them nervous enough to get them into the air. When they flush, they use gravity to their advantage by flying downhill. The birds achieve high speeds with just a few flaps of their wings.

When you flush a covey of chukars, the birds will usually break up into singles or small groups. Watch carefully to see where all the birds go so that you can chase after them. They usually hold a little tighter the second time around, perhaps because they are tired from the initial flight.

It's helpful to have a well-disciplined and close-working dog when hunting chukars, especially for retrieving purposes. If you knock a chukar out of the sky without seriously injuring it, the bird may very well escape by running. A dog is much more likely than you to chase the bird down and catch it. Many hunters use #7½ shot for chukars, but #6 is preferable due to the often long-range shots and the need to deal the birds a solid blow in order to anchor them where they land. Modified and full chokes are good choices.

JOSEPH FURIA, AN OREGON HUNTER, WEIGHS IN ON CHUKAR HUNTING STRATEGIES

"A favorite saying of chukar hunters is 'The first time you hunt chukar is for fun; every time after that is for revenge.' The level of frustration that accompanies any chukar hunt will be familiar to anyone who has fly-fished for steelhead or bowhunted for elk. At times,

it seems impossible. But when you are successful, it can be euphoric.

"It's more about hunting than shooting. Most public land chukar hunting involves long walks on rugged, steep terrain with a gun in your hand and little actual shooting. To that end, it is important to hike smart, travel light, and enjoy the view.

"But shooting **does** matter. After hiking twelve miles in two days, you finally flush your first covey at **inside** 40 yards and then you blow all three **shots** right over the top of them. It's painful. Most shots **at** chukar are crossing or going away from you in a downhill direction—**not** a shot found on the skeet or trap field. To make these shots, keep these three things in mind:

"Feet. When you're expecting **a** chukar to flush, set your feet on stable ground pointed in the direction where you expect to shoot the bird. If you must move, walk slowly and be ready the second you stop—birds get especially nervous when you stop moving.

"Eyes. Prior to the flush, relax your eyes rather than looking at specific spots on the ground; when your eyes are relaxed, you **pick** up movement quicker. Once the birds **flush** and before you mount, focus on the head of an individual bird—this helps avoid flock shooting (which **almost** always results **in** a miss).

"Mount. Practice mounting your gun at home—a bad mount is responsible for **most** missed shots. You **can** tape a flashlight to **the** end of your barrel **and** practice swinging **and** mounting along the edge where the **wall** and ceiling meet. **The** light should show a smooth swing with no up-and-down movement. Let your front arm steer the gun.

"Practice in the terrain. The best practice is hiking with a friend along with a hand thrower and some shooting clays in the **type** of terrain you'll be hunting.

"Early **season,** you'll **find** chukar near water, often lower down in the canyons. **By** midseason you'll find them up **on** top **and** on south-facing **slopes** where they can warm themselves on dark rocks that absorb **sunlight.** In snow **conditions,** look for them in rock bands and sage just on the leeward side of ridges. In light wind, you'll want to hunt quietly and be prepared for long shots. In heavy wind, you'll get much closer, but you'll need to shoot quickly before the birds catch a wingful of wind and get out of range.

"Dogs find chukar, but their success is greatly increased if you hunt them into the wind whenever possible. Put them above the birds when you have an up-canyon wind (which is almost all the time). Also keep your dog well watered. In basalt country, a pair

(continued)

of rubber dog boots will protect the dog's pads and increase the length of your hunt. My favorite hunt with a pointing dog is to run my dog on the ridges from mid- to late season until he points a covey. Then I'll sneak down below the dog and walk uphill in order to flush the birds. My shooting percentage doubles when I can get chukar to fly over me rather than shooting at them when they're flying downhill away from me.

"I know chukar hunters who hunt in spandex leggings and running shoes in order to travel light and cover lots of ground. Chukar hunting isn't about looks; it's about efficiency. Leave your heavy tin-cloth pants and shooting jacket in the truck. Merino wool underlayers, lightweight brush pants, cross-training hiking boots, gloves, a knit hat, a brimmed cap, and a rain jacket will cover 90 percent of your hunts. If it gets really cold, then add heavy wool gloves and gaiters for snow drifts. A warm jacket is nice for when you stop to take breaks.

"I have shot wild chukar with everything from a .410 to a 12-gauge, but I prefer 12-gauge and 16-gauge shotguns with improved-cylinder and modified chokes in the early season. Late season, I use modified and full chokes. A 28-inch barrel helps with the swing and follow-through. Regardless of the gun, my preferred load remains the same: high-brass #6 shot.

"Chukar typically use the same spots as long as conditions remain the same. When you find a covey, make a mental note (or mark it on your GPS) and remember under what conditions you found the birds in that location. Chances are, you'll find them there for years to come.

"Follow wounded birds. If you see a chukar rock or drop a leg after you shoot at it, watch it for as long as you can and then head toward it. Because chukar are often flying downhill, they can sail a long distance before falling dead.

"Chukar country demands respect. Safety needs to be a top priority. Chukar live in rocky, remote locations with poor footing and poorer cell coverage. If possible, always hunt with a partner and carry a basic medical kit and a basic survival kit (space blanket, fire starter, iodine tablets for water purification, energy bar, and a knife). If you're hunting alone, tell someone where you'll hunt and when you'll be home. And solo hunters should stick to stable terrain and, if possible, carry a personal locator beacon. Before you head into a location, ask yourself, 'If I break an ankle, how am I going to survive until someone shows up?'"

HUNGARIAN PARTRIDGE
Perdix perdix
A.K.A.: Hun, gray partridge, English partridge

The Hungarian partridge is a non-native species imported to the United States and Canada primarily from Hungary and Czechoslovakia in the late 1800s and early 1900s. The birds are generally regarded as an incidental species occasionally taken by hunters chasing pheasants and sharp-tailed grouse. The lack of concentrated effort for Hungarian partridge might have something to do with the difficult nature of hunting these birds. Not only are they extremely wary, often jumping well ahead of hunters and their dogs, they can also be very difficult to locate even when they are abundant. The birds are not nearly as predictable in their whereabouts as other upland game birds, and seem just as likely to be in the short stubble of a mowed field as in the more "classic" bird cover along stream

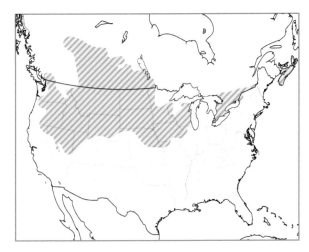

edges and coulees. But the rareness of harvesting a Hun is what makes the event so special, all the more if you actually went into the field with the intention of shooting one. And if you ever manage to bag a legal limit of Hungarian partridge, you will be a member of a small and privileged group of hunters.

BARROOM BANTER: Hungarian partridge produce some of the largest clutches of any bird species, with up to twenty-two eggs.

PHYSICAL DESCRIPTION: Hungarian partridge are grayish brown birds with a dark orange face and throat. Their flanks are barred reddish brown and the tail feathers rusty. The male and female have a chestnut patch on their belly; the patch is much less pronounced or altogether absent on the female. The average Hun weighs just shy of a pound and is about 12 inches long.

HABITAT: Open farmlands and grassy fields. Unlike many other upland game birds, Huns can thrive in extensively cultivated country that offers very little cover.

DIET: A wide variety of agricultural grains as well as wild plant seeds. Will readily eat grasshoppers and other insects as well.

BREEDING AND REPRODUCTION: The female lays a clutch of twelve to eighteen olive-colored eggs, hatching mid-June to late July. The chicks will leave the nest and begin feeding almost immediately after hatching.

LIFE AND DEATH: The eggs and chicks of Huns often fall prey to nest raiders such as raccoons, minks, weasels, and skunks. Adult Huns are preyed upon by foxes, coyotes, and several species of hawks and owls.

TELLTALE SIGN: Almost none during snow-free months. Tracks will be found in snow along field edges and roadsides.

EDIBILITY: The flesh is a little darker than chicken or pheasant, but still mild. Very good quality.

HUNTING OPPORTUNITIES: Moderately available in a range split between Canada and the United States. They are still being introduced into some regions, but their North American numbers are dropping. Seasons typically run from September through January and are often aligned with chukar season. Daily bag limits are usually between four and eight.

HUNTING METHODS: Huns are typically found around intensively managed farmlands, where the majority of the landscape is devoted to grain production. The birds will feed in the morning and again in the afternoon, spending the day in loafing areas. In this way they are

Hungarian partridge, or gray partridge, are generally found in and around intensively farmed country, but sometimes you'll locate them in rawer and more scenic environments. The author has flushed and killed Huns in the Missouri Breaks, miles from the nearest road.

similar to pheasants, but the loafing areas of Huns are far less predictable than those of pheasants. Rather than hunkering down in cattail marshes or creek bottoms, the birds feel comfortable hiding in the relatively sparse cover provided by stubble and short grass. Thus, the birds seem as though they could be virtually anywhere on the landscape. However, Huns do seem to prefer edge-type habitats such as crop borders or windrows, so don't worry so much about covering the centers of large crop fields when trying to find the birds during their early morning and late afternoon feeding periods. Stick to the edges. And despite the difficulty of patterning Huns, you

should still make a permanent note of any coveys that you do find. If the habitat doesn't change, it's quite common to find coveys of Huns in the same basic areas from one year to the next.

Dogs are a good asset for Huns, but only if the dog is willing to work close. Huns are very skittish, and a wide-ranging dog is going to spook far more birds than he'll be able to pin down. Unlike pheasants, Huns will not hold long enough for you to cover 100 yards of distance between you and your dog.

The real key to killing Huns—perhaps more so than with any other game bird—is the ability to stay with a covey of the birds after the initial flush. A covey of Huns might include a dozen or more birds, but they'll break up into several smaller groups once you flush them. These small groups will not travel far, usually landing within a few hundred yards. Watch where each group goes, paying careful attention to the type of ground cover where they land. Huns that set down in sparse cover are likely to run after landing, and they're also likely to flush well outside of range when you approach. Concentrate instead on birds that land in thicker cover, as these birds are less likely to move and more likely to hold tight. If you're persistent, you might flush each subgroup of Huns once or twice after the initial flush. These follow-up flushes are often far more successful than the initial flush, because you're better prepared for the appearance of the birds and because the birds tend to hold tighter and tighter each time you flush them.

Because Huns occur in such large coveys, there's a temptation to fire a lot of rounds in quick succession when you put them up. But flock shooting doesn't work on Huns—nor does it work on anything else. Instead, try to take your time and make one or two shots that count rather than squeezing off a full magazine from your pump or autoloader. High-power shells with #6 or #7½ shot are appropriate. Modified and improved cylinder chokes are good, but a full choke might also come in handy on skittish coveys that flush at the edge of your effective range.

MOURNING DOVE
Zenaida macroura
A.K.A.: Turtledove, rain dove

The mourning dove is America's leading game bird, with some 20 million harvested annually. During years of great abundance, this figure can get as high as 70 million. Doves are warm-weather birds. In much of the United States, open seasons bridge the gap between summer and fall. Thanks to the pleasant weather, easy accessibility of productive hunting grounds, and generous bag limits (typically ten to fifteen doves per day), dove hunting is often a social affair that brings together families, friends, and even entire communities. Since doves are so easy to clean and simple to prepare, they are perfect for post-hunt celebrations. A delicious meal requires nothing more than a mess of doves, an outdoor grill, and some butter seasoned with a pinch of cayenne pepper. A dove shoot is a relaxing and fun-filled way to kick off the long string of hunting seasons that will keep you busy (and often cold and miserable) through the fall and early winter.

BARROOM BANTER: When constructing nests, male and female doves use teamwork.

The male will carry building materials to the female as she weaves the nest, landing on her back to deliver the load.

PHYSICAL DESCRIPTION: Light gray and brown in color, with black spots on the wings; males and females are very similar in appearance. They average 12 inches in length and weigh about 5 ounces.

HABITAT: Widely distributed from coast to coast, mourning doves occupy a great diversity of semi-open habitats, including farm country, prairies, grasslands, deserts, mixed forests, and suburbia.

DIET: Wide variety of seeds, including those of foxtail, ragweed, pigweed, and agricultural crops such as millet, safflower, canola, and corn.

BREEDING AND REPRODUCTION: Mourning doves are prolific breeders. In warmer climates they might raise six broods in a season, with two chicks per brood.

LIFE AND DEATH: Mourning dove eggs are commonly consumed by scavenging birds such as crows, plus house cats, raccoons, opossums, and several species of snakes. Raptors are the primary predators of adult doves. Seventy percent of doves die during their first year of life.

TELLTALE SIGN: Like most upland game birds, doves leave very little sign.

EDIBILITY: Dove meat is dark and rich and generally regarded as excellent.

HUNTING OPPORTUNITIES: Widely avail-

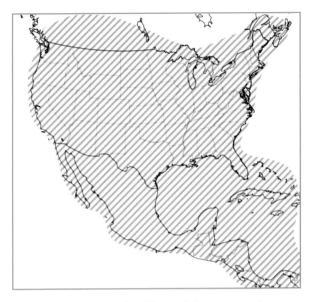

able throughout the United States and some portions of Canada. Usually the first bird season to open in most states, starting in the beginning of September and often running just a few weeks. Depending on number densities, daily limits range from six to fifteen.

HUNTING METHODS: Doves are one of the few upland game birds that are best hunted by using ambush strategies. While it's certainly possible to flush the birds from their feeding locations, it's far better to stay put in a place where you can intercept the birds as they fly to their preferred feeding and watering areas.

The key to success is determining where the doves want to be and when they're likely to show up. This is best done by watching the birds and studying their movements. The species's habit of perching on power lines and in open treetops or dead snags makes them fairly easy to locate. Binoculars come in handy when looking for doves. Once you find a flock, de-

A Virginia hunter's bag limit of fifeen doves.

termine which fields or watering holes the birds are using. They prefer open ground and will not feed in brushy areas where their visibility is compromised. Their most active feeding times are in the morning and late afternoon, but don't take this for granted. Make note of their arrival times, and then plan on getting into position well in advance of that time in order to get set up.

When setting up, keep three things in mind: location, visibility, and concealment.

LOCATION: Basically, you want to set up as close as possible to where you last saw the greatest amount of dove activity. If the birds were favoring a particular corner of a field, you want to set up near that corner. If they were landing in a dead tree before dispersing around the edges of a large watering hole, you want to be near that dead tree. If they were flying through a narrow gap in a tall windrow before landing in a field, set up near that gap.

VISIBILITY: You need to be able to see the doves as they come in, so select an area where you can maximize your field of view. Ideally you'd have 360° of visibility, though in real-world scenarios this usually isn't possible. However, it is essential that you put yourself where you can see where the birds are coming from, and hopefully where they'll be going once they're spooked. For instance, if the doves

Hunt near food when targeting doves. In the late summer, sunflowers are irresistible to the birds.

are approaching a field from the north and your immediate view in that direction is obscured by trees or thick brush, you need to rethink your setup.

CONCEALMENT: Doves are skittish, especially when they've been getting shot at. Wear camouflage clothing that matches your surroundings, and a brimmed hat that shields your face. Face masks are also a good idea. Keep your movements to a minimum when you're waiting for the birds to show. When you need to move in order to have a look around, turn slowly. Try to nestle into some cover in order to break up your outline, but make sure you can still move freely. If you can get your back to a tree, that's a great way to hide. But don't pick a tree that's going to block your view

in a direction that birds are likely to come from. Open-topped ground blinds are a good option as well; you can hunker down into the blind but still see what's happening overhead.

Doves are very difficult to hit. They are small and fast, and they fly erratically. It's been calculated that eight shots are fired for every dove that gets killed. They do not usually give you the necessary time to adjust your posture and calculate leads. Instead, you need to shoot instinctively and quickly. If you're right-handed, keep your left foot pointing in the direction where you expect the birds to come from. Keep your shotgun in the ready position—trigger finger along the trigger guard, hands on the grip and forearm, butt against your hip or rib cage. When a bird appears within shooting range, raise the shotgun to your shoulder in one fluid motion and then, coming from behind the bird, brush the bird out of the sky with the barrel. Pull the trigger just as you pass the bird's head.

Though difficult to hit, mourning doves come down quite easily when you do connect. Target loads in #7½, #8, and #9 shot are appropriate when fired through improved or modified cylinders. A 12-gauge will suffice, though many dove hunters prefer the easier handling and reduced kick of a 20-gauge shotgun. It's not uncommon to shoot up a box or more of shells in a good dove field, so think ahead about how much abuse your shoulder can handle.

WHITE-WINGED DOVE

Although bigger than the mourning dove, the white-winged dove is not always an easier target. With a cruising speed of 40 miles per hour, these birds demand that the shooter have a knack for calculating leads. Historically, white-winged doves were only found in southern Texas and Arizona. But since the 1980s the range and population of this species has increased dramatically. They can now be found in Louisiana, Mississippi, Florida, Kansas, Arkansas, Oklahoma, and New Mexico as well. Hunting for white-winged doves is legal almost everywhere they are found, though there are few hunters who actually target them. Usually they are picked up as a bonus species by hunters gunning for mourning doves. The flesh is excellent.

The ring-necked pheasant is an introduced non-native species that would falter and quickly vanish from much of its habitat if not for constant restocking efforts by humans. Despite the ecological artificiality of the bird, it remains one of our most highly regarded and cherished game species. Many rural communities throughout the pheasant's extensive range have built cottage industries around catering to the massive influxes of pheasant hunters who come in search of birds during the fall months—a welcome bit of commerce in rural areas that are often plagued by economic misfortune. Demand for ringnecks

is so high that many landowners manage their property with an eye toward pheasant production rather than traditional agricultural output—they've found that selling pheasants to hunters pays better than selling beef cattle to feed lots. Even inexperienced hunters have little problem killing a few pheasants if they're willing to pay for access on these productive (and often stocked) lands. Do-it-yourself hunters who are confined to public lands or marginally productive private ground can still find plenty of birds during good years, but it can take work. The payoff, however, is well worth the effort. There's something inherently gratifying about picking up a downed pheasant. The beauty, robust size, and excellent food quality of this creature outweigh its status as an introduced exotic on the American landscape. Your taste buds won't know the difference!

BARROOM BANTER: The ring-necked pheasant was first brought to North America in 1881 by a California judge who imported thirty live birds from China. Four of the birds died during the journey, while the other twenty-six were released in the wild. A decade later, their progeny were abundant enough to support a harvest of fifty thousand birds.

PHYSICAL DESCRIPTION: Females appear to be generally dull beige, mottled with dark spots and bars. Comparatively, males are spectacularly colored. They have a long, orange-colored tail with black bars, a bluish gray rump, bronze-colored flanks, a white neck ring, iridescent head markings, and a patch of reddish facial skin. Females weigh around 2½ pounds and are about 22 inches long. Males weigh up to 3 pounds and measure up to 36 inches.

HABITAT: Predominantly farm country with active croplands and abundant ditches, fence-rows, thickets, undisturbed grasslands, overgrown fields, cattail marshes, or other sources of cover.

DIET: Agricultural crops such as corn, soybeans, and wheat, plus a variety of wild-growing seeds and fruits as well as insects such as grasshoppers.

BREEDING AND REPRODUCTION: Pheasants are highly polygamous; one male can easily breed a dozen or more females. Females lay between eight and twelve eggs in the spring.

LIFE AND DEATH: Pheasants have many predators throughout their life cycle, including skunks, opossums, raccoons, foxes, coyotes, hawks, and owls. They do not live long: 80 percent of all pheasants killed by hunters in the United States are less than one year old. Three-year-old pheasants are a rarity.

TELLTALE SIGN: In snow-free conditions, pheasants leave very little sign beyond the occasional feather and mound of droppings. In snow, look for abundant tracks in well-used areas.

EDIBILITY: Mild and pleasant. This light-colored flesh can be used for many chicken applications.

HUNTING OPPORTUNITIES: Found in most regions of the northeastern, midwestern, and western United States, and in some parts of Canada. Seasons tend to start sometime in

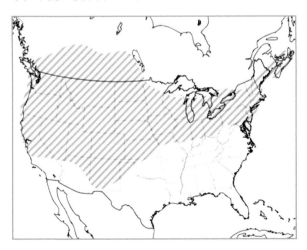

October and run through January, with a daily bag limit of around two or three.

HUNTING METHODS: Pheasants live according to a fairly predictable daily schedule. When hunting, you should consider the time of day when selecting the areas that you want to hit. In the early morning, pheasants will leave their thick roosting cover and head to a gravel source such as a roadside to supply their gizzard with some grit. From there they'll head to a crop field or other prime feeding area. It takes them an hour or two to eat their fill, and then they'll head to what's known as a loafing area—basically a safe place where they can spend their day. It could be the same place where they roost, or else another patch of cover closer to their feeding area. In the evening, they will venture back to their feeding area for another hour or two before heading to roost during the final moments of the day.

The exact places used for roosting, feeding, and loafing will fluctuate throughout the season according to weather and hunting pressure. For this reason, it's helpful to think of pheasant season as occurring in two parts, early and late. During the early season, pheasants are more abundant and more inclined to be following the "natural" movement patterns established before the opening-day influx of hunters. Late-season birds are far less numerous, and they've adjusted their movement patterns in accordance to hunting pressure.

On average, three out of every four pheasants killed by hunters will be killed during the first half of the season.

During the early season, especially on opening day, expect to find birds in the vicinity of the most obvious and productive feeding areas. The birds are likely to loaf in the immediate vicinity of these feeding areas, because they haven't been pressured out of these places yet. Look for them in the tall grass at the edges of crop fields, along ditches that bisect crop fields, in windrows bordering crop fields, or in grassy buffers between gravel roads (good sources of grit) and crop fields.

Once pheasants are subjected to significant hunting pressure, the easy birds get killed off. Those that are left will begin roosting, feeding, and loafing in cover that gets less hunter traffic. These areas tend to be thicker, less accessible, and more difficult to hunt. Think cattail marshes, wide and brushy creek beds, abandoned homesteads, and briar patches. Concentrate especially hard on "sleeper spots," those areas of cover that might have gotten overlooked because they're too small or too far out of the way to have warranted much attention from other hunters. A room-sized patch of weeds growing up around an old junked-out tractor at the back end of a field might hold a farm's worth of pheasants if other hunters have routinely neglected to hit it. Likewise with an island covered in willow and tall grass out in the middle of a river, or with a

Classic Midwest pheasant country: lots of tall grass.

windrow that's guarded by such vicious thorn-bearing vines that none but the most blood-thirsty dogs want to deal with it.

Just as pheasants will alter their preferred hangouts according to hunting pressure, they'll also change the way they respond to intruders. Birds that readily flush within 20 yards of a hunter's gun either are going to get killed or are going to quickly learn to avoid such mistakes. Avoidance typically amounts to holding tight or running. The best way to deal with both is to hunt with a dog that's got a good nose. Not only can the dog detect the presence of tight-holding birds and then flush them, it can detect the trail of birds that have run ahead and then move quickly to stop them, flush them, or turn them back around.

When hunting without dogs, you need to put together a solid plan before you start working the cover. First off, be quiet. If you're slamming truck doors and shouting to your buddies, you're going to send the birds flying or running to distant cover before you ever get within shooting range. Next, try to imagine where the birds will go if they decide to run. Have a stander sneak into position where he or she can block the birds from exiting the area. If hunting alone, enter the cover near the most

A Midwest hunter topples a rooster.

likely exit and then try to "herd" the birds in a direction where they'll be forced to either flush or expose themselves by running across open ground (they'll choose flushing). At all times, behave as though you *know for certain* that birds are holding in your patch of cover. Don't just pass through in blasé fashion, but carefully kick out every last possible hiding place that might be holding a bird that refuses to flush.

When you do flush a pheasant, avoid the temptation to make snap shots. This isn't like ruffed grouse hunting, where you've got only a split second to make your shot before the bird vanishes. Pheasant country tends to be more open, and you can usually afford to make a more careful shot. Patience is especially important because it's illegal to kill hen pheasants. Before you touch the trigger, you need

to make sure you're looking at a rooster. If the bird cackles when it lifts off, kill it. It's a male. If there's no cackle, you need to make a quick assessment based on physical appearance. At close range and in good light, it's simple. Males are brilliantly colored with an iridescent head and a white band around their neck; females are drab brown and relatively uniform in color. In poor light, or when looking at just the silhouette, you need to judge the bird by its tail. A rooster has a long and full-looking tail that measures from about 18 to 26 inches long. A female's tail is narrower and only 8 to 12 inches long. When hunting with friends, do everyone a favor and shout out a bird's sex—"Hen!" or "Rooster!"—as soon as you identify it. This will save others from making mistakes.

Wide-open pheasant country in Kansas. Notice the long line of hunters; it takes a lot of people (or a lot of time) to properly work such a huge expanse of cover.

When a pheasant flushes, it might seem to rise almost straight up out of the ground. It'll rise up to about 12 or 15 feet before leveling out and putting some yardage between itself and the source of its trouble. Let the bird get a little distance before you shoot. If not, you're likely to miss it because your shot pattern hasn't widened out yet. If you do connect, you're likely to destroy the meat because you're connecting with a full load of heavy shot at tight range.

Pheasants are hard to kill and many downed birds are lost to hunters who operate without a good dog. To limit loss, be careful not to overextend your maximum effective range. Sure, it feels great to kill a pheasant at 60 yards. But it feels simply awful to bust a pheasant's wing and lose it in the brush because you were taking a stunt shot. Shot size should be on the heavy side for upland birds—#6 shot is as small as you should use, unless you know for certain that you'll be taking a lot of close-range shots better suited to #7½ shot. When longer shots are more likely, #4 or #5 shot is a good choice because it packs the necessary punch to bring down these big and strong birds. For all-around use, a modified choke is a good choice on pheasants.

When hunting areas where the land is all locked up by private landowners who won't grant access (or who want money for access), you should get creative about finding good spots. Use plat maps or land ownership GPS

Hunting pheasants can be hard work. A good dog will pound a lot of cover for you and deliver more flushes than you'd get on your own. And it will retrieve more birds than you'd find on your own.

cards such as those sold by HuntingGPSMaps .com to identify oddball patches of ground that might be open to public access. It's also a good idea to talk to your state's fish and game agency to determine governing rules on small islands, river access points, railroad right-of-ways, and roadside ditches. Often these patches of public ground are the same kinds of habitat that draw in high-pressure birds like a magnet. Chest waders should be regarded as an essential piece of pheasant hunting gear. Most hunters don't keep a pair in their truck, which means they're not able to hit places that are protected by a defensive moat of water. By wading just a short distance, you can often reach virgin patches of cover that are teeming with birds.

Canoes and chest waders (conspicuously missing from this hunter's feet) can open up a lot of pheasant cover that gets overlooked by the competition.

RYAN CALLAGHAN, AN IDAHO AND MONTANA HUNTER, WEIGHS IN ON THE STRATEGIES AND PHILOSOPHIES OF PHEASANT HUNTING

"Know before you go. Some areas have multiple seasons; check your regulations. If you are hunting a new area, make sure you know the daily limit and possession limit. Does this area require nontoxic shot? Does your area require additional licensing above the upland game validation? Get familiar with your areas, new or old; go through the regulations every year.

"Organize your gear. Most pheasant hunters have a dedicated game vest. Get one and keep it well stocked. Carry water and snack items for both you and your dog, a whistle, a multitool, a basic first-aid kit, and the appropriate ammo. I use only one load for pheasants so as to not complicate things. When I reach into my vest for a shell, I know what I'll be grabbing out: B&P 16-gauge 1-ounce #6 lead. An exception to this rule is when I'm hunting an area that only permits nontoxic shot. In that case I shoot Winchester 2¾-inch #4 shot in 12 gauge. Find a load that works for you and stick with it; that consistency lends itself to more productive shooting.

"Communication. Pheasant hunts are often a group activity that requires planning and communication, both for a successful hunt and for safety. If you are hunting with any new members or if you yourself are new to the group, be sure to establish whether everyone has been on a hunt before or even shot before. It is often a very tough

(continued)

conversation to have on the edge of a field with roosters cackling over your shoulder, but believe me, everyone in your party will be grateful that someone spoke up and laid out both a game plan for the hunt and covered shooting lanes and safety. Don't be afraid to initiate this conversation, especially if you have a dog in the mix.

"I lay out a hierarchy as follows. If it's your hunt—i.e., you have the spot, public or private—it is your job to get your group together prior to the hunt, whether that's days or even weeks ahead of time. Figure things out down to the carpool situation, and if need be, make sure everyone knows not to slam the truck door. If it's a common area you and your buddies have routinely hit, the hunters with the dogs have final say.

"Wear blaze or hunter's orange caps. When hunting in a group you can only move as fast as the next hunter in line. Keep an eye on each other both for safety and for success; you may see something that the hunter next to you did not. Or you may notice that the group is moving a little fast for an older, younger, or out-of-shape hunter. When people get tired, that's when shotgun barrels start to wander; offer to put that hunter at a blocking position next time around.

"Positions. I like to position first-time hunters on the wings or outside of the group. Sometimes these spots can have tougher shooting, but your first-time hunter will only have other hunters to the left or right, not on both sides. If the spot belongs to you, it's advantageous for the entire group if the hunter with prior knowledge is in the middle directing the show. Rotate through positions if possible; if you were a blocker on the first swing, offer to walk the next.

"Do not shoot birds on the ground. 'Ground swatting,' or shooting a rooster before he flies, seems like a great way to get some frustration out and get something in the bag. Beyond the fact that smacking a bird capable of 60 mph flight while it's hunched in the grass is not considered sporting, pulling the trigger while the barrel of a gun is anything less than above level is a good way to kill a dog or make a hunter in the blocking position very uncomfortable.

"Have fun. As we've covered, pheasant hunting involves people; if you discover that someone else has found your spot, move on to the next and swing back through later in the day. Don't be afraid to ask other hunters how they are doing; on occasion they'll let some good information slip."

TEN RULES FOR UPLAND BIRDS

Each species of upland game bird has its own peculiarities, and these peculiarities change according to each bird's whereabouts. From a hunter's perspective, a ruffed grouse in a farm-country thicket of New England has little in common with a ruffed grouse in a mixed spruce and aspen forest outside of Fairbanks, Alaska. While the former bird might be paranoid in the extreme, flushing at the mere sound of a truck door opening in the distance, the latter bird might have such limited experience with humans that it'll walk ahead of a hunter at a distance of 10 or 15 yards and then take a position atop a stump as though offering itself as a sacrifice. Despite the many differences between upland bird species—and the glaring differences between members of the same species across varying habitats—there are still some loose rules and guidelines that can be used by all upland hunters regardless of their particular location and quarry.

1. Hunt near food. Upland game birds are almost strictly diurnal, meaning they rest at night and become active only during daylight hours. While pressured deer might start to feed at night in order to avoid hunters, birds do not. They feed during the day, and will do so every day except in the case of very extreme weather. Once you've identified a food source that is being actively used by upland game birds, the hardest work is behind you.

2. Pay attention to what works, and then do it again. Hunting upland game birds is a numbers game; missed shots are common, and you usually need to generate a lot of flushes in order to put a few birds into your game vest. When you do flush a bird, especially the first one of the day, study the area carefully. Even if you can't figure out why exactly the bird was there, try to understand the look and feel of the place so that you can readily identify similar locations that will hold additional birds. For example, if you flush a pheasant from the cattails along the edge of a slough, start looking for more sloughs.

3. Beware the undisciplined dog. As a general rule, bird dog owners love dogs equally as much as (or more than) they love hunting. That's all fine and dandy, at least until their love of the dog begins to cloud their judgment about whether or not the dog

(continued)

deserves to be taken on a hunt. The majority of "bird dogs" that are out there don't deserve the title. Let them out of the truck and they're flushing birds hundreds of yards away before you can even load your shotgun. And when they do actually execute a retrieve, they so thoroughly maul your bird that it resembles a feathery pâté by the time you get it. When it comes to friends bringing along their undisciplined dogs on an upland hunt, just say, "Thanks, but no thanks." Failing that, leave the dog in its kennel until you're having trouble finding a bird, then bring it over to do a search. Of course, this isn't meant to discredit the many finely tuned dogs that are out there. Watching a good bird dog in action is thrilling and a thing of beauty—and it's a great way to kill birds. But if there really was a great bird dog behind every kennel door, then it wouldn't be such a surprise when you finally meet one.

4. Miles = birds. You should never go into an upland bird hunt thinking that it's going to be a cakewalk. Sure, when hunting the perfect location at the perfect time, upland birds can provide nonstop action with little effort. More often, a productive upland bird hunt requires hard work and dedication. Success comes to the hunters who are willing to keep hitting fresh patches of cover in a relentless pursuit that ends only when the sun sets. When teaming up with another upland bird hunter, ask yourself: Is this person willing to hunt as hard as I am? If not, you might be happier going alone.

5. Walk through cover, not around it. No one actually enjoys busting through thick cover that binds up your legs and scratches at your face, but that's often what it takes to get birds to flush. This is especially true with cover-loving birds such as pheasant, quail, and ruffed grouse. A hunter who merely skirts around the edges of the nastiest briars and thickets is likely missing a lot of birds that have learned to stay safe by holding tight. If a patch of cover really is too thick to penetrate, or if you're hunting alone and can't afford to be in a tight spot that makes shooting impossible, try lingering at the edge of the thicket as a way to unnerve the birds and get them to fly. If that fails, throw a few rocks or sticks into the thicket to stir things up. Often that'll get reluctant birds up and flyin'.

6. Stay ready. Even if you've been hunting for hours without flushing a bird—or rather, *especially* if you've been hunting for hours without flushing a bird—keep your shotgun in the ready position and stay mentally focused on shooting. Upland birds have an uncanny knack for flushing right in front of you as soon as you abandon all hope. You should respond with a rapid shot rather than clumsily fumbling with a shotgun that's slung over your shoulder because you're tired of carrying it.

7. Take a shot. Or, better yet, take two. When an upland bird flushes, things happen very fast. There might just be a whir of wings and a flash of feathers and that's it—the opportunity has come and gone. Many beginning hunters miss these chances because of their reluctance to take what's known as a snap shot. While such shots are generally a bad idea on big game, where accurate shot placement is of utmost importance, it's okay with upland birds. Just one or two pellets can be enough to knock a bird down, and the only way to get those pellets out there is to pull the trigger. And once you've touched off the first round, follow it with another unless you've clearly seen that the bird's body has folded and its neck has dropped. A few extra pellets in the meat aren't going to hurt anything.

8. Pick a bird. Upland game birds often flush in groups ranging in size from two to twenty depending on species and location. Inexperienced hunters have a tendency to "flock shoot" when presented with multiple targets; rather than picking an individual bird, they point their shotgun in the general direction of the flock and then shoot with the idea that surely they'll hit something. This strategy leads to failure. It's imperative that you pick out a single bird and focus on it.

9. A bird in the hand is better than two crippled birds hiding somewhere in the bushes. Sure, nothing feels better than knocking down a pair of birds in quick succession—known as a "double" in hunter's parlance—but nothing feels worse than losing a bird that you've injured or killed. By taking your eyes off the landing place of a bird you've dropped in order to take a shot at a second bird, you risk losing track of the first bird's whereabouts. When you down a bird, it's best to proceed immediately to the last place you saw it and begin searching. If you dilly-dally, a wounded bird can easily walk off. This remains true even when hunting with dogs. Sure, dogs are an invaluable asset when it comes to retrieving birds, but they are not infallible.

10. Don't shoot your buddy. Firearms-related hunting accidents are quite rare, but many of those that do occur involve upland hunters who are swinging on a bird and fail to realize that one of their hunting partners is positioned beyond the target. Such

(continued)

accidents aren't necessarily due to pure negligence. Thick brush, low-flying birds that travel in unpredictable directions, and hunters who inadvertently stray from their position in the lineup can all lead to dangerous scenarios. If you get into a situation where you're unsure about your partner's whereabouts, stop hunting until you've reorganized. If a bird ends up giving you the slip, it's no big deal. That beats hauling your buddy to the hospital to have shotgun pellets picked out of his flesh.

PTARMIGAN

Willow ptarmigan *(Lagopus lagopus)*
Rock ptarmigan *(Lagopus mutus)*
White-tailed ptarmigan *(Lagopus leucurus)*
A.K.A.: Snow grouse

P tarmigan are probably the least appreciated and most underutilized of all North American upland game birds. Many hunters regard them as a novelty item that might be hunted as a side venture while pursuing larger tundra- and alpine-dwelling species such as caribou, moose, and Dall sheep. As long as you're in ptarmigan country, the thinking goes, why not try to bag one of these strange white birds? This is sound reasoning, as ptarmigan meat is a great way to supplement a diet of freeze-dried backpacking food when you're camped in remote country. But don't just think of these birds as a diversion

to more serious pursuits. If you're lucky enough to find yourself in a ptarmigan habitat, these often abundant and easy-to-harvest birds can provide some of the hottest, most fast-paced wingshooting a hunter will ever experience.

BARROOM BANTER: Willow ptarmigan males will help care for their young and will even assume full responsibility for their hatchlings if the female is killed. In this way they are different from all other North American grouse or ptarmigan species.

PHYSICAL CHARACTERISTICS: There are three species of ptarmigan in North America: willow ptarmigan, rock ptarmigan, and white-tailed ptarmigan. All three species have three molts per year, changing from almost pure white in the winter to mixed white and brown in the spring to mostly mottled brown during the snow-free summer months. All have fully feathered feet and other adaptations for extremely cold environments. Willow ptarmigan are the most abundant and largest, weighing well over a pound. They have a thick, heavy bill. Rock ptarmigan are slightly smaller, generally weighing under a pound, and have a relatively thinner bill than willow ptarmigan. Rock and willow ptarmigan both have black-tipped tail feathers, even with their winter plumage, though these tail feathers can be difficult to see at a distance. White-tailed ptarmigan, the smallest and least abundant, have a thin bill and lack black-tipped tail feathers.

HABITAT: Rock ptarmigan and willow ptarmigan occur across much of Alaska, throughout British Columbia, and across much of northern Canada. Their ranges often overlap, with willow ptarmigan in lower, denser vegetation at or below timberline and rock ptarmigan in higher, rockier locations. White-tailed ptarmigan are found mostly in southeast Alaska and British Columbia; they are the only ptarmigan that occurs in the lower forty-eight. A species of the high alpine, they occur in scattered populations on mountaintops south to New Mexico. Of the lower forty-eight, Colorado has the strongest populations.

DIET: Young ptarmigan will readily eat insects, with adults being largely herbivorous. Willow ptarmigan prefer the buds, leaves, and catkins of willow, while rock ptarmigan rely heavily on dwarf birch. However, both species will eat a variety of berries and other plant materials when necessary. White-tailed ptarmigan have the most varied diet of any ptarmigan species, eating grasses, forbs, flowers, berries, pine needles, seeds, and lichens.

LIFE AND DEATH: Roughly 75 percent of all ptarmigan die before they're a year old. About 50 percent of all adults die every year. A four-year-old ptarmigan is a lucky bird. Predators are many and include foxes, bobcats, weasels, hawks, and owls.

BREEDING AND REPRODUCTION: Willow ptarmigan hens lay between six and ten eggs in the late spring; rock ptarmigan lay between seven and eleven eggs; white-tailed ptarmigan, four to eight eggs.

TELLTALE SIGN: Look for feathers and clusters of droppings; in snow, look for abundant tracks. In a well-used area, ptarmigan will form trails in the snow that course through preferred feeding areas.

EDIBILITY: Many hunters describe the flesh of ptarmigan as being like liver, though it is actually quite good. Especially suitable for pâtés and terrines.

HUNTING OPPORTUNITIES: Found predominantly in regions of the arctic tundra and some portions of the continental United States. In some areas, seasons begin in August and run

through May. Depending on the region and species, daily bag limits range from three to ten.

HUNTING METHODS: Ptarmigan are prone to radical fluctuations in population numbers due to weather, predation, and other factors; one year they might seem to be everywhere, the next year it can be hard to find one. Dedicated ptarmigan hunters who live in ptarmigan country learn to follow these population swings and then do the bulk of their hunting during years of abundance. Unlike with most other upland game birds, you can sometimes locate ptarmigan just by looking and listening for them. Willow and white-tailed ptarmigans are especially vocal. Willows make noises that sound more like frog croaks than bird calls, especially in the early morning. Their most common call is often described as *go-back, go-back, go-back*. White-tailed ptarmigan sound like *cuk-cuk-cuk-caak*.

Once you hear the birds, it's usually a simple matter to find them by tromping around in the vicinity of where the noise came from. You can even glass for ptarmigan. Willow ptarmigan prefer thick willow patches along watercourses in semi-open or treeless environments; during winter months, when they are white, they contrast quite strongly when they fly over the reddish-hued vegetation. Rock ptarmigan and white-tailed ptarmigan, which prefer higher, less brushy alpine terrain, can sometimes be found standing out on open hillsides or in the vicinity of scree slides. When you locate distant birds, you can often get pretty close to them by walking at an angle to them that will bring you to within 30 or so yards at the closest point. If you walk directly toward them, they will know

Ptarmigan are often killed by hunters pursuing big game in the far North, such as caribou and Dall sheep. Here, a caribou hunter in Alaska prepares a ptarmigan for dinner.

Serious ptarmigan hunters like to use dogs for flushing and retrieving. Danny Rinella's dog, Tig, enjoyed chasing the white birds. Note the ptarmigan wingprints in the snow next to the dog.

birds while still taking advantage of shots provided by running and standing birds as well. Standing shots are especially common when the birds are gathered in larger winter flocks—at least if they haven't been pressured by other hunters. Even when the bulk of a flock has flushed, a few stragglers might stand around staring at you. As soon as you touch the trigger, though, be ready for action. Other hidden birds might very well take to the air, and you'll have a good chance of pulling a double. (Make sure the first bird is down and retrievable before you shoot a second bird.) Ptarmigan make relatively easy targets for the wingshooter because they fly low and straight. They aren't unpredictable fliers like doves, and they aren't fast fliers like ruffed grouse. An exception to this is during windy conditions, which are common on the open tundra and in the mountains where ptarmigan live. They will catch the wind and be gone like a shot. Keep in mind, though, that ptarmigan (like other game birds) have to take off into the wind in order to get enough resistance to fly. This is important when you're approaching game birds in the wind, as you'll know which direction they're initially going to jump when they lift off, and which direction they'll bank toward once they do.

that you've seen them and they'll be more likely to flush.

Ptarmigan are not difficult to kill, and it's common to be presented with standing shots. Many caribou and Dall sheep hunters have stories of bagging them with thrown rocks. They can be easily taken with a .22 rifle, though the best bet is a shotgun loaded with #7½ pellets. That way, you can capitalize on flushed

DANNY RINELLA, AN ALASKAN HUNTER, WEIGHS IN ON HIS PASSION FOR PTARMIGAN HUNTING

"The first ptarmigan I ever shot was on an icy mountainside on Kodiak Island. I was new to Alaska and had lucked into a month of fall field work on the island, which included some free time for hunting and fishing. I was hiking up the creek behind the ranch where I was staying, and as I crossed the base of a scree slope that ran a thousand feet up the mountainside, I could hear croaking noises coming from the rocks above. It sounded more like a bullfrog than anything else, but I knew that it couldn't be that. I scanned the scree slope with my binoculars and saw, a couple hundred yards above, a dozen plump, white birds staring down at me through black masks. Rock ptarmigan! Their masks—streaks of black on the male's winter plumage that connect the black bill to the black eyes—were what caught my attention in the first place and, in the years since, have betrayed otherwise camouflaged birds several times.

"The ptarmigan were nestled into some treacherous terrain, a steep band of jagged scree about 100 yards wide with a couple of inches of snow on top, all glazed over by freezing rain that had blown in from the Gulf of Alaska a few days before. I could safely climb to the birds' elevation in a band of alder that fringed the scree, but stepping out into that scree to shoot or retrieve a bird would be suicidal. But I realized that if I could connect with a long shot, the dead bird would probably slide down the mountain anyway. I scrambled up through the alder band and found that I could get within about 40 yards of the birds, who were totally unconcerned by the presence of an out-of-breath guy fumbling with a side-by-side 20-gauge. I pointed at the nearest bird and fired the full choke barrel (this was my first shot at a ptarmigan, and I wasn't about to be 'sporting' and flush the birds before shooting). The shot connected and the bird whizzed down the mountainside, coming to rest right where I'd been standing when I spotted them. The remaining birds stood but didn't fly. I reloaded the full choke barrel and again fired

(continued)

at the nearest bird, which in about three seconds was lying next to his flockmate down in the creek bottom. The remaining birds flushed at the second shot, so I slowly but excitedly picked my way down through the alder patch to claim my first two ptarmigan.

"Ptarmigan had been on my mind for a long time before this. When I was a kid I spent a lot of time nosing through the color plates in my dad's old field guide to birds. The plates with game birds were especially intriguing, and I'd imagine tromping through wide-open western country with a shotgun and a dog, scouring prairie or tundra for sporty birds never found in my native habitat of Michigan scrub oak. Of these so-called chicken-like birds, none worked my imagination like the ptarmigan, three species that turned snow white in winter and lived in the continent's wildest and wooliest country. These birds helped feed my childhood fascination with Alaska (the willow ptarmigan is, after all, the state bird), and when I moved to Anchorage in my late twenties, hunting these birds was high on my long to-do list.

"My pursuit has led me to the alpine valleys and windswept arctic tundra where these birds live. Willow ptarmigan, the largest and apparently most abundant of the three, are indeed found mostly in patches of shrub willow, typically on or near the valley floor. From my experience, creek bottoms lined with felt-leaf and other tall shrub willows are especially productive. Rock ptarmigan, true to their name, are usually found above the valley floor on rocky slopes and benches, just like I had found them on Kodiak. White-tailed, the smallest and apparently rarest of the ptarmigan, tend to be found higher than the others, in craggy boulder fields and often near snow fields or glaciers. Friends and I once bagged all three (the ptarmigan grand slam) in a small alpine valley above Anchorage by hunting from the valley floor all the way up to the craggy ridgeline.

"Alaska's hunting regulations (which, incidentally, are bewilderingly complex by midwestern standards) hint at the abundance of ptarmigan in the vast expanses. The season runs most of the year and hunters are allowed ten birds a day around Anchorage and up to fifty birds a day (a hundred in possession!) in other areas. It's even legal to use traps or snares.

"These permissive regulations might lead one to expect a ptarmigan behind every bush, but it didn't take long to discover that this wasn't necessarily the case. Their distribution is patchy, and even when populations are large, hours of birdless hiking are not unusual. In addition, bird numbers seem to fluctuate a lot from year to year, and some years even the most reliable spots are slim pickings. For example, my friend Matt Carlson was caribou hunting on the Kenai Peninsula and discovered an alpine valley that was holding hundreds, maybe thousands, of ptarmigan. We hiked the eight miles into that valley the following September and for three Septembers after that to find a staggering number of willow ptarmigan, so many that the din of their *go-back go-back go-back* calls could be heard for the last half mile of the hike. Over the past few years, though, this valley has been devoid of ptarmigan.

"I do most of my ptarmigan hunting during winter in the mountains above Anchorage. Winter can be a good time to hunt because snow buries a lot of the available cover, concentrating the birds in whatever cover remains exposed. On skis with climbing skins, we travel alpine valleys with our shotguns disassembled and tucked in our packs until we find some promising sign. Ptarmigan can leave a lot of sign. Flocks of them crisscross the valleys, often in the predawn hours, leaving feathery snowshoe tracks that zigzag between patches of cover and piles of droppings that could easily pass for All-Bran cereal. Sign can be everywhere, but birds may or may not be anywhere nearby. Binoculars can be helpful for spotting distant sign or exposed birds, and the strange pink tint that they sometimes get during the late winter makes them easier to spot. Once a flock of ptarmigan is located and flushed, they may only fly a couple hundred yards or to the nearest patch of cover before landing again, giving hunters multiple opportunities for shots. Sometimes, however, they decide to leave the valley before a single shot is fired.

"When I skinned that first ptarmigan back on Kodiak, I was surprised at the darkness of the flesh, which was closer in color and flavor to wild duck than I'd expected. Also like duck, ptarmigan breast meat is darker than leg meat due to their physiological adaptation for sustained flight. Some friends say that ptarmigan meat is best in the fall but that it takes on a liver flavor as the winter winds on. Others I know think it tastes like liver all the time. My favorite ptarmigan meals have been those shared with my brothers on Dall sheep hunts. Some fresh meat, salted with leftover ramen noodle flavoring and fried in oil, is heavenly after days of mountain hiking and freeze-dried dinners."

RUFFED GROUSE
Bonasa umbelluss
A.K.A.: Drummers, ruffs, partridge, pat

The ruffed grouse is the most widely available upland game bird in North America, occurring in approximately thirty-eight states and all Canadian provinces. The fast-flying bird is universally respected and admired among hunters who live within its range, both because of its fine-tasting flesh and the exceedingly difficult nature of knocking it out of the sky with a shotgun. The males are fiercely territorial; they announce their presence to other grouse by standing atop a stump or log and "drumming" their wings, something that sounds like an old lawnmower firing up and then sputtering out. For non-hunters, hearing this noise might be as close as they'll ever come to "seeing" a ruffed grouse, as the birds are otherwise very cautious and quiet and exceptionally well camouflaged—at least until you happen to flush one. When they explode into flight from cover, often from right beneath your feet, the noise and suddenness of the bird's appearance can leave you gasping for air. Hunters who can connect on a mere 25 percent of their shots at ruffed grouse are rare indeed. Many will average just one or two grouse for every box of shells fired, and might regard killing just a single bird as the makings for an exceptionally productive—and tasty—day.

BARROOM BANTER: Once he finds a suitable territory, a male ruffed grouse can live his entire life on just 10 acres of ground. A female's home range will be four times as large.

PHYSICAL DESCRIPTION: Mature ruffed grouse are about 17 inches long and weigh up to 1½ pounds. They have a distinctive black collar, or "ruff," of feathers on their neck, as well as a slight crest on the top of their head. There are two common color phases, gray and red. Grays are more common in the north and at high altitudes; reds are more common in the south.

HABITAT: Mixed woodlands with abundant edge habitats and younger tree growth. The birds are especially common in the vicinity of young aspen. In the Southeast, ruffed grouse are generally found above 2,000 feet. In the West, they are typically found between 3,500 and 8,500 feet. In other areas, elevation does not play much of a factor in grouse distribution.

DIET: Widely varied according to location and time of year. Favorite foods include buds and catkins of aspen, birch, and ironwood, plus fruits and berries from cherry, hawthorn, wintergreen, rose, holly, mountain laurel, apple, snowberry, and a great many other fruit-bearing trees and shrubs. Will also eat insects, seeds, and young green leaves from a variety of plants.

BREEDING AND REPRODUCTION: Hens lay between eight and fourteen buff-colored eggs in the spring. Incubation doesn't begin until the last egg is laid; all eggs hatch about twenty-five days after incubation begins. The chicks can fly when they're five days old.

LIFE AND DEATH: Ruffed grouse are heavily preyed upon by foxes, bobcats, hawks, owls, and many other predators. Severe weather and in-flight collisions with trees kill many as well. Half of all ruffed grouse that are successfully hatched in late May or early June will be dead by mid-August. Only about 18 percent will live to see their first breeding season. Of those that do survive, over half will be dead before their second breeding season. Of every 2,000 ruffed grouse that are hatched, one might live to be eight years old.

TELLTALE SIGN: Like most upland game birds, ruffed grouse leave very little sign during the snow-free months beyond a shed feather here and there or a pile of droppings where it may have lain for an extended period of time. When there is snow on the ground, you can often find zigzagging trails of three-toed tracks left by the birds as they forage through cover.

EDIBILITY: Very mild and good, quite similar to well-exercised free-range chicken.

HUNTING OPPORTUNITIES: Fairly common and widespread throughout Canada and northern portions of the United States. Seasons usually start sometime in September and tend to run through January. Daily bag limits are usually five in combination with other grouse types.

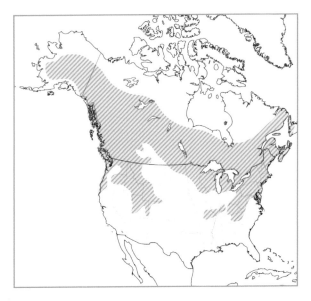

HUNTING METHODS: Even though ruffed grouse occupy a huge range, good grouse cover has a certain look and feel regardless of where you happen to be hunting. Once you learn how to recognize it through experience, you can readily find ruffed grouse pretty much anywhere that the birds live. Basically, they like "broken" habitats that provide plenty of thick cover and an array of foods. The birds are typically found near the edges of woods rather than in the middle. Edges provide overhead cover from avian predators, yet the ground gets enough sunlight to stimulate a lush undergrowth of vegetation that provides both cover and food. Appropriate edge habitats can be found along power lines, stream bottoms, old orchards, gas lines, brushy draws, conifer "islands" amid stands of hardwood, clear-cuts, logging roads, swamp and slough edges, islands of brush or timber within cattail marshes, willow and alder thickets, and stands of young and old aspen or poplar.

Many hunters regard the ruffed grouse season as occurring in two segments: leaves on and leaves off. When the leaves are still on the trees, visibility is greatly diminished but there are more birds around (simply because they haven't been killed by hunters or predators) and they're less likely to be easily spooked. Visibility, and therefore the ability

After killing a ruffed grouse (or any bird), open its crop to examine the contents. You'll find clues about where to find more birds. On left: This Michigan ruffed grouse was feeding on ironwood. On right: Another Michigan bird; this one had nineteen thorn apples in its crop.

A Wisconsin hunter works a patch of classic-looking ruffed grouse cover. In this terrain, shots happen fast. Be ready to shoulder your gun and fire in a hurry.

to see the birds well enough to shoot them, improves dramatically when the leaves drop. But by then there are fewer birds around and they've usually learned the importance of getting up and flying as soon as they hear even a hint of an approaching hunter. Late-season conditions improve once there's snow on the ground, as you can effectively track the birds. When following a set of fresh tracks in the snow, don't expect to catch the bird standing on the ground unless you're hunting in a relatively undisturbed wilderness setting such as Alaska, the Rockies, or the northern Great Lakes, where the birds tend to be much less shy. Even though you're fully expecting to flush one of the birds, it'll still startle you when it

bursts up from the ground in an explosion of wingbeats.

Because ruffed grouse are easily spooked, and because they don't run ahead of you like pheasants do, it's unlikely that you'll pass within range of a ruffed grouse without flushing it. This means you can cover likely habitat at a fairly brisk pace without having to worry about missing birds. In exceptionally thick or great-looking cover, it pays to pause now and then as you walk along in order to unnerve any hiding birds and inspire them to jump up.

It's possible for a lone hunter, working without a dog, to kill ruffed grouse. In fact, many grouse hunters enjoy great success by going solo. However, grouse hunting is highly con-

Ruffed grouse hunting is a great family activity: lots of walking, but not too rugged or strenuous. Here are the author's father and two brothers on a December ruffed grouse hunt in Michigan. I'm almost certain that this was the last grouse my father ever killed; he died the following winter.

ducive to group efforts. The lineup is a great approach. Whether you've got two hunters or six, form a line with about 20 or 30 yards between each hunter and systematically "push" any and all available cover. Grouse often fly in a crosswise direction away from the approaching line of hunters, allowing multiple hunters to get shots at the same bird. Another benefit of group hunting is that you can position a stander along known escape routes that are used by ruffed grouse when flushed from reliable patches of cover. It might take several seasons before you identify these escape routes, but once you do you'll want to make sure to exploit them.

Because ruffed grouse occupy such dense cover, a close-working dog is very helpful. When hunting with a flushing dog, you want it to stay within half the distance of your total effective shooting range; in other words, if you can only see 40 yards through the brush, the dog shouldn't work past 20 yards. That way, you still have a reasonable amount of space in which to shoot a flushed bird before it vanishes from sight. Pointing dogs work well for ruffed grouse, because knowing that a bird is present allows you to ready your shotgun before it actually flushes—this can shave a second or two off your shooting time, which is an eternity when it comes to hitting these speedy birds. Another advantage of having a dog is that they are way better than humans at finding downed grouse—especially wounded birds that hit the ground running.

It is difficult to hit ruffed grouse, mainly because they fly fast and they are found in such thick cover. There are a lot of trees and brush that obscure the flying birds, and which also absorb shotgun pellets that might otherwise have found their mark. Waterfowl or pheasant hunters who are used to the "swing-through" method of wingshooting will likely have to abandon that strategy when hunting ruffed grouse. Many shots are snap shots by necessity, and speed is the most important thing. In one fluid motion, you have to shoulder your gun, point it toward where you think the grouse might be in a second's time, and then pull the trigger. It all happens on a deeply instinctive level. Good grouse hunters will tell you that they hardly ever take notice of their shotgun bead, and that they sometimes shoot without ever shouldering the gun. In many cases, you either do it that way or you won't get a shot at all. For ruffed grouse, 20-gauge and 12-gauge shotguns are appropriate. For chokes, use improved-cylinder and modified. Ruffed grouse hunters are generally divided on whether #6 or #7½ shot is best for ruffed grouse. As a general rule of thumb, go with #7½ when the leaves are on the trees. When leaves are off, go with #6.

RUFFED GROUSE TIPS

1. Ruffed grouse are mostly solitary birds, with the exception of females tending to young hatchlings. However, the birds will often form loose congregations in the vicinity of a prime source for food or shelter. So when you flush a ruffed grouse, be prepared for a second or even third bird to follow.

2. Ruffed grouse hunters use the term *covert* to describe a patch of cover that holds ruffed grouse. A prime covert will often produce again and again, year after year. When you jump a bird, remember the spot (or take a GPS waypoint) in order to hit it again next year.

3. Dress appropriately when hunting ruffed grouse. Be prepared for thick, thorny cover by bringing along leather gloves, protective leggings or chaps, a sturdy jacket and game vest, and a tight-fitting hat that won't be snagged off your head by grabby tree limbs.

4. When there is ample snow cover on the ground, ruffed grouse will bury themselves beneath the snow to ride out extreme cold or high wind. In the absence of snow, look for the birds to be roosted in thickets of conifers—especially toward the outer edges.

SHARP-TAILED GROUSE
Tympanuchus phasianellus
A.K.A.: Prairie grouse, sharptail, sharpy

Sharp-tailed grouse are best known for their leks, or traditional breeding sites, where as many as fifteen males will congregate on the wide-open prairie to compete for female attention by strutting, cackling, and stomping their feet in a strangely synchronized dance. The spring breeding season isn't the only time when sharp-tailed grouse will gather into large flocks. During the late fall and early winter, it's not uncommon for hunters to flush flocks of over a hundred sharp-tailed grouse—or to see that many birds feeding on buds while perched 20 feet up in a tree.

In this way sharp-tailed grouse are much different from their solitary ruffed grouse cousins, which occupy forested terrain. The gregariousness of the sharp-tailed grouse should put hunting them on the to-do list of any easterner who's spent his or her life chasing ruffed grouse, as it's possible that you could flush more sharp-tailed grouse in a single outing than all the ruffed grouse that you'll flush in a decade of stomping brush at home. But don't make the mistake of thinking that sharp-tailed grouse are easy. You might get lucky enough to flush a flock of a hundred, but you'll still

only get off one or two shots before they're long gone. Bagging a limit of these extremely wary birds is a feat to be proud of.

BARROOM BANTER: Sharp-tailed grouse were once common in the Great Lakes states of Michigan, Illinois, Wisconsin, and Minnesota, though their numbers and distribution have fallen greatly due to habitat loss. Prior to European settlement, wildfires helped create suitable mosaics of open habitat where the birds were able to thrive. Wetland edges also provided superb habitat. In the centuries since European contact, a combination of factors including fire suppression, development, high-intensity agriculture, and wetlands destruction have resulted in the disappearance of the birds across much of their historic range.

PHYSICAL DESCRIPTION: Sharp-tailed grouse are mottled brown, beige, and white, and appear to be spotted. Undersides are lighter than upper portions, with small, dark V-shaped patterns. The tail is short—much shorter than that of a hen pheasant—and on a flying bird it appears to be sharply pointed. The head is slightly crested. Males have an eye comb and reach 2½ pounds. Females are slightly smaller.

HABITAT: Open grasslands (natural or agricultural), particularly the short-grassed prairie of the Central Plains. Habitat must include brushy draws and coulees. The species will not usually tolerate areas where more than 50 percent of the land is forested.

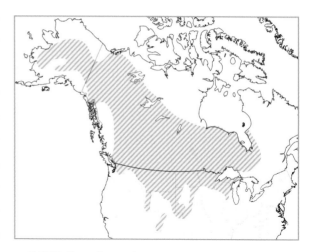

DIET: Rose hips, berries, herbaceous plants, agricultural grain crops, catkins and buds from shrubs and trees, and insects such as grasshoppers.

BREEDING AND REPRODUCTION: Polygamous. Females nest on the ground and will lay nine to twelve eggs.

LIFE AND DEATH: Predation on sharp-tailed eggs is very common. Of those birds that hatch, most die within a year. Adults often live to be three years old. Avian predators such as hawks are a leading killer of sharp-tailed grouse. Extreme winter weather also kills many.

TELLTALE SIGN: Very little during snow-free conditions besides piles of droppings. In winter, look for tracks.

EDIBILITY: Quite good. The flesh is dark, though it lacks the livery quality of ptarmigan.

HUNTING OPPORTUNITIES: Common throughout Canada, Alaska, and some areas in the middle of the United States. As with other grouse, the usual season lasts from September until January, with longer seasons in

Alaska. Limits range from three to five and are often counted toward a combined limit total.

HUNTING METHODS: The best way to locate sharp-tailed grouse is to hunt within a couple of miles of a known lek. It's also smart to stay in the vicinity of active roosting areas, as sharp-tailed grouse will typically feed within a couple miles of their roost. When hunting mornings and late afternoons, look for the birds around crop fields of grain or alfalfa, or else in the vicinity of preferred natural foods such as berries, rose hips, or seed-bearing wild plants that can be found along brushy fencerows, coulee bottoms, abandoned farmsteads, and stream channels. Between feeding sessions, sharp-tailed grouse will move to loafing areas. Unpressured birds will loaf in sparse grasslands, with just enough cover to conceal them from avian predators. In windy conditions, look for the birds to be concentrated on the lee side of hills. Heavily hunted birds, on the other hand, will seek shelter in much denser grass or they'll hide in areas that might be more readily recognized as pheasant cover. As hunting season progresses and weather conditions deteriorate, sharp-tailed grouse will begin to spend more and more time in the vicinity of sheltering windbreaks such as clusters of

Ed Arnett, from the Theodore Roosevelt Conservation Partnership, hunting some classic sharp-tailed grouse country in the Sand Hills of Nebraska.

The author's first sharp-tailed grouse, killed years ago on an antelope hunt. On this morning, it was too foggy to glass for antelope, so we picked up the shotguns.

brushy trees and stands of conifers. In deep snow, the birds will roost beneath the snow. During a storm, they might stay under the snow for so long that any trace of their presence on the snow's surface will be erased. The unsuspecting hunter who flushes one of the snow-roosted birds is likely to get so startled by the explosion of feathers and snow that they'll miss their chance to take a shot.

Sharp-tailed grouse are exceptionally wary, and the relative openness of their habitat allows them to see and hear you coming from a long way off. You should keep quiet and avoid talking and yelling. An added bonus of keeping quiet is that you might hear the birds—they make a host of sounds while feeding in the morning, including clucks and whines. The birds might hold well for a pointing dog in the early season, but heavily pressured birds will typically flush before you can catch up with your dog if it works far out. During late season, it's better to have a close-working dog that hunts within shotgun range. Sometimes sharp-tailed grouse will become so wary that it's virtually impossible to approach them within shotgun distance. Under these conditions, try hunting them as early in the morning as possible. For whatever reason, they often hold tighter in the morning. Also consider the possibility of pass-shooting as the birds travel from their roosting areas to feeding areas, or from feeding areas to loafing areas. This can work well, though it takes considerable scouting effort to identify the exact travel routes used by the birds as they go about their day.

When you do flush a flock of sharp-tailed grouse, watch where they go—especially if the flock breaks up into several smaller flocks. Mark their locations and then try to flush them again. The birds tend to hold a little tighter the second time around, perhaps because they are tired from flying and are thus more reluctant to get back up. Pheasant hunters often miss opportunities on sharp-tailed grouse because they mistakenly think that the birds are hen pheasants and then pass them up. Don't let this happen to you. A sharp-tailed grouse's tail is much shorter than a hen pheasant's, and on a flushing bird it appears to be sharply pointed. Also, sharp-tailed grouse will often make an urgent sounding *kuk-kuk-kuk-kuk* call upon flushing. If you hear that, get ready to shoot. (As long as it's open season for sharp-tailed grouse in your hunting area, of course.)

During the early season, when the birds are likely to hold tighter, a modified choke with #6 pellets is a wise choice. During the late season, it's not a bad idea to bump up to a full choke and #4 or #5 shot if the birds are flushing way out ahead of you.

SPRUCE GROUSE
Falcipennis canadensis
A.K.A.: Canada grouse, spruce hen, fool hen, Franklin's grouse, black grouse, swamp grouse

Big game hunters looking for deer, moose, or elk in the northern forests are often surprised to notice a spruce grouse perched in a tree just a few feet away. It's no wonder that the birds are one of the several species to have picked up the monikers "fool's hen" and "stupid chicken." But for every spruce grouse that you see, there are many more that you pass by without noticing, thanks to this bird's remarkable camouflage and its ability to freeze in place despite what must be an unnerving level of fear. When you do find a spruce grouse, avoid making disparaging judgments about the bird's intelligence or survival instinct. Instead, you should feel hon-ored to have the encounter—especially if it leads to a memorable meal of this bird's dis-tinctive flesh.

BARROOM BANTER: Similar to other grouse species, spruce grouse have features called pectinations on their toes. These are lateral extensions that increase the surface area of the bird's feet, enabling them to stay afloat when walking on soft surfaces of snow.

PHYSICAL DESCRIPTION: Males are barred gray to black on the upper parts, with a black throat and breast patches; tail is brown, with chestnut tips; throat patch is bordered by white feathers; eye combs are red. Females are duller in appearance, lacking the male's conspicuous eye comb and throat and breast patches. They average 15 to 17 inches long, weighing about 1¼ pounds.

HABITAT: Spruce grouse prefer boreal and conifer-dominated forests of fir, spruce, and pine.

DIET: Conifer needles primarily, including tamarack. Also some fruit during summer months.

BREEDING AND REPRODUCTION: Hens typically lay between four and ten eggs in the spring; incubation period is twenty-four days.

LIFE AND DEATH: Weasels, fishers, pine martens, crows, ravens, and magpies will all raid spruce grouse nests. Adult spruce grouse fall prey to many species, including owls, hawks, coyotes, bobcats, pine martens, fishers, and foxes. Spruce grouse are more likely than most other upland game birds to survive their first year of life. They commonly live to be more than six years old.

TELLTALE SIGN: Three-toed tracks in the snow, usually zigzagging as they forage.

EDIBILITY: Fair to good. Spruce grouse flesh is sometimes described as piney or gamey, though it makes for an unusual and interesting treat. Perfect for terrines and pâtés.

HUNTING OPPORTUNITIES: Very common throughout Canada, Alaska, and some areas in the northwestern and northeastern United States. May be considered rare or threatened in some states at the edge of its range. Seasons in Alaska run from August until March, and usually align

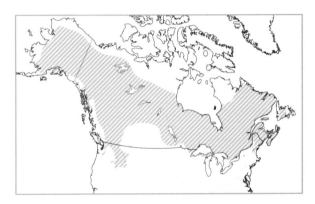

with other grouse species in other states where they are available. The bag limit is usually five in combination with other grouse species.

HUNTING METHODS: Before heading out on a spruce grouse hunt, you need to decide how you feel about shooting a standing bird. Many upland hunters believe that it's an unforgivable sin to kill a game bird that's not flying, while others hold the view that flushing a bird just to have a challenging shot is like playing with your food. Standing birds provide opportunities for quick and humane kills, they'll say, which should be prioritized over "sport."

If you fall into the take-what-you-can-get camp, then you might seriously consider using a .22 pistol or rifle when hunting spruce grouse. If you fall into the flush-'em-first camp, then you need a shotgun loaded with #7½ pellets and a pocket full of rocks to throw at the birds in order to get them to fly.

Regardless of your personal preferences, you'll still need to work hard if you want to reliably find spruce grouse. The key is pacing. You could take hours to cover a mile of trail and not find a single bird because there are none on that patch of ground, or you could cover six miles and miss a dozen birds because you weren't taking the time to look carefully. Hitting the proper balance of fast walking and careful looking comes from experience; you have to get a sense for how finely tuned your game eye is. Some hunters could spot a grouse at 30 yards from the window of a moving truck that other hunters wouldn't be able to spot even if they were standing just 10 yards away from the bird.

When looking for spruce grouse, consider that the birds usually have endless acres of viable food sources at their disposal but often only limited places where they can replenish their gizzards with grit. It makes sense to concentrate your efforts on grit sources such as logging trails, stream banks, gravel roads, well-worn footpaths, and ATV trails. Such features also make walking fairly easy, as you can concentrate on looking up in the trees for birds rather than looking down at the ground for obstacles that might cause you to trip.

What's more, trails and roads create edge habitats where sunlight is able to penetrate to the forest floor and allow the growth of favorite early-season spruce grouse foods such as cranberry and blueberry.

In the absence of roads or gravel stream banks, seek out edge habitats such as meadows, marsh edges, or just openings amid dense conifer forests. These places allow the growth of berries and other potential food sources and also tend to "open up" the trees enough to allow for at least moderate visibility through otherwise dense cover.

If you decide to take a standing shot at a spruce grouse (or any other game bird) with a shotgun, consider the effects of your pellets before you shoot. Don't aim dead center at a bird's body at 10 yards and expect there to be much usable meat left. Instead, hold on the bird's head or just above it in order to minimize meat damage. It also works to position yourself so that there are limbs or other heavy vegetation protecting the breast of the bird before you shoot.

Matt Rinella carries a blunt-tipped arrow while elk hunting in the fall in case he runs into spruce grouse. They can be a welcome addition to freeze-dried food.

STREET PIGEON

Columba livia

A.K.A.: Rock dove, common pigeon, street pigeon, city pigeon, flying rat

The common street pigeon is not generally regarded as a game bird, probably because so many of them live in urban environments where the discharge of a firearm is prohibited. In farm country, though, pigeons are well worth going after. Farmers typically have an adversarial relationship with these destructive birds, which can cause sanitation problems and destruction to both harvested and unharvested crops. Safely removing the birds around barns and silos is a good way to score points with a landowner on whose ground you hunt. Another benefit to hunting pigeons is that they're regarded on state and federal levels as a non-native pest, meaning there are no closed seasons and no bag limits. Once you marinate a few grain-fed pigeons and cook them to medium rare on a hot charcoal grill, you'll never look at these birds in the same way again.

BARROOM BANTER: The common street pigeon is the descendant of the rock dove, native to Europe, North Africa, and western Asia. It may have been the first bird to ever be domesticated by man; Egyptians had domesticated pigeons by at least five thousand years ago. French settlers in Canada first introduced the birds to North America in the early 1600s.

PHYSICAL DESCRIPTION: The common pigeon comes in many different shades and plumage patterns, thanks to centuries of selective breeding. The most common plumage pattern is the blue-bar—dark, usually iridescent head with a bluish gray body, black bands on the wings, and a black-tipped tail.

HABITAT: Farm country, urban landscapes.

DIET: Wild seeds and fruits, agricultural grain crops, food scraps left intentionally and unintentionally by humans.

BREEDING AND REPRODUCTION: In mild climates pigeons will breed year-round, laying up to six clutches annually with one to three eggs per nesting period.

LIFE AND DEATH: Avian predators ranging in size from American kestrels up to peregrine falcons take a great toll on common pigeons, usually striking the birds in midflight. In captivity, pigeons can live well into their teens. In the wild, life expectancy is much shorter.

TELLTALE SIGN: Nesting sites are very obvious, marked by nest mounds, deposits of droppings, and feathers.

EDIBILITY: Pigeons are a common food item in many cultures and can even be found in fine American restaurants. Professional cooks use only squabs, a term for a young, flightless pigeons less than a year old. Squabs are admittedly much better than adult pigeons, being light-fleshed and very tender. However, adult pigeons make perfectly ac-

ceptable table fare. The flesh is dark and a tad livery, so it's well suited for use in pâtés and terrines.

HUNTING OPPORTUNITIES: They are essentially everywhere in the United States and Canada. Because of their status as a pest species, there are no closed seasons and no bag limits.

HUNTING METHODS: In farm country, any pigeons that you see are almost certainly roosting and nesting at a man-made structure such as a grain silo, barn, bridge, or abandoned homestead. (Exceptions are found in cliffy country, where the birds will sometimes roost and nest on high cliff faces beneath overhanging ledges of rock and within narrow crevices.) Hunting them is as simple as finding an actively used structure (or cliff face) and then securing permission from the landowner to shoot in close proximity to the structure. The

Most folks associate pigeons with cityscapes, which is hardly inaccurate. But the birds can also be found in more picturesque and hunter-friendly environs, such as this beautiful farm in Wisconsin's Driftless Area. Look for the birds in and around silos and old barns. Any farmer who's overwintering cattle is bound to have pigeons lurking about in search of spilled grain.

simplest way is to wait for the birds to fly into the structure and then position one or more hunters with shotguns directly beneath the access point used by the birds as they come and go. Then you bang on the structure with a stick, or else have someone go inside to rile them up, and the shooter makes his shots as the birds leave the structure and fly away. Shooting too fast is a common mistake. Let the pigeons get out a ways before shooting. And don't forget to lead them.

This sounds much easier than it actually is, as pigeons hit very high speeds in short order. It's common for three or four hunters to get all lined up beneath a grain silo, so confident that they're giggly with anticipation, only to miss their shots when the birds come blasting out in erratic directions. For easier shooting, wait for the birds to leave the structure on their own and then get set up beneath their access point. You don't need to get too serious about camouflage, but you will probably make the pigeons nervous and less cooperative if you're standing right out in the open beneath their roost. If possible, hide behind a piece of farm equipment or inside an open barn door. Then wait. As the pigeons come into their roost, they'll be flying considerably slower. To get multiple shots, allow a bird or two to enter before you fire the first round. That way you'll get a second crack as the other birds exit.

For pigeons, #7½ shot works very well. Use modified and improved cylinder chokes.

BAND-TAILED PIGEON (*PATAGIOENAS FASCIATA*)

The band-tailed pigeon is a seldom-hunted bird that is easily confused with the common street pigeon. Though their ranges do overlap in places, the band-tailed pigeon shies away from urban areas. The birds are found along the West Coast and in the southern Rocky Mountain interior, where they feed on berries, pine nuts, and the buds and flowers of trees and shrubs. The birds have a particular fondness for acorns and will readily gorge themselves on the ripe mast. Their flesh is nutty and quite excellent.

WESTERN QUAIL

"Western quail" is an admittedly broad category, as it includes a total of five quail species that live west of the Mississippi: Gambel's, valley, Mearns's, scaled, and mountain. To the newcomer, distinguishing the various western quail species is made somewhat difficult by a confusion of common names. (Two species share the common name "blue quail," and several species are known by completely different names in different areas.) What's more, the ranges of several western quails do overlap, and the introduction of quail outside of their natural ranges has further muddied the picture. While each of the species has its own rigidly peculiar behaviors and habitat requirements, it is convenient to lump them together for organizational purposes, as they share a number of key attributes: (1) they live in coveys that typically break up into smaller groups when flushed; (2) coveys are widely scattered, and you sometimes have to walk long distances between flushes; (3) they live in rugged country, which demands good physical fitness on the part of the hunter; (4) they are runners and will often put a lot of distance between themselves and a hunter before flushing; and (5) they all make excellent table fare and are regarded by many hunters as the absolute finest-tasting game birds.

BARROOM BANTER: The Western quail species (as well as the bobwhite quail) are all monogamous. Unlike most other upland game birds, they do not engage in elaborate mating rituals and they are not as viciously territorial.

Found in the desert regions of Arizona, California, Colorado, New Mexico, Nevada, Utah, Texas, and Sonora, Mexico—typically in areas that receive fewer than 10 inches of precipitation a year. This species prefers river bottoms and dry washes lined by an abundance of thick, thorny vegetation. Gambel's quail have a curved black plume jutting from their foreheads and lightly scaled white and brown plumage on their undersides. They are often mistaken for California quail. Mating occurs in the spring, with females laying ten to twelve eggs. They feed on mesquite seeds, cacti flowers, leaves, grains, fruit, and insects.

HUNTING METHODS: Hunt for Gambel's quail in grassy feeding areas in the morning and evening, and in thick, thorny loafing areas at midday. The best locations are stream channels or arroyos with brushy bottoms that lead up to grassy slopes. Hunt the slopes during feeding time, the floor during loafing time. In areas with heavy cattle grazing, pay close at-

New Mexico hunter and biologist Karl Malcolm works a patch of cover that is ideal for Gambel's quail.

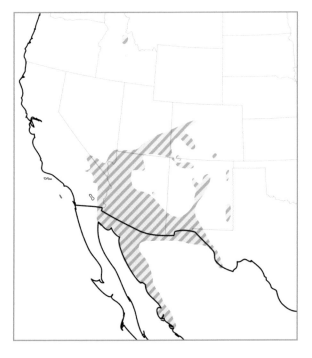

tention to areas with plenty of prickly pear cactus. The thorns keep cattle at bay and allow the quail some access to ungrazed grasses for food and cover. Gambel's quail will visit permanent water sources such as stock tanks and guzzlers on a regular basis. Pointing dogs are preferable over flushing dogs, though each certainly has its benefits when chasing Gambel's quail. Wear heavy boots and protective clothing that can withstand thorns. Target loads in #7½ and #8 work well when fired through improved-cylinder and modified chokes.

VALLEY QUAIL
Callipepla californica
A.K.A.: California quail, blue quail

Valley quail are found in the extreme West, from the southern tip of Mexico's Baja peninsula to southern British Columbia. They are commonly confused with Gambel's quail because both birds have a black topknot, though valley quail have a coarsely scaled buff-colored abdomen and a generally more bluish coloration. They are widely distributed within their range; suitable habitat includes open woodlands, shrubby areas, and mixed habitats in and around urban areas. These birds are brown on the back with gray-blue chests and light brown undersides; their flanks are accented by white streaks. Males have a black face and brown cap from which the black crest rises. The crest is brown on females. Mating occurs in spring and early summer; the female lays twelve eggs. Feeds on grasses, seeds, buds, acorns, insects, and fruit.

HUNTING METHODS: Valley quail can be found in a variety of habitats, but pay special attention to open grassy areas with scatterings

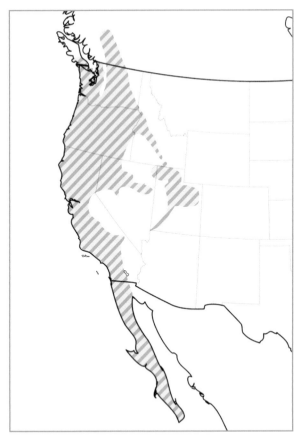

of brush and larger trees suitable for roosting. Can be especially abundant where farm country joins up to thick, brushy habitats. A nearby water source, especially one that supports a surrounding growth of succulent plants, is ideal. Hunt ridges and canyon rims during the morning hours, then work lower toward the bottoms during midday. Valley quail will hold tight, especially when they have thick brushy areas to hide in. Send in a hunter (or, preferably, a dog) to bust out the large thickets. If you see birds head into a thicket, don't give up if they don't flush. They are probably in there and will need some coaxing to get them up into the air. Wear good boots and protective clothing. Shot sizes of #7½ and #8 work well when fired through improved-cylinder or modified chokes.

It's beyond debate: quail, regardless of the species, are some of the finest-tasting birds on the planet. Here's a valley quail that was killed in California. #1, plucked and ready; #2, grilled hobo-style; #3, ready to eat; #4, breaking the wishbone.

MEARNS'S QUAIL
Cyrtonyx montezumae
A.K.A.: Montezuma quail, harlequin quail, painted quail

Found in interior Mexico and in the mountains of West Texas and southern Arizona and New Mexico, typically at altitudes from 3,000 to 9,000 feet, this bird prefers grassy and rocky slopes interspersed with oak. It is easily recognized by the intricate black-and-white patterning on the face, which brings to mind a clown's mask. The underside is tawny brown and the flanks have a black-and-white polka dot appearance. Nesting does not occur until July or August. The female lays six to twelve eggs in a nest resembling a grass dome with a single entrance. It feeds on bulbs, roots, tubers, insects, and fruit; it gets adequate water from food and does not need to visit standing water.

HUNTING METHODS: Mearns's quail are known for holding very tight and being ex-

tremely well camouflaged. Sometimes you almost need to step on them to get them to flush. Hunters who specialize in Mearns's will tell you that dogs are essential for finding and flushing the birds. The problem is that Mearns's country is rugged and hot, and poorly conditioned dogs get exhausted well before a hunter is ready to give up. Mearns's quail like to eat bulbs and tubers that they scratch from the ground, and you will sometimes find evidence of their feeding activities on soft ground. Also look for their chalky white droppings, which are more visible than the droppings of other quail. If you find fresh sign, hunt it; the birds are probably nearby. Shots tend to be close, so #7½ and #8 shot fired through an improved-cylinder choke works well.

A pair of Mearns's quail (a.k.a. Montezuma quail), killed by New Mexico hunter Cody Lujan.

SCALED QUAIL
Callipepla squamata
A.K.A.: Scalie, cottontop quail, blue quail

Found in the arid regions of Arizona, New Mexico, Texas, Colorado, Kansas, Oklahoma, and central Mexico. Prefers open areas of dry grassland with mixed cactus and shrubbery. Pale gray overall, with a distinctive scaled pattern on the neck, chest, and underside. Lacks a plume, but does have a crest that resembles a tuft of cotton, hence the commonly used nickname. Breeding occurs from April through September, depending on location; two broods are often produced in a single season. The female lays nine to sixteen eggs. Feeds on insects, seeds from mesquite and ragweed, and also agricultural grains such as sunflower, sorghum, and corn.

HUNTING METHODS: Populations of scaled quail fluctuate with rainfall. A series of dry years can devastate the birds. Typically, look for them in the vicinity of water, which they will visit daily. If you see fresh tracks but no birds near water sources, hunt the surrounding cover. Scaled quail will travel long distances when stressed, but are usually homebodies that can be located with methodical searching once you find the general area where they are hanging out. Often the birds will find overhead

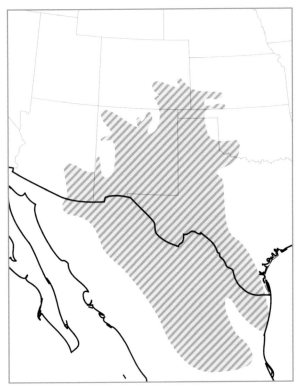

shelter by tucking themselves beneath cacti, yucca plants, or even old farm equipment or other debris left by humans. They are runners, and sometimes seem almost unable to fly. Many hunters prefer to use wide-ranging breeds of pointing dogs, which have a chance of running these birds down. A truly talented dog might turn the birds and herd them back in your direction, but that's asking a lot of a dog. Another way to deal with running scaled quail is to place other hunters along routes that might be used by fleeing quail. Often they will flush when they encounter an un-expected stander. Use #7½ or #8 shot fired from improved-cylinder or modified chokes.

Western quail inhabit some nasty, thorny country. On left: This scaled quail hunter, Karl Malcolm, shows off a thorn in his arm. On right: He also has to remove one from his dog.

MOUNTAIN QUAIL
Oreortyx pictus
A.K.A.: Plumed quail

Found in the mountainous regions of the West Coast, from northern Baja to Washington and eastward into Idaho, the mountain quail prefers thick, brushy mountainous areas ranging in elevation from 2,000 to 10,000 feet. The largest quail species, it is identifiable by two long, straight plumes that jut slightly backward from the top of the head. It has a gray-blue breast and neck, a brown throat patch, and flanks that are heavily barred with white. Breeding occurs in spring, with females laying nine or ten eggs. Feeds on bulbs, pine nuts, berries, insects, and wild legumes.

HUNTING METHODS: Regarded as the absolute toughest quail species to hunt, thanks to the ruggedness and verticality of their preferred habitats. They like the high country and are sometimes found at over 10,000 feet above sea level in the Pacific coastal mountains. They will come to water every day, and are usually found within half a mile of standing water. The

ing slopes, you and your partners should spread out vertically on hillsides and work in a cross-slope direction. Mountain quail will run uphill and then fly downhill, so multiple hunters might have a chance at the same covey of birds. Mountain quail will run if you catch them out in the open, so be prepared for a chase across rough ground if you want to get them up into the air. Use heavy game loads with #6 or #7½ shot fired through modified chokes.

WESTERN QUAIL HUNTING OPPORTUNI-TIES: With five species of western quail, hunting opportunities are widespread in the West and particularly in the Southwest. Some quail seasons begin in September and run into late January. Daily bag limits range from eight to ten.

GENERAL TIPS FOR WESTERN QUAIL

1. Stay with a covey. When flushed, quail coveys will bust up into small groups and singles. Watch carefully to see where these small groups land, and then mark the location. Typically, these smaller groups hold tighter than full coveys. You will typically kill more western quail on secondary flushes than you do on initial flushes.

2. Distance equals chilled-out birds. Western quail respond to hunting pressure by becoming flighty. They run more and flush sooner, offering far fewer shooting opportunities. Coveys that reside closer to roads and access points should be chased early in the season,

birds like berries and will frequent areas that produce wild grape, hackberry, blackberry, snowberry, poison oak, manzanita, and other species. They will often be found in areas that are virtually too thick to hunt, so keep in mind accessibility when choosing locations. Look for places where the thick cover is broken up by openings, and consider bringing along a close-working pointer that's not afraid to dive into the thickets and pinpoint coveys of birds. Flushing dogs also works, but you'll want to keep the dog close at hand so that he's not busting birds that are out of range. When hunt-

before they get educated. Once the season has progressed and the birds turn spooky, plan on doing some walking. By getting a couple of miles away from the roads, you'll find quail that are still holding on to their opening-day naïveté.

3. Make them fly. Several of the western quail species are marathon-grade runners, preferring to escape by foot rather than wing. Try the following tricks to get them to flush:

   a. Fire a shot into the air.

   b. Let out a war-whoop, or blow a quail call. (The latter might make them stop, allowing you to catch up and flush them.)

   c. Rush the birds on foot—while exercising extreme care with your firearm, obviously.

   d. Shout to your companions, directing them on a route to intercept birds and hopefully flush them.

4. Get in shape. Western quail country is often rugged and unforgiving, so you need to be in good shape before embarking on a western quail hunt. Treat it like an elk hunt in this regard, not like a stroll through pheasant country.

5. A bird in the hand . . . Quail are small, well camouflaged, and capable of covering a lot of ground on foot. When you hit a bird from the sky, go immediately to the place where it landed and begin searching for the bird. If you can't find it, start zigzagging in a direction that leads away from your shooting position. A quail with a busted wing will usually run in the same direction that it was flying. If you're fast and you don't waste a lot of time trying to score a double or triple, you stand a greater chance of catching wounded birds.

A large take of mountain quail from the Idaho high country.

The woodcock is easily North America's strangest-looking game bird. Their ridiculously long and flexible bill (used to extract worms and invertebrates from the soft and muddy ground where they hang out) looks especially odd in the broader physical context of this squat and bug-eyed bird with just a handful of stubby tail feathers adorning its backside. Yet the woodcock is also a bird of great beauty, as anyone who's witnessed the elaborate ritual of its spring mating flight will tell you. They are also beautiful when properly presented on a dinner table. The birds can be plucked and left entirely whole, then trussed by piercing the bird's probe-like beak through its thighs. (See illustration on page 304.) It's a stunning display, and certain to make a memorable impression on your friends or family. The primary thing that stands between you and this glorious meal is the difficulty of hitting a woodcock. The birds are famous for holding tight and flushing very close, but they fly in such fast and erratic patterns that many shotgunners are left wanting to throw their shotgun into a swamp after a day of missing these explosive flyers.

BARROOM BANTER: A little-known fact is that the woodcock is a migratory bird. They abandon the northern latitudes when the ground becomes crusted or frozen enough to thwart the intrusion of their beaks. They migrate singly or in small groups, seldom flying higher than 50 feet above the ground.

PHYSICAL CHARACTERISTICS: A small, robin-sized bird measuring 10 to 12 inches and weighing less than half a pound. Coloration is an overall gray-brown with a buff cinnamon breast. The head is accented by black bars; wings are mottled with black spots; tail feathers are black and white. Sexes can be differentiated by bill length. Females' bills are over 3 inches (the width of a dollar bill); the bills of males are shorter, at around 2½ inches.

HABITAT: Found near soft, loamy soils in or around bogs, brushy stream channels, moist woodlands, alder thickets, aspen clear-cuts aged between five and fifteen years, edges of wet hay meadows, grassy ponds, etc. Often encountered in typical ruffed grouse country.

DIET: Mainly earthworms, with various grubs and insects rounding out the menu. Seeds of sedges and grasses may be eaten as well.

BREEDING AND REPRODUCTION: Males court females with an elaborate "sky dance." Nesting occurs from April to June, with females laying four eggs in a shallow, leaf-lined depression.

LIFE AND DEATH: House cats, skunks, opossums, raccoons, ravens, and snakes will raid woodcock nests and often kill the hens. Adults are preyed upon by a variety of predators including foxes, coyotes, hawks, and owls.

TELLTALE SIGN: Look for droppings, which resemble splotches of spilled white paint. Also holes bored into soft soil by the woodcock's bill.

EDIBILITY: Fine-dining enthusiasts with sophisticated palates often regard woodcock as the single best American game bird. Others might find the bird to be livery in taste and texture. Excellent roasted whole, and very good in pâtés and terrines.

HUNTING OPPORTUNITIES: Widely available in eastern and southeastern states. These

A common mixed bag: woodcock and ruffed grouse. If you find woodcock, you will usually find ruffies as well; the opposite is not nearly so true.

birds tend to have a shorter season starting sometime in late September or early October and lasting until mid- or late November. Daily bag limits are commonly three.

HUNTING METHODS: Many woodcock are killed by hunters targeting ruffed grouse, as the two birds are quite often found in the same habitats during the early part of grouse season. In fact, ruffed grouse strategies are perfectly well suited for woodcock hunting. However, there is one huge difference between hunting these two birds: ruffed grouse stay put year-round, and woodcock migrate. The exact timing of the woodcock migration is tricky, though hard frozen ground will certainly send them southward from their summering grounds in the upper Great Lakes, New En-

gland, and southeastern Canada. They will also migrate in the absence of freezing temperatures if they achieve the proper fat-to-weight ratio.

In September, look for the birds in young aspen or poplar stands. As the season progresses and frosts set in, hunt them in the more frost-resistant lowlands around beaver ponds, alder bottoms, and boggy areas with spruce and fir. Suitable habitat along stream corridors or logging trails and gravel roads can be especially good, as the birds like to fly the openings provided by these features and will be concentrated in these areas. The best woodcock hunting conditions come during periods of nasty fall weather, when the birds are prevented from flying at night and they begin to stack up in good habitat like grounded airplanes. Find a good area during such conditions, and you'll be able to hunt the birds for a few days straight.

Pay very close attention to where you find woodcock, and then try to locate other areas with the same attributes. The birds are finicky about soil moisture and other conditions; just because you found them along alder-choked creek bottoms last week doesn't mean they'll be there this week. The migration also tends to shuffle the deck constantly, meaning a bad area yesterday might be dynamite today.

Dog lovers will tell you that you can't hunt woodcock without a good pointer or flusher, but they're only partially correct. These tight-holding birds are perfect for dogs, as woodcock put off a strong odor and dogs seem to locate them quite easily. (It's often said that the cocker spaniel takes its name from the bird, as the dogs were originally bred to be woodcock specialists.) However, a couple of hunters who know how to identify woodcock habitat can be quite effective by lining up shoulder to shoulder about 15 yards apart and working the cover.

When you flush a woodcock, you don't typically have time to check your form and calculate your lead. It's a point-and-shoot game; rapidly shoulder your shotgun and try to swing through the rising bird, firing just above it. It sounds a lot easier than it actually is, so be prepared for many misses and much frustration. If you do connect, the bird will come down easily. A good choice for the often short-range shooting opportunities is #8 or #9 shot fired through an improved-cylinder choke.

As with all game, you need to look hard and long for any woodcock that you manage to knock out of the sky. Birds this small can be very difficult to find, even with the help of a dog. This woodcock was killed by Ronny Boehme. After hitting the bird, he and his dogs simply could not find any trace of it except for a small speck of blood. Eventually someone was lucky enough to look up and notice that the bird had gotten hung up in a tree. It was with a relieved smile that Ronny finally made this retrieve.

RONNY BOEHME, A MICHIGAN-BASED HUNTER, WEIGHS IN ON STRATEGIES FOR WOODCOCK AND RUFFED GROUSE

"Woodcock and grouse both love heavy cover. Although I have shot some grouse on logging roads or trails, I have never flushed a woodcock from a trail. If you're hunting with a partner, have one of you bust the cover. The other guy should flank the edge, where a clearer shot might be had.

"When hunting with a partner, always call or yell out 'Bird!' whenever you see or hear one. The bird could flush toward your buddy, who may not know it's coming.

"Hunt with your ears open, especially early in the season, when the cover is so dense. A grouse flush is loud and easily heard, but a woodcock makes a quieter, more subtle *peep-peep-peep* sound that is produced by its wing feathers. Listen for this sound.

"Even when hunting with a dog, always stop now and then to take a careful look around you. Upland birds will sometimes sit tight and let both you and your dog pass them by. Stopping makes them nervous and will often cause a bird to flush.

"Always reload and be ready when approaching what you think is a downed woodcock, as it might not be injured. Woodcock fly very erratically and land the same way, usually about 50 yards from where they were flushed. Many hunters will think they hit a woodcock and run toward it, only to have the perfectly healthy bird jump up and fly away.

"If you miss a long or otherwise tough shot on a grouse, hunt in the direction that the bird flew unless you actually saw the bird flying away long after your shot was fired. Grouse fly so fast and hard that you can't always see the impact of your shot. It only takes one pellet to kill a bird, and your 'miss' might have been a hit.

"Grouse and woodcock don't use their nostrils for anything but breathing, but when you hunt smaller patches of cover you should still hunt with the wind in your face. This gives your dogs an advantage, as the wind will be blowing toward them, and it reduces the amount of sound that will travel to the birds.

"When you flush a grouse, pay attention to the particular habitat you're standing in. Does it have any particular type of fruit, such as thorn apple or wild grape? If so, look for more of that same plant. If there's no favorite grouse food present, you may have caught the bird passing from a roost area to a feeding area. If you killed the bird, check its crop to see what it's been eating. If you can find the food source, you're likely to find more birds.

"Grouse can be found in a variety of habitats, but woodcock can only eat worms and other bugs that they pull from soft, wet soils with their long beak. If you want to find both grouse and woodcock, hunt the brushy edges of swamps and creek bottoms where woodcock feed. Grouse will usually be there, too.

"No one except Elmer Fudd walks with a gun mounted to his shoulder. If you're new to wingshooting, you need to practice snap shooting. This is where your gun is lowered and you do not know when the target will fly. Have some friends throw target clays for you while you're walking or facing away from them, so it's a surprise when the target flies. This really helps to tune your senses.

"Always anticipate a second bird. Early-season grouse stay in family groups, and woodcock are usually concentrated in particular areas. Shoot, reload, and get ready.

"When you miss, don't dwell on it. You have to put it out of your mind as quick as you can. Even great baseball pitchers throw some in the dirt. If they couldn't let that go, they would never win a game.

"One last thing. Never tell your hunting partners that you miss your spouse; never tell your spouse that you miss your hunting partners."

WATERFOWL

Waterfowl hunting is the outdoor equivalent of chess. Luck plays only a very minor role in waterfowl hunting, and patience isn't entirely helpful, either. Instead, success typically comes down to planning and execution. Ducks and geese are both highly mobile and incredibly wary. They often don't show up where you want them to, and when they do show up they're likely to use their aerial perspective and excellent vision to decipher your plans and then thwart them. A common refrain at the end of many duck and goose hunts goes like this: "Well, what we probably should have tried is . . ."

Thankfully, there's hardly any limit to the number of waterfowl opportunities that await an American hunter. There are literally dozens of duck and geese species nationwide, and you can hunt them in all fifty states. Most hunters will readily divide these disparate waterfowl species into three main categories: geese, puddle ducks, and diver ducks. Each group has its most sought-after species, whose popularity has to do with abundance, quality of flesh, challenge of hunting, and physical beauty. Canada geese and snow geese are the most commonly hunted geese; mallards, wood ducks, and teal are the most beloved puddle ducks; and scaup (greater and lesser) and canvasbacks are two of the most highly favored diver ducks. Though virtually all waterfowl species have their own devotees and experts, it's possible to understand the methodology of waterfowl hunting by looking at these key species and then studying the tactics and strategies used to hunt each group.

GEESE

Hunters are attracted to geese partly because of size—both the size of the birds themselves and also the size of their flocks. A big Canada weighs around 15 pounds, and to have a flock of a hundred of these birds swarming into your decoy spread as they call loudly enough to drown out shotgun fire is something that you will never forget even if you continue to hunt for another hundred years. North American goose species include the Canada goose, snow goose, white-fronted goose, and brant, though the Canada and snow geese are the most commonly sought. Understanding these two goose species will allow you to successfully target all the others.

CANADA GOOSE
Branta canadensis
A.K.A.: Canadas, Canadians, honkers

The Canada goose is the most common—and most commonly encountered—goose species. Their availability is extremely high, and they can be found everywhere from golf courses to grain fields to backwoods marshes. Seasons for Canada geese are long and are often divided into early seasons (when local geese are targeted) and late seasons (when migrating geese are targeted). Bag limits are also generous, allowing a hunter to bag upward of five or six geese—a haul that can easily amount to 50 or 60 pounds of birds that can be plucked and gutted and converted into a host of goose goodies ranging from pastrami to pickled hearts. Due to their generous size, geese are where big game and waterfowl hunting collide.

BARROOM BANTER: Between 1914 and 2004, almost 3 million wild Canada geese have been fitted with ankle bands by waterfowl researchers; of those, 715,000 were killed by hunters who then reported the band numbers along with the date and place of harvest to authorities. Everyone from air traffic controllers to farmers has utilized the resulting information about the movements and life histories of Canada geese.

PHYSICAL CHARACTERISTICS: The Canada goose has extremely distinct features, including a long black neck, white face patch, and black bill, legs, and feet. The rump is black with a white V; lower parts are white; wings and back are dark brown; breast feathers are dark gray to light gray. The sexes are similar in appearance. The number of Canada goose subspecies that exist in North America varies

with whom you ask. Arguments range from five to eleven, with the primary differences among these "subspecies" being size and range. A greater Canada goose can weigh up to 15 pounds and stretch to almost 4 feet, while smaller varieties weigh as little as 3 or 4 pounds and measure less than 2 feet. Family flocks are typically five to eight birds; migrating flocks can number over a hundred.

HABITAT: Canada geese breed throughout Canada and much of Alaska, migrating to the central and southern United States and also Mexico. Many areas in the United States have local populations as well; many of these never migrate. The birds are found on all manner of lakes, rivers, ponds, and marshes, and they feed primarily in agricultural fields or other cultivated landscapes. They are never far from open water, where they rest during the day and roost at night.

DIET: Aquatic plants, wild and domestic grasses, and agricultural crops such as corn, wheat, and alfalfa.

LIFE AND DEATH: A slew of predators and rodents will harvest eggs from unguarded nests, and many predators will target the young. Adults are much less susceptible to predation. Canada geese are long-lived and can survive from ten to twenty-five years.

BREEDING AND REPRODUCTION: Canada geese typically nest in the early spring; females lay two to eight eggs.

TELLTALE SIGN: Look for cylindrical droppings, the size and shape of bent and half-smoked cigarettes. Heavily used areas will be littered with many, many droppings. Also look for tracks in soft shoreline mud. Another giveaway is the Canada goose's distinctive *her-honk* call, which can be heard at a great distance.

EDIBILITY: Canada geese have a mild flavor that results in good eating; done properly, it resembles lean beef in texture. If they are not prepared properly (overcooking the breast meat is a common mistake), the meat can be tough and almost unpalatable.

Canada geese are big, and you're allowed a lot of them. Danny Rinella and Brandt Meixel (left and center), use geese for pastrami, confit, sausage, jerky, pâté, and simple grilled preparations.

SNOW GEESE
Chen caerulescens
A.K.A.: Blue geese, snows

Snow geese are an ecological winner of the modern age. They've adapted so well to contemporary agricultural practices in their southern wintering grounds that their populations have exploded wildly in recent decades; today, they stand to severely damage their Arctic breeding grounds with overgrazing. Government game managers across the snow goose's wintering grounds and along its migratory corridors have basically pulled out all obstacles that stand in the way of hunters being able to harvest as many of the birds as possible. Bag limits are extremely high to nonexistent, seasons extend well into the spring migration season, capacity-limiting plugs are not required on shotguns, and you can even use electronic calling devices (a formerly taboo practice) in the pursuit of snow geese. While the flesh is not as good as that of Canada geese, it is still a wonderful thing to have at your disposal.

BARROOM BANTER: Female snow geese will build their nests on the tundra in areas protected by shrubs and rocks. Rather than building her nest all at once, a female will expand the nest size prior to dropping each individual egg.

PHYSICAL CHARACTERISTICS: Snow geese are usually white with black wingtips.

The "blue goose," often regarded as a separate species, is simply a color phase of the snow goose. These have grayish or slate-colored wings and body with a white head and tail. (The Ross's goose looks very similar to the snow goose, but it is smaller and has a shorter, stubbier bill.) Snow geese measure about 28 inches long and weigh up to 6½ pounds.

HABITAT: Snow geese breed high on the Arctic tundra in the summer months, then begin migrating southward in September. Their migration corridors spread them throughout the United States; the birds congregate for the winter in the mid-Atlantic states, along the Gulf Coast, and in Mexico. On their wintering grounds, they are closely associated with agricultural fields.

DIET: Aquatic plants and tubers, a variety of grasses and forbs, and agricultural crops such as rice, corn, alfalfa, and wheat.

LIFE AND DEATH: Predators such as Arctic foxes and weasels will raid snow goose nests, though adults are much less susceptible to predation. Snow geese can live to be well beyond ten years of age in the wild.

BREEDING AND REPRODUCTION: A female snow goose will lay two to six eggs during the early summer breeding season.

TELLTALE SIGN: Similar to Canada geese—look for concentrations of droppings in active feeding areas.

EDIBILITY: Snow geese have dark, strong-tasting meat that is generally regarded less highly than that of Canada geese. Using brine or a similar soaking solution can help with their overall flavor and tenderness. Great for sausages and cured dishes such as confit, corned goose, and pastrami.

GOOSE HUNTING METHODS

Geese roost on the water at night and then leave the water early in the morning in order to fly to their feeding areas. They will often return to their roosting areas in the late morn-

Snow geese and Canada geese are extremely wary when approaching feeding areas, especially when they've been pressured by hunters. Here the author used a military surplus snow camo outfit while sitting among a decoy spread that was laid out in a cut corn field. All he had to do was lie down in order to disappear. `

ing and then spend the middle part of the day resting on the water. In the afternoon, they will head back out for another feeding session and then return to the water again at dusk. During cold weather, they might make additional feeding trips throughout the day.

The most effective way to hunt geese is to ambush them at their feeding grounds with the aid of decoys and calling. The key to this strategy—typically called field hunting—is to locate active feeding grounds. In this case,

"active" does not mean that geese were using the area last month or even last week. Active means that geese were using the area during their most recent feeding session. (If you're hunting on Sunday morning, you want to be where the geese were feeding Saturday night; if you're hunting Sunday evening, you want to be where the geese were feeding Sunday morning.) While there's no guarantee that the flocks will use this place again, you might as well operate under the assumption that they will. Beyond selecting the proper field, you should strive to place your decoys in the exact same part of the field that the geese were using. They were there because of something that they liked, and they'll feel comfortable landing there again.

When planning your decoy setup, be mindful of concealment. When pressured, geese become extremely wary. Hunters should take every possible precaution to make sure they are well hidden. Geese will make multiple overhead passes to scrutinize their landing areas before committing. If anything looks out of the ordinary, they will refuse to touch down no matter how enticing the decoys look and how provocative the calling sounds. In a picked corn field with lots of stubble lying about (known as a "dirty" field), concealment is made easy because you can use the debris to your advantage, piling it up around your layout blind or weaving it into the cover of your pit blind. But in a field of newly sprouting winter wheat there is little natural cover that can be put into use. In these situations you need to get creative. Field edges are sometimes suitable for blind placement, but remember that geese don't like to land near cover that they can't see over. Irrigation ditches sometimes make great blind locations. So do grassy divider strips between fields. Snow is an asset as well. A white layout blind on a field of snow might give the hunter all the advantage he needs.

If you are spooking geese, there's a reason why. The problem might seem very minor, but in the eyes of a wary goose it makes all the difference. Fresh dirt scattered around the edges of an otherwise well-constructed pit blind might be to blame. Corn stubble used to construct a blind in a wheat field might be suspicious-looking enough to scare them off. So might a wrong-colored glove, a bit of uncovered skin, or a shotgun shell box that's been left lying outside of the blind. Keep making adjustments until you figure out what's going wrong. If the last four flocks of geese have spooked without attempting to land, the fifth is going to spook as well unless you correct the issue.

When hunting over decoys for geese, use a 12-gauge shotgun with a modified choke. Shoot 3- or 3½-inch shells in either #1 or BB.

Pass-shooting—ambushing flying birds along their natural travelways without the aid of decoys—can also be deadly on geese. The strategy is especially useful when you don't have legal access to the birds' feeding areas. The key is to set up in an area where the birds are going to be flying low enough to reach them with a shotgun as they pass overhead, which generally means setting up in a place that's close to either their roosting area or their feeding area so that they're either still climbing to their cruising altitude or descending from it. Observation of the birds' movements should reveal the proper place. As they go about their routines, geese will utilize the aerial equivalent of game trails. Geese leaving a large lake might funnel through a gap in the trees along the water's edge. Geese following a wide river corridor will funnel through narrow gaps formed where the river valley is pinched by natural features. Scouting will also reveal the best times to set up, as geese follow a fairly predictable clock. Blind construction isn't nearly as important for pass-shooting as it is for decoy hunting, mostly because the birds aren't looking for trouble as diligently when traveling as they are when preparing to land. You still need to be careful, as heavily hunted birds will veer off course to avoid anything that looks fishy, but you shouldn't need to actually construct a blind. Just put yourself under the best source of cover you can find beneath the center of the travel corridor and then stay low until it's time to pop up and shoot. And be careful not to jump up too soon in advance of the birds' arrival. Geese are masters at evasive flying. They can simultaneously veer to the sides and gain elevation, quickly turning a sure thing into a total failure.

When pass-shooting geese, use a 12-gauge shotgun with a modified or full choke. Shoot 3- or 3½-inch shells in BB or BBB.

WHEN TO SAY "TAKE 'EM!"

There are some days that go perfectly. Birds will respond to calls without any hesitation and fly into your decoys like long-lost friends. On days like this, you can wait until the very last second—just before their feet touch the water—to stand up and fire. A duck's retreat to the sky from the cupped-wing and feet-out landing position is that of an aerial backpedal. This makes them easier targets at close range and gives you time to make careful selections of gender. If it's been an off day, one where the birds are hesitating before moving in toward the decoys, shooting earlier may be necessary. If midrange shots have been the daily norm, try to anticipate how close the birds will come before

(continued)

shooting. Try to draw them as close as possible with calling, perhaps allowing them to circle a few times to encourage confidence in the idea of landing. If they start to bail, shoot before they are out of range. And of course, some days will be terrible. The birds will not respond to calls, the decoys won't look inviting, an odd wind will blow, or any number of other things will happen that can create a bad hunt. If you see a bird that is within range and you have only had a few shooting opportunities, attempt the long shot. Sometimes it is better to shoot and miss than not shoot at all and wish you had. But beware the risk of crippling birds. Shots beyond 40 yards should be limited only to experienced wingshooters who understand how to lead birds.

PUDDLE DUCKS

Puddle ducks, also known as dabbler ducks, are ducks that feed primarily in shallow water and do not dive beneath the water's surface. Mallards, teal, wood ducks, widgeons, gadwalls, pintails, and shovelers are all puddle ducks. They have large wings relative to their body size, which enables them to lift off from land or water vertically rather than needing the long horizontal takeoff "runway" required of deep-feeding diver ducks. Puddle ducks generally have colored wing patches, or speculum feathers. Their calls are generally coarse and gravelly compared with the whistles and croaks of many diver species. Their legs are positioned in the center of their body, enabling them to walk and feed competently on land—though not as well as geese. When feeding on submerged vegetation, puddle ducks dip their head beneath the surface in a motion known as dabbling. They cannot feed in water much deeper than 75 percent of their total length. Puddle ducks have a primarily vegetarian diet. Their flesh is milder and better-tasting than that of diver ducks, which feed heavily on fish, shellfish, aquatic insects, and other animal matter. There are exceptions. The shoveler is a puddle duck that feeds heavily on animal matter, and it is one of the poorest-tasting puddle duck species. In certain places and at certain times of year, otherwise excellent species of puddle ducks will develop an "off" flavor from feeding on crustaceans and other animal matter. Such is the case with mallards in many areas of southeast Alaska, where they taste as bad as most diver ducks. Below we will cover mallards, wood ducks, and teal. Familiarize yourself with these puddle duck species and you'll be prepared to target all the others.

Puddle duck country is a beautiful place to be in the morning.

MALLARDS
Anas platyrhynchos
A.K.A.: Greenheads (males), susies (females)

Mallards are the most common North American duck species, and the most commonly hunted. They can be found in most every state and are widely available through Canada and Mexico as well. Besides the ready availability of mallards, they are popular with hunters because of the relative predictability of their movements and the fine quality of their meat.

BARROOM BANTER: Since 1914, over six million mallards have been fitted with ankle bands by waterfowl researchers; of those, over 1 million were killed by hunters who then reported the band numbers along with the date and place of harvest to authorities. These data have helped wildlife managers and other scientists understand the complex migratory patterns of North American waterfowl.

PHYSICAL CHARACTERISTICS: Males, or drakes, have iridescent green heads with a white ring on the neck and a yellow bill; back and wings are gray-brown; bellies are light gray; feet are orange. Females, or hens, are mottled brown with a light brown head and belly. Both drakes and hens have blue speculum feathers that are outlined in white. Mallards weigh upward of 3½ pounds.

HABITAT: Mallards can be found in almost any wetland habitat, including rivers, streams, lakes, reservoirs, prairie potholes, beaver ponds, farm ponds, irrigation ditches, flooded timber and crop fields, and urban park ponds. They breed throughout the northern United States, Canada, and Alaska, and generally migrate southward when water sources begin to freeze. Huge numbers winter across the American South.

DIET: Mallards will eat a variety of aquatic plants and agricultural crops. During breeding season, they feed readily on aquatic protein sources.

LIFE AND DEATH: All puddle ducks can fall victim to numerous dangers. A host of predators, including snakes and rodents, will steal eggs from nests. Avian predators, large fish, and aquatic and terrestrial predatory mammals will kill juvenile and adult mallards. Despite their substantial predator load, a mallard can

live to be well over ten years old in the wild. (One captive mallard lived to be twenty-seven years old.)

BREEDING AND REPRODUCTION: Mallard hens typically nest in shoreline grasses or cattails, laying one to thirteen eggs.

TELLTALE SIGN: Look for feathers and tracks around shorelines and muddy banks.

EDIBILITY: Excellent when cooked to medium rare. Overcooked mallard has an off-putting livery quality.

Mallards are the king of the puddle ducks. They are big, abundant, and fun to hunt. They are also excellent to eat. This Alaskan mallard has been plucked and gutted. Now it's getting slow-roasted over a fire.

Regarded by most hunters as the most beautiful species of North American waterfowl, wood duck males, or drakes, are colorful enough to be mistaken for some exotic jungle species. The places that wood ducks call home are equally pretty. They prefer small, heavily wooded bodies of water such as beaver ponds, creeks, marshes, and small lakes. Wood ducks are one of North America's great conservation stories. The ducks nest in tree cavities, and the destruction of suitable nesting sites nearly drove the species to extinction in the 1920s. Aggressive efforts by hunter-conservationists—particularly the construction of artificial nesting boxes—brought the species back from the brink of extinction. Today they are widely abundant.

BARROOM BANTER: The wood duck's scientific name, *Aix sponsa*, translates into "waterbird in bridal dress."

PHYSICAL CHARACTERISTICS: Wood duck males are easily distinguished by their crested purple and green head, which is accented by white lines running from their bill to their crest; eyes are ringed by red; white chin and throat; maroon chest; tail is dark purple and black. The female has a gray-brown head with a small crest; white chin, throat, and eye patches; whitish-gray belly; the tail is long and gray. Both sexes have dark brown wings with white frosting and blue markings.

HABITAT: Wood ducks live in wooded wetland areas with plenty of vegetative cover, particularly in the vicinity of mast-bearing hardwood trees. They can weave through unbelievably thick limbs and vegetation in order to reach watery landing areas. They breed throughout their northern range and winter in the southeastern United States.

DIET: Acorns, hickory nuts, beechnuts, and wild rice, plus a variety of other nuts and seeds as well as aquatic vegetation and aquatic insects.

LIFE AND DEATH: Raccoons, mink, opossums, and other predators will rob wood duck eggs from nests in tree cavities. Juvenile and adult wood ducks fall prey to predatory fish, birds, and mammals. Wood ducks can live to be over ten years old.

BREEDING AND REPRODUCTION: Wood duck hens lay six to sixteen eggs in tree cav-

ities or artificial nesting boxes placed by conservationists.

TELLTALE SIGN: Besides the occasional feather, wood ducks leave very little physical evidence of their presence.

EDIBILITY: Excellent, unless it is overcooked. On par with mallard.

If you don't pause to appreciate the beauty of a wood duck after a successful hunt, there's something wrong with you. The birds taste as good as they look.

TEAL

North America has three teal species: blue-winged teal, cinnamon teal, and green-winged teal. They are the smallest of the puddle ducks, with most teal topping out at well under a pound. They can also be one of the toughest ducks to hit with a shotgun. Many hunters try to explain away their inability to hit teal by citing the birds' fantastic flying speeds. While teal are actually incapable of approaching the top flight speeds achieved by many larger ducks, they do seem to do everything at an accelerated pace. Mallards might approach a decoy spread by slowly dropping from the sky like an Airbus, but teal will usually come in like F-16s. They materialize out of nowhere, buzzing low and fast across the water in a wild zigzagging pattern, and then vanish from sight without ever offering a plausible shooting opportunity. This is especially frustrating because a missed teal is a missed meal—and a damn fine meal at that. These small, agile birds are among the finest-tasting ducks.

BARROOM BANTER: Hunters sometimes refer to teal, particularly blue-winged teal and cinnamon teal, as "summer ducks." The birds are early migrators and leave their summer nesting grounds well ahead of other duck species—and sometimes well ahead of the general waterfowl hunting season. Some states accommodate teal hunters by offering an early teal-only duck season.

GREEN-WINGED TEAL
Anas crecca
A.K.A.: Greenwings

PHYSICAL DESCRIPTION AND RANGE: Green-winged teal are the smallest puddle duck, weighing only ¾ pound and measuring just 13 to 15 inches. Drakes have a chestnut-colored head with a dark green ear patch. Sides are barred gray and white; wings are light brown. Hens are mottled brown and generally similar in appearance to the hens of both blue-winged and cinnamon teal. However, hens can be readily identified by their emerald-colored speculum feathers. Green-winged teal breed throughout Alaska, Canada, and the prairie pothole region of the Great Plains and upper Midwest. The species has widespread wintering grounds, ranging across the southern tier of the United States and throughout Mexico and much of Central America. They are particularly abundant in Louisiana and Texas.

BLUE-WINGED TEAL
Anas discors
A.K.A.: Bluewings

PHYSICAL DESCRIPTION AND RANGE:
Blue-winged teal are slightly larger than green-winged teal, weighing up to a pound. Drakes have a slate-blue to purple head with a distinctive white facial crescent that runs from the jawline upward past the eye. The bill is long and black, and the body has an overall polka-dotted appearance of black on brown. Speculum feathers are blue. While hens are mottled brown and very similar in appearance to the hens of green-winged teal, their blue speculum feathers can distinguish them. Blue-winged teal nest throughout Alaska, across much of Canada, and in most of the United States excluding the Pacific Coast and extreme south. They winter in the southern United States, Mexico, Central America, and South America.

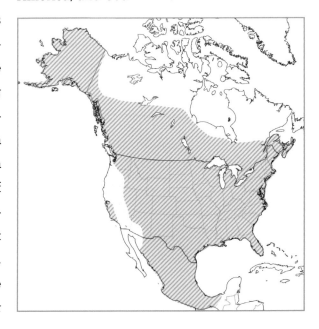

CINNAMON TEAL
Anas cyanaptera
A.K.A.: Red teal

PHYSICAL DESCRIPTION AND RANGE: Cinnamon teal weigh up to a pound. Drakes have a cinnamon-colored head, neck, breast, and belly. Feet are orange. The bill is wider and more shovel-shaped than in other teal. Cinnamon teal hens are virtually indistinguishable from the hens of blue-winged teal; they are mottled brown, with blue shoulder patches and dark green or emerald speculum feathers. Cinnamon teal nest in the western United States, particularly along the Pacific Coast and the Great Salt Lake. They winter in the southern portions of California, Arizona, and New Mexico, as well as in Mexico, Central America, and South America.

HABITAT: There is some variation among the three teal species, but the birds are generally found in shallow, heavily vegetated wetlands where food is easily accessible near or above the water's surface.

DIET: Teal are particularly fond of aquatic plants, including algae, duckweeds, and pond-

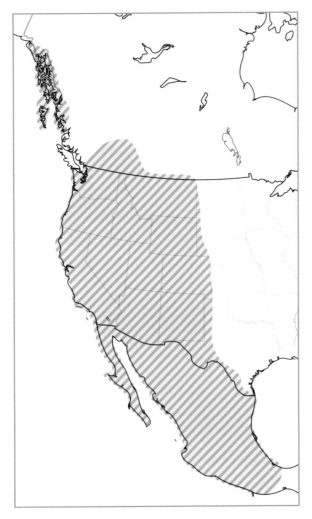

weeds. They will also eat the seeds of various grasses and sedges, as well as a wide variety of aquatic invertebrates.

LIFE AND DEATH: Like all puddle ducks, teal are hunted by a variety of terrestrial, avian, and aquatic predators. Blue-winged teal have the highest mortality rates of any puddle ducks, perhaps due to long migrations.

BREEDING AND REPRODUCTION: Teal hens typically nest in heavily vegetated, waterside areas, including small islands. Hens lay eight to ten eggs.

TELLTALE SIGN: Like most duck species, teal leave very little evidence of themselves. Look for feathers and the distinct webbed-foot pattern from their movements around the muddy edges of bodies of water.

EDIBILITY: Teal flesh is generally milder and tenderer than many other duck species. An excellent way to introduce the uninitiated to the joys of eating waterfowl.

A chocolate Lab brings in a green-winged teal in Louisiana.

PUDDLE DUCK HUNTING STRATEGIES

It's difficult to list all the scenarios that one might encounter when hunting puddle ducks. The birds use so many different habitat types in so many different ways that the possibilities are endless. In one week you could feasibly kill mallards on a bedroom-sized beaver pond, along a drainage ditch, in a dry cornfield, and on an island in the middle of a large lake without ever traveling more than a few miles from your home. Scouting and flexibility are the keys to success. You need to scout to find out what the puddle ducks are doing, and you need to be flexible in order to exploit that information.

The most thrilling way to hunt puddle ducks is to decoy them. The surest recipe for success is to set out your decoys right where you've seen ducks landing in the past few days, though this is hardly the only way to do it. Ducks are highly social critters, and they will readily abandon their day's plan in order to investigate a new flock of "ducks" that you've positioned in a likely-looking area. Puddle ducks can be decoyed effectively all day, but early morning is perhaps the optimal time. Ducks coming off their roosting area and heading toward an early morning feeding area will often commit to a spread of decoys much more readily than they will in the middle of the day when they've been shot at a time or two. Evening is a close second, especially when hunt-

A decoy spread on a marsh that worked for both puddle ducks and divers. This is a J-shaped decoy pattern. With the wind blowing from right to left, birds will approach from the left and try to settle in the immediate foreground. See "A Primer on Decoys and Decoy Spreads" on page 283 for a broader explanation of decoy use.

ing roosting water. In general, the best duck hunting happens in the worst weather. Ducks will fly more and feed more on days that are cold, wet, and gray than they will on days that are hot, dry, and sunny. When setting puddle duck decoys, don't crowd the birds together. Puddle ducks feed in looser configurations than diver ducks. It's common for hunters to leave as much as 10 feet of space between decoys. Keep the decoys facing into the wind, as that's what real ducks generally do. Puddle ducks are as wary as geese, so take camouflage very seriously. For hunting puddle ducks over decoys, use a 12-gauge shotgun loaded with 2¾- or 3-inch shells with #2, #3, or #4 shot (use #2 and #3 for longer shots, #3 and #4 for closer shots). When exclusively targeting smaller puddle ducks like wood ducks and teal, an improved-cylinder choke with #4 shot is a good bet.

For information on pass-shooting puddle ducks, consider the earlier section on pass-shooting geese. While it might seem counterintuitive, the best locations for pass-shooting ducks are those that receive the heaviest hunting pressure. Positioning yourself along a narrow channel between two lakes that get heavy hunting pressure allows you to capitalize on birds that will be getting bounced back and forth between hunters. Another strategy is to locate a roosting area where ducks are congregating at night. In the predawn darkness, slip into position along the typical route that the birds fly when they lift off to visit their feeding areas. This is a quick and fairly effortless way to secure a duck for the dinner table before you head off to work. For pass-shooting ducks, use a 12-gauge shotgun loaded with 3-inch shells with #2 or #3 shot.

A few puddle ducks killed by a jump-shooter who was working the shoreline of a small lake in Alaska's Brooks Range. In extremely remote areas with no hunting pressure, puddle ducks are very easy to hunt.

Jump-shooting works really well with puddle ducks thanks to their habit of feeding and loafing in shallow water close to shorelines. This is not the most challenging form of duck hunting, but it's great when you're hunting for food or teaching a youngster the fundamentals of hunting. The method shares a lot in common with grouse and pheasant hunting, because you're basically taking a quiet walk through likely habitats in hopes of flushing birds within shotgun range. Wearing a pair of waders or hip boots, work the edges of narrow creeks, ponds, sloughs, or brushy lakeshores, or wade through marshes, swamps, or flooded timber. You'll sometimes see ducks before they flush, or you'll see ducks land in the distance. In this case, the hunt turns into a stalk as you try to sneak within range before they flush. A lot of jump-shooting jaunts begin when you're sitting in your blind on a slow day and see a flock of ducks land a couple hundred yards away. These side trips often reveal new locations where you'll want to set decoys in the future.

If you see ducks in range before they flush, you can either jump the birds by walking toward them or shouting, or you can shoot a bird off the water. If you do the latter, chamber a second round in a hurry, because you're almost sure to get a second shot as birds start to flush. When jump-shooting, always be mindful of the surrounding cover. The ducks are flying away from you, and they'll be even farther away when they land. Don't shoot birds over impenetrable cover where finding them will be too difficult unless you've got a good retrieving dog with a reliable nose. A variation on jump-shooting is to team up with a buddy and use a canoe to float down rivers and streams. The paddler in the back guides the boat, and the hunter in the front does the shooting. If you're quiet, you'll often drift right up on ducks before they flush. When floating, use the contours of the shoreline to help conceal your approach. Ducks and geese will often lie

A good retriever is an invaluable duck hunting tool. If you're hunting without a dog, be very careful about the shots you take. Keep retrieval in mind *before* you shoot.

A jump-shooter's boat. Notice the veil of vegetation placed in the bow. Even a little bit of camouflage can improve your odds when trying to approach ducks in a boat. The key to getting close is to move slow, low, and quiet.

at the lower end of islands and sandbars, so be ready when approaching these features. This can be an action-packed and highly productive way to hunt both ducks and geese.

When jump-shooting ducks, use a 12-gauge loaded with 2¾- or 3-inch shells. It's a good idea to have a shell with #4 shot chambered and then have a pair of shells with #2 shot in the magazine. This makes you ready for a close shot as the birds flush followed by longer shots as the remainder of the birds hightail it away.

SAM TERRELL, A LOUISIANA AND CALIFORNIA HUNTER, WEIGHS IN ON THE LANGUAGE OF DUCKS

"The first difficult word I ever learned was *gregarious*. It's an adjective with two definitions. The first is in reference to people being fond of company, and the second is in relation to animals living in flocks or loosely organized communities. As a duck hunter coming from a family out of New Orleans, the second meaning has vital importance. Ducks are as sociable as people; they seek connections with others and communicate specifically about food, friends, and danger. I spent hours when I was younger talking with my uncle Tim and his close friend Jim about how to use calls and decoys to convince these birds that the water in front of our blind was safe to land in. I found out early that ducks, just like people, are gregarious. They want good food, good friends, and a place to relax.

"If you really want birds to come down out of the sky and into your decoys, learning to call is going to be supremely important. When it comes to choosing a call, if you have never used one before, there are quite a few companies that produce entry-

(continued)

level calls for nominal prices. Some even come in package deals that include the recordings of what various calls should sound like so you can practice. Practice is going to help really polish the way your calling sounds. It's important to note that a duck call is a tool just like a gun. Using your tools properly will help bag your daily limit, while improper use will keep birds out of range.

"When people first start calling there is a tendency to 'overcall,' or get excited and call too aggressively. This has a negative effect. Calling needs to be done with distinct intentions: get the birds' attention, bring them in close, and convince them to land. To do this effectively, you should have a group of practiced calls to tap into. For mallards, my top five are the quack, greeting call, feeding call, comeback call, and hailing call.

"The quack is the essential first step of duck calling; mastering the basic quack will help you move forward in your calls as well as aid you as a duck hunter. You can blend individual quacks into a mixture of calls that will help add realism to your calling. There should be a sharp and clean ending to a proper quack, focusing on a crisp *-ck* rather than a soft *qua-* sound.

"The greeting call is a welcome invitation to birds flying by at a distance. The structure of the call is a string of sounds five to seven notes long using a ***knack-knack-knack-knack-knack*** pattern. The notes should be blown in an even rhythm that sounds very certain and steady. You can use a greeting call to get birds interested in your decoys as they start toward your blind and come into view.

"The feeding call is a fast, garbled sound that is produced by making a ***tika-tika-tika*** pattern. Using a feeding call adds variety to your calling and makes decoys sound happy and alive. Ducks have clearer feeding calls when they are flying than they do when they are in the water. Use speed and volume control to help keep birds interested without getting too loud to scare them. The quack can also be inserted to break up a feeding call.

"The comeback call is used when birds are not accepting your greeting call or they are not responding well to the calls you are providing. This a speedy, urgent, and simple call that makes a succession of sounds similar to ***quanckanck-kanck-kanck-kanck.*** Make this call fast and with force in a string of four to seven notes. Use this to help birds turn back and come down into your decoys.

"Finally, the hailing call is one to use sparingly. This is a loud, in-your-face call that helps bring high-flying birds down using a long *aaaaick* sound **twenty** or more times in succession, fading off as you reach the end. This string of *aaaaick*s should start slower than it ends, speeding up **as** you run **out** of breath so the sounds start blending together slightly.

"If you practice these **five** calls, you will have a great start to your calling arsenal. There are more specific calls that can be purchased later on, as your involvement with duck hunting increases, which impersonate geese, whistling ducks, and other specific duck sounds. But to simply get started, buy a call you like the look and feel of, one that is priced right for you, and one that makes you wish it was fall. And if the birds **are** coming in and you are wondering if you should keep calling or start shooting, put the call down and paint the sky with feathers."

Top left: Ken Martin Canada goose call. Top right: Down-N-Dirty Outdoors mallard call. Bottom: Tim Grounds mallard call.

A PRIMER ON WATERFOWL REGULATIONS

Make sure to report all banded birds that you recover. The information that these bands reveal is integral to waterfowl conservation.

Unlike most game animals, which are managed on the state level, waterfowl is managed both on the state and federal levels. As a waterfowl hunter, it is your responsibility to know and follow all the laws that pertain to the activity. These rules change every year, so check them thoroughly each season before you hunt.

Federally, all of the nation's duck and geese are regarded as belonging to one of four flyways, based on their particular migration corridor: Atlantic, Mississippi, Central, or Pacific. Each flyway has an administrative council with one member from each state within that flyway to help formulate state/regional regulations with the U.S. Fish and Wildlife Service. (Other North American countries have a say as well.) The states and their associated flyways are listed below.

Atlantic Flyway: Connecticut, Delaware, Florida, Georgia, Maine, Maryland, Massachusetts, New Hampshire, New Jersey, New York, North Carolina, Pennsylvania, Rhode Island, South Carolina, Vermont, Virginia, and West Virginia.

Mississippi Flyway: Alabama, Arkansas, Indiana, Illinois, Iowa, Kentucky, Louisiana, Michigan, Minnesota, Mississippi, Missouri, Ohio, Tennessee, and Wisconsin.

Central Flyway: Montana, Wyoming, Colorado, New Mexico, Texas, Oklahoma, Kansas, Nebraska, North Dakota, and South Dakota.

Pacific Flyway: Alaska, Arizona, California, Idaho, Nevada, Oregon, Utah, Washington, and those portions of Colorado, Montana, New Mexico, and Wyoming west of the Continental Divide.

OVERVIEW OF BASIC FEDERAL TERMS AND REGULATIONS

Shooting hours: You can only hunt waterfowl during open shooting hours, usually starting half an hour before sunrise and ending at sunset.

Closed season: You cannot hunt waterfowl during the closed season.

Daily bag limit: You can take only one daily bag limit in any one day. This limit determines the number of waterfowl you may legally have in your possession while in the field or while en route back to your car, hunting camp, home, or other destination.

Wanton waste: You must make a reasonable effort to retrieve all waterfowl that you kill or cripple and keep these birds in your actual custody while in the field. You must immediately kill any wounded birds that you retrieve and count those birds toward your daily bag limit.

Tagging: You cannot put or leave waterfowl at any place or in the custody of another person unless you tag the birds with your signature, address, number of birds identified by species, and the date you killed them.

Rallying: You cannot hunt waterfowl that have been concentrated, driven, rallied, or stirred up with a motorized vehicle or sailboat.

Dressing: You cannot completely field-dress waterfowl before taking them from the field. The head or one fully feathered wing must remain attached to the birds while you transport them to your home or to a facility that processes waterfowl.

Dual violation: A violation of a state waterfowl hunting regulation is also a violation of federal regulations.

(continued)

Duck stamp: If you are **sixteen** or older, you must carry on your person an unexpired federal migratory bird hunting and conservation stamp. You must validate your duck stamp by signing it in ink across the face before hunting.

Migratory Bird Harvest Information Program (HIP): Unless exempt from license requirements in the state where you are hunting, you must enroll in the HIP and carry proof of current enrollment while hunting.

Protected birds: Federal law prohibits the killing of non-game migratory birds. Protected birds that you could encounter while waterfowl hunting include songbirds, eagles, hawks, owls, vultures, herons, egrets, and woodpeckers.

You may *not* hunt waterfowl:

- With a trap, snare, net, rifle, pistol, swivel gun, shotgun larger than 10-gauge, punt gun, **battery gun**, machine gun, fish hook, poison, drug, explosive, or stupefying substance.
- From any low-floating device that conceals you beneath the surface of the water.
- From a motorboat or sailboat, unless the motor is off or the sail is furled and the vessel is no longer in motion.
- Using live birds as decoys.
- While possessing any projectile other than nontoxic shot.
- From or by means, aid, or use of any motor vehicle, motor-driven land conveyance, or aircraft.
- Using recorded or electrically **amplified** bird calls or sounds, or imitations of these calls and sounds. (Does not apply during light-goose-only seasons in certain authorized areas of the Central and Mississippi flyways.)
- With a shotgun that can hold more than three shells, unless you plug it with a one-piece filler that cannot be removed without disassembling the gun. (Does not apply during light-goose-only seasons in certain authorized areas of the Central and Mississippi flyways.)
- Over bait. The act of baiting is the direct or indirect depositing or exposing of salt or feed that could attract waterfowl to specific areas for hunters to take. If an area has been intentionally or unintentionally baited, it is off-limits to hunting for ten

days. "Bait" or "baiting" includes any crop that has not been harvested but that has been rolled or disked; crops that have been harvested outside of recommended harvest dates; crops that have been damaged by livestock or by other types of manipulation that expose feed. You may not hunt any area where grain is present and stored (grain elevators, grain bins, etc.); any area where grain is present for the purpose of feeding livestock; freshly planted wildlife food plots that contain exposed grain; or croplands where a crop has been harvested and the removed grain is redistributed to the same lands.

You may:

• Hunt waterfowl in unharvested standing crops and flooded fields; where grains are scattered solely as a result of agricultural planting, harvesting, or post-harvest processes; lands where top-sown seeds are scattered as a result of a normal agricultural planting; and where non-agricultural, native, or naturalized plant species are growing in response to planting or from existing seeds.

If you have additional questions about waterfowl hunting and the law, contact the nearest U.S. Fish and Wildlife Service law enforcement office or one of the service's regional law enforcement offices.

THE ART OF HIDING: BLINDS AND CAMOUFLAGE

Camouflage clothing is essential for waterfowl hunting, unless you've got a good blind that keeps you entirely hidden. Wear clothes (and waders) that match the vegetation or ground cover where you hunt. But camouflage can't work miracles; you also need to employ some tactics of stealth when trying to get wary ducks or geese into shotgun range. Use a backdrop when you can, such as a large tree trunk. Keep a low profile at all times, except when you rise to shoot. Avoid nylon and acrylic clothes that have a shine to them. Keep your face low and covered with a mask or face paint when

(continued)

watching circling birds. Check your hunting partners to make sure they aren't making clothing mistakes. If your buddy is wearing a reversible hunting jacket with hunter's orange on the inside, make sure none of the orange is showing around the collar or cuffs. Avoid horizontal lines. A set of horizontally oriented shoulders in a stand of vertical cattails can easily give you away.

Waterfowl blinds come in myriad forms, from simple painter's suits for field hunting in the snow to expensive and elaborate layout boats for hunting diver ducks on vast ocean bays. Here are a handful of options to consider when trying to vanish from the prying eyes of waterfowl.

A goose hunter in a layout blind. His dog can climb in there with him. Notice the wing-shaped flag, used to get a flock's attention from a long way off.

• Layout blinds are fantastic for field hunters. These allow you to lie down and hide in a field that provides little or no natural cover. Commercially produced versions are quite nice and come in a variety of camouflage patterns ranging from corn stubble to pure white. Some layout blinds are even made to look like gigantic geese. For the water-fowler on a budget, you can make do with less expensive materials. Try laying burlap sacks over your body to mimic dirt, or use a net draped with corn stalks to mimic corn stubble. A white bedsheet can work well in snowy conditions.

This gang of hunters killed a limit of geese using pit blinds, which are visible behind them. Cover the holes with light-duty fencing into which grass has been woven; you can push this cover away as you rise to shoot.

• Pit blinds serve the same purpose as layout blinds—to hide you in a landscape offering little or no cover. Here the recipe is simple: dig a hole and get in it. The larger the hole, the more comfortable it will be to hunt out of. If you want to get fancy, build a bench into the hole for sitting and a dugout shelf for spare shells and coffee. To improve your camouflage, take a section of wire fence big enough to cover the hole and weave dead grasses and sticks into it. Once inside, use it as a lid and fling it open when the birds are close.

Montana hunter Kent Undlin killed a bunch of tasty geese by using a coverall suit to blend in with the snow.

• Coverall suits are simple and often quite effective. Since you're wearing your "blind," moving it is as easy as standing up and walking away. Ghillie suits are great when trying to hide in low brush. Painter's suits work well for snow camo. Simple Carhartt coveralls are often adequate for hiding on bare dirt.

• Some variation of the brush blind is probably the most common way to conceal yourself from waterfowl. For the simplest approach, start with a framework of logs and sticks and then fill in the gaps with nearby vegetation, such as brush, grass, cornstalks, cattails, or leaves. An-

An Alaska hunter constructs a brush blind at the water's edge.

other method is to pound in four chest-high stakes and then wrap the stakes in hog-wire fencing. Weave the fencing with vegetation. When hunting soggy areas, put down a piece of plywood for a floor.

A well-camouflaged boat was used to kill eleven Canada geese on the Tennessee River.

• Boats can be turned into blinds by covering them with textured camouflage covers or brushing them out with natural materials woven into netting. You can also get manufactured boat coverings with doors that swing open for fast shooting.

DIVER DUCKS

Diver ducks, also known as diving ducks, are capable of diving beneath the water's surface in order to feed. They are generally associated with larger and deeper waterways than puddle ducks are. Because they have proportionally smaller wings than puddle ducks, they are incapable of lifting directly into the air from a standstill and must run across the water's surface in order to take flight. When flying, they have much shorter and faster wing-beats than puddle ducks. They are very clumsy on land but are adept underwater swimmers, with legs positioned toward the rear of their bodies and relatively large feet. Many divers can feed at depths of 20 to 30 feet, with the king eider going all the way down to 150 feet. Diver ducks are primarily meat eaters, consuming small fish, clams, crayfish, aquatic insects, snails, et cetera. In general, their flesh is inferior to that of geese and puddle ducks. It can be oily and strong, and often tastes of fish. A few diver duck species, including canvasbacks and redheads, do have predominantly plant-based diets. These are the best-tasting diver ducks. Greater and lesser scaup also have passable flesh, despite their protein-rich diets. Other diver species, particularly mergansers, are nearly unpalatable and should be avoided. Below we'll cover two diver species: canvasbacks, the most respected of the divers; and lesser scaup, a fairly common and fine-tasting diver.

A wet and very happy California hunter, Sam Terrell, with a mixed bag of divers, puddlers, and geese. Divers are not the best-tasting waterfowl, but with the proper cooking methods they can begin to hold their own against the more desirable species.

CANVASBACKS
(Aythya valisineria)
A.K.A.: Can, king of ducks

While diver ducks are generally of poorer quality than puddle ducks, many people prize the meat of canvasbacks above all other waterfowl species. In the early 1900s, when a canvasback meal fetched today's equivalent of about $100 in a restaurant, market hunters nearly shot these birds to extinction. Thanks to modern-day conservation practices, canvasbacks have rebounded to levels that can once again withstand hunting, but bag limits are necessarily low. These ducks can be tough to hit, as they regularly cruise at speeds exceeding 60 miles per hour. But because of their size—up to 3½ pounds—and the exceptional quality of their meat, they are well worth the effort.

BARROOM BANTER: Canvasbacks have been clocked at top speeds of 72 miles per hour, but the speed record for ducks is held by a merganser that was clocked at 100 miles per hour.

PHYSICAL CHARACTERISTICS: Canvasback drakes have a reddish or chestnut-colored neck and a head with a long, black beak. The chest is black; the belly and breast are white; the back is light gray and heavily flecked with white. Hen canvasbacks have an overall light dirty-brown appearance with a whitish belly.

Their beak is similar to a drake's—long, black, and sloped. The wings of hens and drakes both have a frosted-brown appearance.

HABITAT: Primarily large lakes, bays, and saltwater estuaries, though canvasbacks will also land on prairie potholes, rivers, marshes, and smaller lakes. They breed primarily in Alaska, central and western Canada, the prairie pothole region of the Great Plains and upper Midwest, and a scattering of locations in the western United States. They winter in California, Mexico, and the southeastern United States, extending northward along the Atlantic coast through Chesapeake Bay and New England.

DIET: A favorite food is wild celery, though canvasbacks feed on a wide variety of submerged aquatic vegetation. They will also eat aquatic insects and small crustaceans.

LIFE AND DEATH: Ducklings and nesting adults are vulnerable to predation from a wide variety of predators.

BREEDING AND REPRODUCTION: Canvasback hens nest in shoreline vegetation. They typically lay five to eleven eggs.

TELLTALE SIGN: Little to none.

EDIBILITY: Excellent, the best of the diver ducks.

SCAUP
Greater scaup *(Aythya marila)*
Lesser scaup *(Aythya affinis)*
A.K.A.: Bluebills

The great thing about scaup is that they are good to eat, easy to hunt, and plentiful. Both lesser and greater scaup are suckers for decoy spreads—even decoys intended for other species—and they are not very cautious. It's common to have these birds come piling into your decoys even when you're standing in the middle of the spread trying to set them up or collect them. Many otherwise unsuccessful waterfowl outings have been saved by a flock of scaup that happened to come along at just the right moment. While many hunters who pursue diver ducks might dream of someday decoying a flock of canvas-backs, scaup are what they eat in the meantime. And it's hardly a compromise. Many diver duck critics have been turned into believers after a meal of carefully prepared scaup.

BARROOM BANTER: On their wintering grounds, greater and lesser scaup will often collect on the water into flocks of thousands. For many hunters, these "rafts" of scaup are the greatest concentrations of waterfowl they'll ever see.

PHYSICAL CHARACTERISTICS: Drakes of both species have a black head and chest with purple or green hues and a light blue bill; back and sides are mottled white and black; belly

is white; tail is black. Hens of both species have an overall brownish body and a head with a whitish blotch around the base of the bill and light-gray mottling on the breast and back. Hens and drakes of both species have white speculum feathers, though the wings of greater scaup have whitish primary feathers as well as speculum feathers. Lesser scaup weigh around 2 pounds; greater scaup weigh around 2½ to 3 pounds.

HABITAT: Scaup breed from the prairie pothole region of the Great Plains and upper Midwest northward through Canada and into Alaska. Lesser scaup winter along the West and East coasts and throughout the Great Lakes. Greater scaup winter along the West, East, and Gulf coasts as well as the Great Lakes. Lesser scaup are frequently found on both small and large waterways, while greater scaup typically prefer large waterways.

DIET: A wide variety of aquatic crustaceans and insects. Also submerged vegetation including wild rice, wild celery, and coontail.

LIFE AND DEATH: Most diving ducks will live to be around eighteen years of age at the oldest, if they survive through hatching and into their juvenile years. Lesser scaup have developed the ability to play dead, becoming rigid, wide-eyed, and immobile. This can fool their predators, commonly red foxes, into putting them down and allowing for escape.

BREEDING AND REPRODUCTION: Greater scaup lay between six and nine eggs, while lesser scaup lay nine to eleven. Brood parasitism (eggs dumped by other females in the same nest) is common, resulting in clutches of twenty-four or more eggs.

TELLTALE SIGN: Little to none.

EDIBILITY: Quite good, one of the better divers.

DIVER DUCK HUNTING METHODS

Hunting diver ducks can be cold and miserable. Michigan hunter Craig Jones had to chip ice off his equipment on this Lake Michigan trip.

Divers are generally not as spooky as geese and puddle ducks. If a duck lands among your decoys and doesn't flush when you stand up, there's a good chance it's a diver. Unlike other waterfowl, these birds don't circle your spread from high above while scrutinizing every square inch for trouble. Instead, they're likely to lock on to a spread of decoys from a distance and, if they buy it, come directly in for a landing.

Despite their relative lack of wariness, decoy spreads set for divers need to be accurate. It is not smart to think that you can just set out a bunch of mallard decoys and lure in some divers. For maximum success, you need to use appropriate decoys (divers for divers) and set

A collection of North Carolina redheads.

your spread in a way that mimics the ways in which real birds sit on the water.

While divers can often be found close to shore, a serious hunter will find himself chasing birds that are in deep water far from land. Basic puddle duck anchoring systems, in which each decoy is attached to a hunk of lead by a short cord, will not cut it. Instead, two or three dozen diver decoys are clipped to main lines that are 60 to 70 yards long. The main lines are then anchored, and the floating decoys are allowed to play out in a downwind direction. A typical spread might include hundreds of decoys. It can be cold, expensive work to create the perfect diver setup in the freezing predawn darkness of a December morning.

Being far from shore also means that you can't always build a standard cattail blind and stand on firm ground. If you want to get serious about diver ducks, you need to rig up a floating blind that can be driven or towed into position. Setups vary according to budgets and the severity of the weather you're likely to encounter. Layout boats, sculling boats, and low-lying johnboats can all be used effectively. When hunting diver ducks over decoys, use a 12-gauge shotgun with a modified choke. Shoot 3-inch shells with #2 or #3 shot.

BRANDT MEIXELL, AN ALASKA AND MINNESOTA HUNTER, WEIGHS IN WITH WATERFOWL HUNTING ADVICE

"Location, location, location. Waterfowl tend to feed in spots they've fed before, roost in places they've roosted before, and travel flight paths they've flown before. Of course, you want to pick a general location where birds are present, but more important, you want to pick the precise spot the birds like. It may be a small channel through the cattails, a slight depression in a field, or a not-so-obvious spot in the middle of a marsh. Identify a flight pattern or a specific location birds tend to use, and you will tend to have success.

"Play the wind. Waterfowl land into the wind. Set up your decoy spread with the wind at your back or at your side. This is critical for a couple of reasons. First, when a bird is landing toward you, the softer flesh of the breast is exposed for easier penetration by your pellets. Second, the wind at your back tends to keep birds out in front of you, where they are less likely to spot you and your hunting buddy.

"If it looks like a blind to you, it looks like a blind to a duck. If a blind conceals you and your movement, it's serving its purpose. Plenty of birds are killed from stupid-looking

(continued)

blinds. But, especially in pressured areas, birds can be as good at picking out blinds as they are at seeing some guy wearing blaze orange who's standing up in the middle of a marsh. Some extra effort to conceal your ambush spot with natural vegetation, or a little sacrifice of comfort for extra concealment, can often make a big difference.

"You decide where they land. Decoying waterfowl generally attempt to land in holes or open spots within the decoys. Once you've determined a location for your blind, determine your X, or that precise spot you want the birds to be when you shoot. This should be close enough to the blind to provide for those ideal 20- to 30-yard shots, but far enough out that attention isn't drawn to you. Leave an obvious opening in the decoys on your X to increase your chances for close, clean kills.

"Increase the visibility of your spread. For a decoy spread to attract birds, the birds have to see it. White and black are the most visible colors, so don't be afraid to mix in some drake diving ducks or Canada goose decoys to your dabbler spread for some added visibility. You can also increase the visibility of your spread through larger-than-life magnum decoys and by adding some motion with spinning-wing decoys, flags, and decoys connected to jerk cords.

"Calling is a great tool for attracting the birds' attention and for coaxing them in for that final approach. On some days, all you need is a few soft quacks or honks and they'll drop in on a string. On other days, you'll need to stay on that call with every bit of your lungs from start to finish. Pay attention to how the birds are responding, and give them what they seem to like. When in doubt, call as little as is necessary. Once you have the birds coming, let them come. Wailing on the call at the wrong time may just ruin your chances for that feast of roasted duck.

"Observe and adapt. If the first flock flares at 80 yards, or lands to the outside of your spread, there's a good chance the next flock will, too. This could be a result of someone's shiny face, an insufficiently concealed blind, or the fact that you're not where the birds want to be. Getting out 100 yards from your setup and taking a bird's-eye view can often reveal these small, but important, mistakes. Figure out the problem and keep modifying things until the birds start cooperating.

"In short, be where the birds want to be and give them what they like. If what you're doing isn't working, mix things up until it does."

A PRIMER ON DECOYS AND DECOY SPREADS

Waterfowl decoys are visual aids that serve to attract ducks and geese and convince them that an area is safe for landing. The placement and number of decoys that one uses is highly situational, but wind direction is always a major factor. Like airplanes, ducks and geese approach their landing areas by flying into the wind. They cup their wings to create drag, and then touch down feet first. When setting out decoys, always make sure to position yourself with your back to the wind or with the wind coming from an angle over one shoulder. This will ensure that the birds make their final approach from a direction where you can clearly see them.

None of the following information should be taken as the final answer to decoy setup. While these are time-tested and proven methods, there are many other ways to go about it. As you hunt the same areas again and again, you'll gain a better understanding of what spreads work best in your particular areas. When it comes to decoys, an ounce of experience is better than a pound of reading.

PUDDLE DUCK SPREADS (WATER)

Slot pattern 1 utilizes twenty-four decoys, but this can be adjusted up or down according to the specifics of the area or the limits of how many decoys you own. With the wind approaching from behind your position, place twelve decoys to the left of your blind about 15 yards out. Do the same on the right side. (Avoid grouping the ducks too close, as ducks clump up when they are frightened and you don't want to send that message.) The separation between the two sets of decoys creates the "slot," and that is where the majority of ducks will attempt to land.

When hunting with two or three hunters in the same blind (*slot pattern 2*), you can create multiple slots by dividing the twenty-four decoys into groups of eight. This makes three major groups of decoys that can be spread

SLOT PATTERN #1

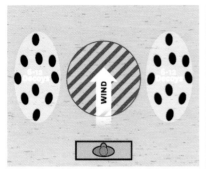

SLOT PATTERN #2

SLOT PATTERN #3

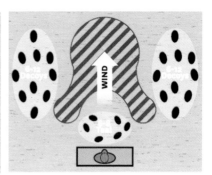

J HOOK SPREAD #1

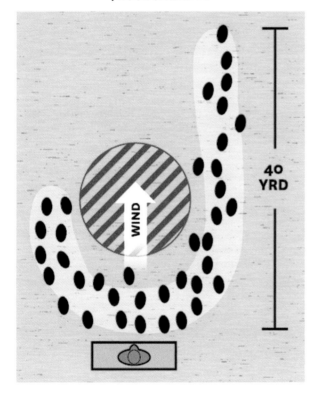

J HOOK SPREAD #2

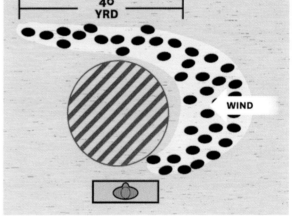

evenly, creating additional slots. These slots become shooting zones wherein multiple hunters can shoot safely without crossing each other. This makes the hunt safer.

For extra encouragement, placing a group of teal decoys five or so yards out in the water in front of the blind helps (*slot pattern 3*). Depending on the size of water you are hunting, anywhere from six to twelve teal decoys will work. Teal are very nervous birds, scattering whenever there is a threat. When teal are in the water, other ducks will have a heightened sense of safety when trying to land. It also makes the decoy spread larger and will be seen more easily by high-flying birds.

J Hook spread patterns can be used for puddle ducks in a strong wind or with diving ducks on open water when hunting from a blind or

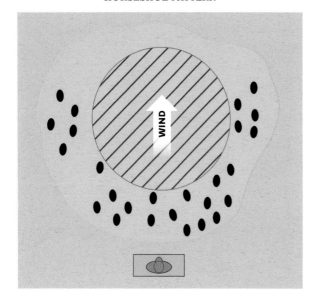

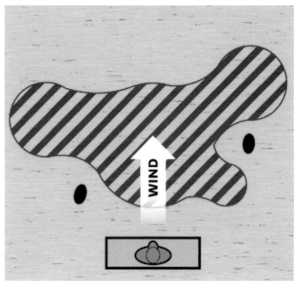

boat. A J pattern is just what it sounds like—a string of decoys that starts in a long single line and stretches out into a hook. This creates something similar to a landing strip with an open pocket of water in the middle as a landing pad. When setting up a J pattern, place the straight line of decoys into the wind, rounding it away from the wind. This forces the birds to follow the string of decoys into the opening at the bottom of the J. This pattern can be moved around a large pond or open water depending on what direction the wind is coming from, creating freedom to hunt a stationary blind or boat in various wind situations. The J should always hook toward the blind or boat, since birds will land to fill in the open space

and add to the end of the hook. Being near the end of the hook will create more shooting opportunities.

Slot patterns and J patterns can also be combined in pond areas into *horseshoe patterns*, creating a curved landing zone that encourages birds to land in the open shooting area in the middle.

Sometimes spreads with fewer decoys are better. This is especially true on small ponds or when hunting highly pressured ducks that have grown suspicious after seeing many conventional decoy spreads containing a couple of dozen decoys. Such minimalist spreads are sometimes known as "*confidence patterns.*"

DIVER DUCK (OR OPEN WATER) SPREADS

When hunting diving ducks on open water from a boat, a *parallel decoy spread* is used. This is a setup using four dozen to six dozen decoys placed in lines parallel to the wind direction. It helps to diversify your spread with a mixture of birds that can be found in the area you are hunting, to add variety and entice birds to land. The blind or boats should be facing away from the wind and toward the opening between the two sections of decoys. This will allow shooters to hit birds over open water without hitting decoys or losing sight of downed birds in choppy water.

A *gapped line pattern* is great for hunting diver ducks from a position where circum-

PARALLEL DECOY SPREAD

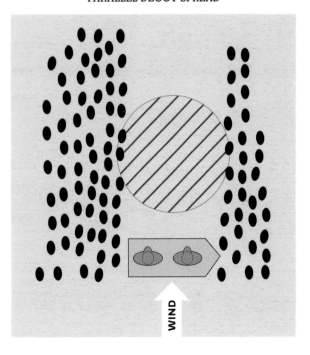

WIND

GAPPED LINE PATTERN

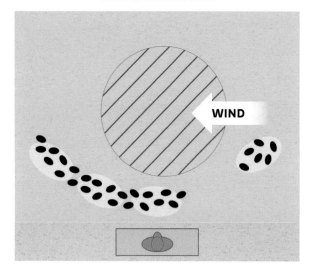

RESERVOIR PATTERN

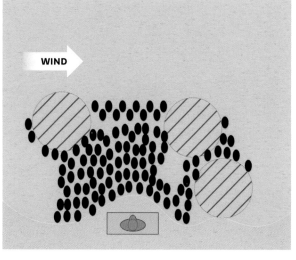

stances dictate that you are facing a crosswind. This can be used in open water when hunting from a boat or from a shoreline blind. Place a small pod of six to twelve decoys about 15 yards out from your blind and about 30 yards in an upwind direction. Allow for a gap, and then place a string of the remaining decoys in a line that starts in front of your blind and extends in an outward and downwind arc for a distance of about 30 yards. Birds will land either in the open space on the far side of the decoys or in the gap.

The *reservoir pattern* is a spread for both divers and puddle ducks on large bodies of open water. Place a large group of four dozen to seven dozen decoys tightly along the shore 15 to 20 yards in front of your blind. Create several small pockets on the outward side of the decoys to allow landing areas for birds. If the wind is exceptionally strong, group the decoys a little more tightly to better mimic the positioning of real ducks.

GEESE SPREADS (FIELD)

The H pattern is useful when field hunting for geese in a crosswind. Place about three dozen decoys around your blind in rows, spreading outward about 35 yards on either side of your blind. Place another single row of decoys about 75 yards out from the blind in order to act as an outside bracket. Use sentry decoys at the ends of the lines to help add realism to the pattern. Place a few feeding-position decoys between the outward line and the main cluster on the upwind side of the spread in order to encourage approaching birds to land in the middle of the pattern.

THE H PATTERN

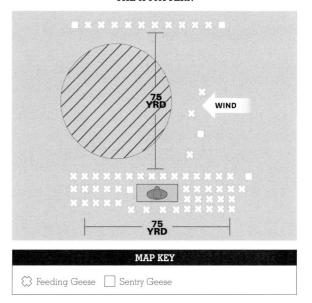

MAP KEY	
⬦ Feeding Geese	☐ Sentry Geese

THE U PATTERN

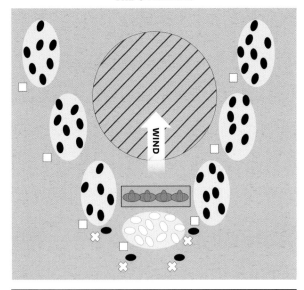

MAP KEY
☐ Sentry Ducks ● Resting Ducks ✗ Feeding Ducks
◯ Feeding Geese

Another field setup, *the U pattern,* is good for hunting with the wind at your back. Place a dozen resting decoys behind (or upwind from) the blind. Those decoys form the bottom of the U. Using several dozen more decoys, build out the arms of the U in downwind directions to the right and left of the blind. Geese will land into the wind all over the open middle section, so try to keep the entire spread within range, approximately 60 yards. Consider using some feeding-posture mallard decoys to help add realism to the pattern.

GOOSE AND DUCK SPREADS (WATER)

This setup creates the illusion of a waterfowl feeding frenzy, with decoys on both land and water. The blind is positioned on the shore with the wind at your back. Surround the blind with a mix of feeding and resting decoys. A narrow band of floating decoys is then positioned in the near-shore water in front of the blind, with an arm of decoys extending outward on the right-hand side. This creates an open pocket of water within easy shooting range. When hunting geese on ponds, it is often a good idea to include some duck decoys as well.

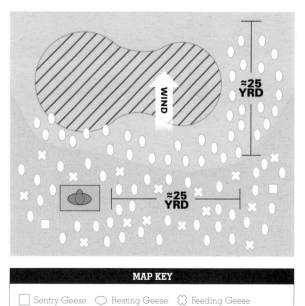

MAP KEY

▢ Sentry Geese ◯ Resting Geese ✕ Feeding Geese

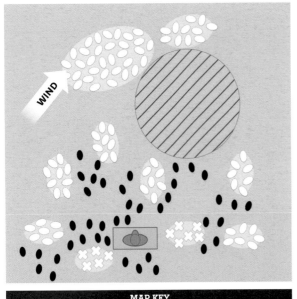

MAP KEY

● Resting Ducks

○ Resting Geese   ✕ Feeding Geese

This is a good spread for rivers and large lakes where there's the possibility of ducks and geese. It's similar to the traditional goose pond setup in that it uses decoys on both land and water. In this case, you want to use a combination of both duck and geese decoys. It's suitable for use when the wind is coming from your back or at an angle over your shoulder. Approaching birds will try to land in the gaps between the floating decoys.

A FEW EXTRA THINGS TO KEEP IN MIND WHEN HUNTING WITH DECOYS

1. When setting up with geese as your primary target, you can use geese decoys exclusively or mix them up with duck decoys. Geese and puddle ducks are often found together, but not always. Depending on your area, one may work better than the other.

2. Decoy postures are another thing to consider when placing geese decoys. Feeding-posture, resting-posture, and sentry-posture decoys all send a different message to geese, and their placement should be carefully considered. Study real concentrations of waterfowl to get a sense of how sentry birds and resting birds position themselves relative to the flock.

3. Experiment with different numbers of decoys. Decoys are generally sold by the dozen. Over time, ducks and geese see a lot of spreads that include one or two dozen decoys, and they grow suspicious of such configurations. It pays to experiment with spreads that include a lot fewer decoys and a lot more decoys. If you have access to them, several hundred decoys in a spread is not too many, especially with diver ducks and geese. Use any of the setups outlined here; just add more decoys to the configurations.

4. Utilize moving decoys. They can be motorized, wind-powered, or powered by a length of fishing line tied to a stick in your blind. Movement, including ripples on the water near feeding decoys, will convince birds to come dropping in.

5. Make or buy a small flag with the prominent colors of your target species (white, gray, and black for Canada geese, for instance). Stand up and wave the flag over your decoy spread to get the attention of faraway birds. But once the birds turn in your direction, get back into the blind before they realize what you are.

6. Confidence decoys are a great way to add a touch of reality to your spreads. Think outside the box of waterfowl species and use decoys of wary non-game species. A crane or blue heron decoy outside of a duck spread can make a world of difference. Likewise with a couple of turkey or crow decoys set near geese in a field.

7. Avoid old, chipped, worn-out, or low-quality decoys when hunting highly pressured birds. A duck knows what a duck oughta look like, so give him the credit he deserves. Your grandpa's tricks worked on yesterday's ducks; it takes today's tricks to fool today's ducks.

BUTCHERING

FEATHERED SMALL GAME

You might not expect it, but gutting small game is a controversial subject. Many guys like to hang, or age, their small game with the guts inside. I've never heard a good argument for this beyond the fact that it saves time in the field. This is the usual perspective of hunters who simply "breast-out" their game birds, a term for just filleting away the breast meat and discarding the smaller, more difficult-to-use wings, legs, and thighs. That's because these hunters have no intention of salvaging the organs or cooking with the whole carcass, so a little internal spoilage is of no concern to them.

Not only do I generally dislike the practice of breasting birds from a culinary standpoint, but I hate the practice of discarding usable meat and organs from an ethical standpoint. And while you can get away with leaving the guts in a bird for a day or two without having them rot, I don't like to risk it. That's why I try to gut all of my game birds within an hour or two of killing them—even sooner in hot weather.

Note: When it comes to butchering, many of the procedures that you use on one class of birds can be used on another. Beyond issues of size, there is honestly very little difference between how I handle a quail and a turkey. Keep this in mind as you study the following pages; what you see in one place can be adapted for use somewhere else.

Begin the gutting incision below the point of the breastbone and continue through to the cloaca (anus).

You need only enough of an incision to allow a couple of fingers in there. On smaller birds such as quail, the incision will run all the way to the point of the breast bone. On geese and turkeys, it'll extend just a little bit forward of the cloaca.

Insert two fingers all the way into the chest cavity; reach forward until you reach the heart.

Grab hold and pull the guts back out of the bird.

After the initial pull, put your fingers back in and make sure you got everything out. Then scrape the lungs away from the back of the bird.

Thoroughly wash the cavity with water or handfuls of snow.

Remove the giblets—heart, liver, and gizzard—and wash them if possible. The gizzard (this one is from a turkey) needs to be opened with a knife and emptied of gravel. Bag the giblets, or place them back into the cavity for safekeeping.

The poet and novelist Jim Harrison once said that skinning a bird is a sin against God and man. The skin holds flavor, provides fat, protects the meat from drying out during cooking, and provides a wonderful crispness when properly cooked. Retaining the skin of a bird requires you to pluck it. Harrison's warning should be taken especially to heart by turkey hunters, who handle only one or two of these birds per year if they're lucky. It takes minimal time and effort to do the job right; the reward is better-looking, better-tasting wild game dishes that will leave you feeling proud of the fact that you utilized your resources to their maximum potential. (Exception: Skin diver ducks, as the fat tastes a little fishy on most.)

While I advocate gutting birds soon after killing them, it can be helpful if you hold off on gutting the bird so long as you're going to pluck it within a few hours. This makes plucking easier, as the edges of the gutting incision are a tad bit harder to pluck otherwise.

(If you decide not to heed Mr. Harrison's warning, little instruction is required for skinning a bird. Just pluck a small area above the cloaca, slice through the skin, and start peeling. The job goes quickly.)

Hang the bird by the neck.

Work slowly and carefully, removing just pinchfuls of feathers at a time by tugging upward and away from the bird.

Be careful not to tear the skin, especially in the vicinity of the breast, where it's most fragile.

Keep plucking! The most difficult parts to pluck are along the wing bones and in the bird's "armpit" beneath the wing.

Once the turkey is completely plucked, you can gut the bird while it's still hanging. Start the gutting incision at the cloaca and slice toward the point of the breastbone.

Reach into the cavity all the way up to the bird's windpipe. Take a firm hold of the guts and draw them out.

Retain the heart, liver, and gizzard. They are edible and good.

Next you want to remove the breast sponge, a sack-like collection of fatty tissue that sits above the bird's breast and beneath its crop. To do so, cut up each side of the wishbone, through the skin.

Carefully slice the sack away, leaving just clean meat and bone.

Next, remove the bird's head. If you plucked the wings all the way to the end, they can remain on the carcass. If not, pluck them at least to the first major joint beyond the body and then sever that joint to remove the remainder of the unplucked wing.

To remove the legs, cut around the skin that covers the joint where the rubbery, scaly skin meets the feathered skin.

Snap the joint like a stick, then cut the tendons to free the leg. (Don't just chop through the bone with a hatchet; the sharp edges of broken bone are annoying to deal with and they puncture vacuum-sealed bags.)

At this point, the turkey can be used for any whole preparations, such as stuffed and roasted Thanksgiving-style turkey.

What I generally like to do, though, is split the bird in half so that I've got two manageable-sized pieces. This lets me enjoy the turkey in parts, rather than all at once, and it takes up a lot less space in the freezer (or cooler, if you're a traveling hunter). Though you seldom see this procedure undertaken by modern-day hunters, splitting the bird is quite simple.

Note: You can take the breakdown one step further by removing the turkey's thighs and legs. Now you've got a boneless, skin-on breast fillet that can be baked, grilled, or sliced into schnitzel. (Turkey schnitzel is unbelievably good.) The leg and thigh pieces can be smoked, or else braised until they are so tender that if you flick the leg bone, all the meat will come flying off. Handled this way, the leg and thigh flesh is perfect for soups, stews, pulled-turkey sandwiches, and all kinds of other preparations.

Slice down each side of the ridge-like breast bone and begin slicing and peeling the breast meat away from the bone.

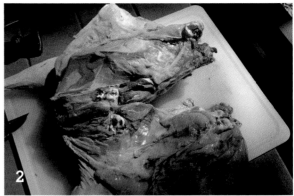

Cut through the thigh joint and finish removing the half.

Two halves, ready for the grill or transport. Notice that the leg is still on this bird; that (the spur, particularly) serves as legal evidence of sex should the bird need to be transported. This one, however, went immediately to the grill.

A wild turkey half, vacuum-sealed, labeled, and ready for the freezer.

As I have said, handling upland game birds is similar to handling turkeys, just on a smaller scale. Here are some images that show my favorite way to deal with grouse, pheasants, quail, chukar, and just about every other bird that produces mild and delicate white flesh. It's called spatchcocking, and it's perfect for grilling and smoking.

As with turkeys, start by carefully plucking the bird's body.

Sever the neck, wings, and feet, leaving only the bird's edible portions.

Using game shears or a sharp knife, split the bird's backbone from the tail-bone all the way up to the neck. Then flatten the bird out. It's ready for a marinade or a dry rub (or nothing) and then the grill, pan, or oven.

There's no law saying that you have to **remove** a bird's head and feet. You can **be** creative and experiment with a variety of presentations. Here, for instance, is a pair of whole plucked woodcock **that** have been trussed with their **own** beaks. It's a startlingly beautiful way to serve birds.

EXPERT WILD GAME CHEF AND AUTHOR HANK SHAW WEIGHS IN ON HANDLING GEESE AND DUCKS

"Don't let your birds heat up. Most waterfowlers don't really think about meat care in the marsh, probably because they associate the season with cold, nasty weather—even when it isn't. But teal hunters, southern hunters, Californians, and really anyone hunting the early season must take into account the heat or your birds will spoil. Ducks and geese have a layer of down that insulates their body heat, and waterfowl run warmer than most other game animals, about 107.5°F. That means even temperatures in the 60s can wreck the meat if you are hunting all day.

"First, keep your birds in the shade. Second, don't stack them, as this will prevent them from cooling off. If you are just hunting the dawn, there's no need to bring an ice chest, but if you have a long drive home or you are hunting into the late morning, keep a cooler with ice in your truck. Once chilled, your birds can safely age for up to several days.

"Consider aging. This one's controversial in our antiseptic age, but aging game birds has historically been the norm. I often age ducks and geese for a few days. I find they come out more tender and with a duckier flavor I really like. If you like dry-aged beef, it's the same process. Hang well-shot birds—that is, those that are not gut-shot—between 35° and 55°F for a day or more in the feathers and ungutted. Then you can pluck or skin them.

"A general rule is the larger the bird, the longer the hang. An old, lean Canada goose can use a full five days to a week. A teal, maybe overnight. The fatter the bird, the shorter the hang time, too; the fat can go rancid.

"When to skin, when to pluck? Every duck or goose can be delicious, but you need to know what they'll be good in. Roasting a scoter whole will send everyone screaming out of the kitchen—once the heat hits these clam-eaters, it'll stink like low tide in

(continued)

August. But roasting a pintail or green-winged teal whole can be a sublime eating experience. There is a lot of nuance to choosing whether to skin or pluck, but here are some quick tips.

"Sea ducks: skin. Always. I skin most divers, unless they are canvasbacks, which are almost always excellent plucked. I also skin most snow geese, as they have weird blue skin and unusually hard-to-pluck feathers. Ditto for Canada geese, although that's mostly a question of effort—ever pluck a limit of Canada geese? Ouch.

"Pluck specklebelly geese, green-winged and blue-winged teal, pintails, wood ducks, and most mallards. They are your 'money ducks' and will usually be fat and tasty.

"Break 'em down. Everyone loves a roast duck or goose, but it's more of an idea than a reality. Fact is, roasting whole waterfowl is immensely tricky if you want nice medium-rare breast meat and well-cooked legs and wings. It is doable, but not easy. I do save a few whole birds each year for the smoker or for special occasions, but I find I use my duck meat more when it's broken down and separated into packets of leg, wings, and breasts. You will, too.

"Storage method matters. I swear by my vacuum sealer. It is a game changer, literally. Vac-sealed game keeps longer and is cleaner than game stored in freezer bags or butcher paper. If I had a dollar for every time someone asked me to cook his duck, then brings out nasty freezer bags with globs of duck breasts all stuck together, encased by an iceberg of blood, I'd be able to afford a fancy duck blind. It's a terrible thing, folks. Don't do it.

"Giblets rock. I save all the giblets from my ducks. In some cases, the gizzard alone can weigh a pound, and that's good meat. At the very least, save the hearts and gizzards for stock (though don't forget to clean the gizzards before doing so), but there are all kinds of great recipes for them. Slow-cooked gizzards done in the style of corned beef are magical, and even if you hate the idea of liver and onions with calf's liver, you may well love it with duck livers. Hearts are great in stir-fries or grilled on a very hot fire. Don't like the look of them? Mince them fine in sausages or in Cajun dirty rice.

"Make stock. People pay good money for store-bought stock, and duck hunters have a ready supply of the carcasses you need to make superior broths and stocks at home. Whether you skin or pluck, save the carcass to make stock. Just make sure to trim all the fat if you are **doing** this with sea ducks **or** stinky divers. Roast your bones, then simmer them very gently—the pot shouldn't bubble **too** much—for as **many** hours as you can stand (I go overnight) and then add the vegetables and spices. Go for another two hours **and** strain. Store your stock a week in the fridge or **a** year in the freezer or pantry if you know how to pressure-can your stock.

"Render fat. Yep, you heard **right**. Duck fat is God's gift, especially in agricultural areas. Some of the best-tasting fat I've ever eaten was rendered off rice-eating pintails and teal in California's Sacramento Valley. Most duck fat is under the **skin,** and you will get lots of it in the tail (the pope's nose), the neck, and around the gizzard. Obviously, skip this with sea ducks and most divers. Pintails, teal, specklebelly geese, and most mallards will have good fat, as will other birds that have been eating grain.

"Color is your guide. White fat is always good. Orange fat is always bad. Yellow fat can be good, but only if it's from corn. If you shoot **fat** birds where there's **no** corn for 100 miles, you might want to **skip** it.

"Your nose never fails you. Chop up the tail (after cleaning it well), put it in a little pan with **some** water, and **set** it on the burner. As it renders, you'll smell it. If it smells nice and ducky, you're good. If it stinks, toss it.

"Don't overcook breasts. If you've ever heard someone saying they don't like duck because it's 'livery,' they probably have been **eating** the breast meat well done or worse. Duck and goose **breasts** are like steaks: cook them as you would your steak, which for me is medium rare. It's perfectly safe to **eat** and will increase your enjoyment of eating waterfowl **by** 100 percent. **Trust** me on this one.

"Conversely, it's nearly **impossible** to overcook legs and wings. They are perfect candidates for the slow cooker or Dutch oven. **Slow and** low moist **heat is** the way to **go.** Some people just leave the bones in, but I like to take the extra step of fishing them all out and separating the meat. It makes the stew or braise easier to eat, and your family will thank you for it."

Hank Shaw runs the wild foods website Hunter Angler Gardener Cook (honest-food.net) and is the author of the cookbooks *Hunt Gather Cook* and *Duck, Duck, Goose.*

REMOVING THOSE ANNOYING LEG TENDONS

The edibility of bird legs improves dramatically when you remove the tendons. This makes the legs more tender and user friendly. Below are a few photos showing the process on a mallard. On birds bigger than mallards, this becomes a two-person job as the tendons are quite strong. Removing the tendons from a turkey leg requires a pair of pliers and nearly Herculean strength.

Using a sharp knife, cut through the rubbery skin on the duck's leg, right over the leg joint. Be very careful not to nick the meat or tendons beneath the skin.

Pop the joint, like snapping a stick. Wiggle the leg a bit to work the tendons clear of the popped joint.

Take a firm hold of the bird's thigh with one hand and of the foot with the other. Now pull slowly and firmly. The tendons should separate from the hip joint and pull out with the foot.

A GREAT WAY TO PREP DUCKS

Here's a favorite way of mine to handle ducks, especially puddle ducks and the better-tasting divers such as scaup. It also works well with upland game birds, and I've even done street pigeons this way.

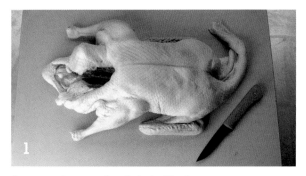

Start out with a gutted and plucked bird.

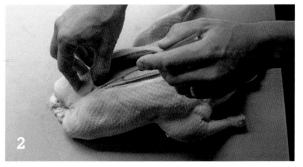

Slice down each side of the ridge-like breastbone, from the top of the breast to the bottom.

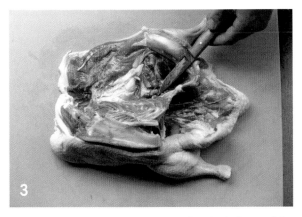

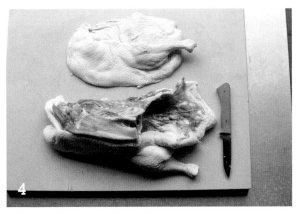

Continue filleting the breast downward. Pop the ball joint of the hip bone, then work your way down to the skin of the back and slice through that, freeing half of the bird from the breast plate.

This half is ready to cook. Proceed to the second half.

A FEW MORE TIPS AND SUGGESTIONS FOR HANDLING WILD BIRDS

1. After plucking a bird, particularly ducks, you might find hard-to-remove pin feathers and also small hairlike feathers that are difficult to grab with your fingers. These become especially apparent on ducks once you begin the cooking process, as the

(continued)

skin tightens and they stand up on end. A great way to remove these is by burning them off with a lighter or kitchen torch, or simply by using your stove burner.

2. All game birds, whether upland or waterfowl, can benefit from a little aging. This improves the flavor and tenderizes the meat. Gut the bird, and then thoroughly rinse and dry the body cavity. Place the gutted bird in a paper grocery bag and let it sit on the shelf of your refrigerator for a few days. You can then pluck the bird and cook it, or freeze it for later.

3. Shotgun pellets often grab feathers on their way into a bird and then carry them deep into the flesh. You'll notice these feathers as dark blotches beneath the skin after you pluck the bird. A great way to remove them is to insert a wooden toothpick into the wound channel and then twist it. When you pull the toothpick back, the feather will come with it. (This also works well for removing tufts of hair from shotgun-killed squirrels and rabbits.)

4. When packaging birds for the freezer, two methods are equally acceptable. They can be vacuum-sealed or double-wrapped in layers of plastic wrap and waxed freezer paper. Smaller birds, such as quail, do well when frozen inside a container filled with water. Giblets are best retained in the same manner, by submerging them in water and freezing them.

FURRED SMALL GAME

You should gut furred small game as soon as possible, especially rabbits and hares, because there's something about their innards that allows them to sour very quickly. In warm weather, it only takes an hour or so for the thin abdominal muscles to start turning greenish blue. It's easier to skin rabbits or squirrels before they're gutted, as the hide comes off more easily if the animal is completely intact. But leaving the hide in place is a great way to keep the meat clean, so it's generally better to gut an animal immediately after harvest and delay skinning until you're in an environment suitable for processing.

I handle squirrels and rabbits in only one way, by parting them into five pieces—four legs and a ribless back. Virtually all species of furred small game, including oddballs such as muskrats and porcupines, can be parted out in similar fashion. Remove the back legs at the ball joint that sits on the upper end of the femur. The front legs are connected by ligaments; there are no ball joints, so they slice away easily. The legless body can then be chopped crosswise into two pieces. Make the cut just below the rib cage.

Here's how to do a squirrel:

Start with a sharp knife.

Girdle the squirrel around the waist, careful to slice just through the hide and not nick the muscle beneath.

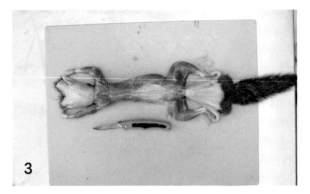

Pull the hide off the squirrel like removing a shirt and a pair of pants. The tissue that binds a squirrel's hide to its muscle is very strong. You'll need to pull hard. Stop pulling when the hide meets the ankles and base of the tail and neck.

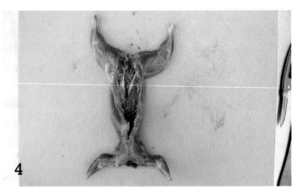

Sever the ankles, tail, and head by chopping through the joints with a heavy knife, a cleaver, or a pair of game shears.

Cut the squirrel into five pieces. Discard the ribs and that portion of the spine that sits above the loins. Trying to get meat off that section of the carcass is like trying to get meat off a small rattlesnake—hardly worth the effort.

Rabbits and hares are done a little differently from squirrels, primarily because the skin pulls so easily. The rabbit in the following photos was not gutted before it was skinned, only because the skinning took place almost immediately after it was killed.

You can skin rabbits without the use of a knife, but it helps if you pinch a handful of skin on the back and snip a hole into it with a knife or game shears.

Start pulling the hide: the front half pulls forward, the back half pulls rearward.

Strip the hide off until it's connected to the rabbit at the ankles and head. You can pull it free from the tail without needing to cut anything.

Sever the ankle joints and neck with a heavy knife, cleaver, or game shears.

Make a gutting incision and split the pelvis bone.

Pull out the innards. Now you can part the rabbit out, just like the squirrel method shown above.

THE SLOW AND MIGHTY PORCUPINE

Porcupine are not fast movers, which causes them a lot of trouble. They are deceptively easy targets for inexperienced dogs, who inevitably end up with a mouth full of quills. And they are easy targets for landowners and pet owners, who often kill them as pests. It should be known that porcupine meat is actually quite good. The flesh is fatty and rich. However, dealing with the quills during the skinning job can be a nuisance. Many indigenous hunters simply tossed porcupines whole into a fire to burn off the quills, which makes them much easier to deal with. Because of its lethargic gait, the porcupine is one of the only mammals on our continent that a human can easily chase down and kill with a stick. In the old days, it was considered poor etiquette to kill a porcupine outside of dire survival situations. Best to leave the animal for someone who might really need it.

A FEW MORE TIPS FOR HANDLING FURRED SMALL GAME

1. You'll often find a lot of small hairs on your rabbit and squirrel meat after skinning. You can wash them away with cold running water. If the meat is really hairy, you can burn off the hair with a lighter, kitchen torch, or stove burner—but do try the water first. Or better yet, do a more careful job with skinning.

2. Many people soak rabbit and squirrel meat in water overnight before freezing or cooking. (My mother always did this when I was a kid.) There's no reason for it, though. If storing meat overnight in the fridge, just cover it with a tight wrapping of plastic wrap.

3. For removing hairs that are dragged into the meat by shotgun pellets, see the section on game bird tips for the very excellent toothpick trick.

4. Not only are rabbit and squirrel organs edible, they are excellent. Cook the heart, liver, and kidneys right along with the rest of the animal in stews and other preparations.

5. Always sever joints on small game by popping the ball joints, not by breaking the bones. Broken bones are very sharp. They are dangerous to kids eating the meat, and they poke holes in vacuum bags.

6. When freezing small furred game, you'll get the best results by either vacuum-sealing the meat or submerging the pieces in water before freezing. This will keep the meat in fine condition for a year or so. Suitable freezing containers can be made from recycled milk cartons or plastic soda bottles with the upper portion cut away.

RECIPES

MINI SQUIRREL OR RABBIT POT PIES

My friend Andrew Radzialowski, a chef from San Juan Island, developed this simple and fun potpie recipe a few years back when he and I did a couple of elaborate wild game dinners for folks who had only limited experiences with wild food. The pies were a huge hit, and left everyone asking for how-to information about squirrel hunting. While I like the mini versions, you could just as easily make a large pie if you wanted to.

SERVES: 8

- 4 squirrels or 2 rabbits, skinned and cut into 4 legs and 2 loins each (about 2 pounds total)
- Kosher salt
- Freshly ground black pepper

- 3 tablespoons extra-virgin olive oil
- 1 large onion, peeled and diced (about 2 cups)
- 2 cups peeled and diced butternut squash

- 7 ounces shitake mushrooms or morels, cleaned and with stems removed, diced (about 2 cups)
- 1 garlic clove, minced
- ½ cup dry white wine (optional)
- 6 cups game stock (or chicken stock)
- 1 bay leaf
- 1½ sticks unsalted butter
- ¾ cup all-purpose flour
- 3 tablespoons brandy (optional)
- 1 tablespoon chopped fresh thyme leaves
- ¼ cup heavy cream
- 1 egg, beaten
- 1 package puff pastry, thawed

Season the meat with salt and pepper on both sides. Heat the oil in a large heavy-bottomed pot or Dutch oven over medium-high heat. Working in batches, brown the meat on both sides. Remove the meat to a plate and set side.

Add the onion and squash to the pan and cook until just tender. Season with salt, remove from the pan, and set aside. Add the mushrooms and cook until soft. Add the garlic and cook for another 30 seconds until fragrant. Deglaze the pan with the wine (or a splash of stock or water), scraping up any brown bits with a wooden spoon. Remove the mushrooms and set aside.

Return the meat to the pot and add 5 cups of stock (the liquid should just barely cover the meat). Bring to a boil, then reduce heat to a simmer. Skim off and discard any scum. Add the bay leaf and cook at a low simmer for 1½–2 hours, until the meat is very tender but not quite falling off the bone. (Squirrel and rabbit have different cooking times. Rabbit joints will become flexible at the point of doneness. Both meats are done when they no longer spring back when pressed with your finger or a fork.)

When the meat is tender, remove the pot from heat. Remove the meat from the pot and set aside to cool, reserving the cooking liquid. When the meat is cool enough to handle, remove the meat from the bones and discard the bones. Chop or tear the meat into bite-sized pieces. Cover and set aside.

Heat the remaining 1 cup of stock in a 4-quart pot. Using a fine-mesh sieve, strain the reserved cooking liquid into the pot with the stock and keep warm.

Preheat the oven to 400°.

Melt the butter over medium heat in a heavy-bottomed pot. Add the flour and stir to make a roux. Let cook for 2–3 minutes. Add the cooked vegetables and stir. Off the heat, add the brandy if using, then return to the heat and cook until it has mostly evaporated, stirring constantly so the mixture doesn't burn. Whisk in the hot stock one ladleful at a time. Keep stirring until the sauce becomes thick. Add thyme and season with salt and pepper to taste. Reduce the heat to low and stir in the cream. Add the reserved meat. Adjust the seasonings if needed.

Divide the stew mixture among eight ramekins. Brush the outside rim of the vessels with the beaten egg. Lay out the puff pastry and cut out 8 rounds slightly larger than the diameter of the ramekins. Top the ramekins with the pastry and press the outer edge so it adheres. Brush the tops of the pot pies with the remaining beaten egg. With a paring knife, make three small slits in the pastry. Bake until golden brown, about 30 minutes.

HASENPFEFFER (FOR SQUIRREL OR RABBIT)

My mom originally got a version of this recipe from her mother, who found it on the back of a box containing a frozen domestic rabbit. Growing up, my brothers and I ate countless squirrels and rabbits prepared in this fashion, and it remains one of our favorite small game preparations today. I've made a few changes to the recipe over the years, particularly to tone down the vinegar and to thicken the sauce, though it still serves as a pleasant and vivid reminder of chasing small game with my brothers. If you know someone who's reluctant to try squirrel, this timeless classic is likely to change their mind.

SERVES: 4

- 1½ cups cider vinegar
- 1 teaspoon whole cloves
- 3 bay leaves
- 1 medium onion, peeled and sliced
- 2 teaspoons kosher salt

- 2 teaspoons sugar
- ¼ teaspoon freshly ground black pepper
- ⅛ teaspoon allspice
- 4 squirrels or 2 rabbits, skinned and cut

into 4 legs and 2 loins each (about 2 pounds total)

- Vegetable oil for cooking
- ½ cup flour
- 3 cups low-sodium chicken stock
- 5 or 6 gingerbread cookies, crushed (about ½ cup)

Make a brine by combining the vinegar, cloves, bay leaves, onion, salt, sugar, pepper, and allspice. Place the meat in a food-safe tub, pour the brine over, and set a heavy plate on top of the meat to keep it submerged. Refrigerate for two or three days.

When ready to cook, remove the meat and pat it dry with paper towels. Reserve 1 cup of the leftover brine and discard the rest. Heat ¼ inch oil in a large heavy-bottomed pot or Dutch oven over medium-high heat. Dredge the meat in the flour. Working in batches, brown the meat in the hot oil. Remove the meat to a plate and set aside.

Drain the excess oil and return the meat to the pot, arranging it in a single layer. Add the stock and the reserved 1 cup brine; it should be enough to just barely cover the meat. Bring to a boil. Lower the heat, skim off and discard any scum, and simmer for 1–1½ hours until the meat is tender but is not falling off the bone. (Squirrel and rabbit have different cooking times. Rabbit joints will become flexible at the point of doneness. Both meats are done when they no longer spring back when pressed with your finger or a fork.)

Remove the meat and set aside. Thicken the remaining liquid in the pan with the crushed gingersnaps. Return the meat to the thickened sauce to warm through.

Serve over a bed of mashed potatoes.

CHICKEN-FRIED SQUIRREL OR RABBIT

Pretty much everyone loves fried chicken, so why not apply that method to small game? My brother Matt asked himself that question years ago, and he became a huge advocate of browning squirrels and rabbits in a pan and then finishing them in the oven. The biggest risk with chicken-frying small game is that the meat will be too chewy. Vigorously tenderizing the meat with a sharp-tined fork and then soaking it in buttermilk will solve that problem. This recipe will have you skipping work in order to hit the woods with your .22 rifle in search of more ingredients.

SERVES: 4–6

- 4 squirrels or 2 rabbits, skinned and cut into 4 legs and 2 loins each (about 2 pounds total)
- 1 quart buttermilk
- 2 tablespoons hot sauce (I like Frank's)
- Peanut or canola oil
- ½ cup all-purpose flour
- 1 teaspoon cayenne
- Kosher salt
- Freshly ground black pepper

Using a two-tined fork, pierce the quartered squirrels or rabbits many times. Lay the meat in a baking dish or a food-safe tub. Pour the buttermilk over the meat and add the hot sauce, stirring to combine. Cover and refrigerate for 4 hours or overnight.

Heat 3 inches of oil in a deep cast-iron pan over low to medium heat until it reaches 325°–350°. Use a deep fry thermometer to measure the temperature.

In a pie plate or baking dish, combine the flour and the cayenne pepper. Remove the meat out of the marinade, let the excess liquid drip off, and set the meat on a plate. Season the meat with salt and pepper, then dredge the meat in the flour.

Working in batches, fry the meat on one side until golden brown and crispy. Using tongs, turn each piece over and fry on the second side until browned and crispy.

Lift out a piece of meat and place it on a rack set into a baking sheet or on a baking sheet lined with paper towels. Use an instant-read thermometer to check the internal temperature of the meat; it should be at least 160°. When all the meat is cooked, let the pieces drain. Season with additional salt as soon as they come out of the oil.

RABBIT RAGU

This is the perfect cold-weather meal, the kind of dish you want to make when it's snowing outside and you're settling in for a long winter. I make mine with Chianti or another dry Italian red. The wine doesn't have to be fancy; as long as it's something you'd want to drink from a glass, it's good enough for the ragù. Tuck into this one, and for at least a few hours you'll be thinking that winter ain't so bad after all.

My favorite way to serve this is on top of some fresh pappardelle, but it is also good when served over a nice batch of soft polenta.

SERVES: 8–10

MARINADE

- 2 cups dry red wine
- ½ onion, peeled and sliced
- 5 garlic cloves, smashed
- 2 bay leaves
- 1 sprig rosemary
- 1 tablespoon juniper berries

RAGÙ

- 2 rabbits, skinned and cut into 4 legs and 2 loins each (about 2 pounds total)
- Kosher salt
- Freshly ground black pepper
- ½ cup extra-virgin olive oil
- 1 large onion, peeled and diced small
- 2 carrots, peeled, cut in half lengthwise, and sliced into ¼-inch half-moons
- 2 stalks celery, cut into ¼-inch slices
- 4 cloves garlic, minced
- ½ cup dry red wine
- 1½ cups chicken broth
- 2 cups tomato sauce
- 2 bay leaves
- 2 sprigs thyme
- 1½ pounds fresh pappardelle (or 1½ pounds dry lasagna noodles—see note)
- ¼ cup chopped flat-leaf parsley
- 2 tablespoons chopped fresh mint
- Freshly grated Parmigiano Reggiano or Pecorino cheese

QUICK AND EASY "HOMEMADE" FRESH PAPPARDELLE

Get fresh pasta sheets from a grocery or specialty store (some sell them for lasagna) and cut them into large, wide, irregular strips. Wonton wrappers can be made to work. No luck finding these? Break up dry lasagna noodles into 3-inch pieces and cook according to the package instructions. Any way you do it, it's delicious!

In a large bowl, combine the marinade ingredients. Add the meat and refrigerate for at least 1 hour or overnight.

When ready to cook, remove the meat from the marinade and set aside. Discard the marinade. Pat the rabbit dry with paper towels. Season the rabbit pieces liberally with salt and pepper.

Heat the oil in a large heavy-bottomed pot or Dutch oven over medium-high heat. Working in batches, sear the rabbit pieces on all sides until light golden brown, about 2 minutes per side. Remove the meat to a plate.

Add the onion to the pan and cook until just softened. Add the carrots and celery. Cook, stirring occasionally, until the vegetables are lightly caramelized, about 5 minutes. Add the garlic and cook for another 30 seconds. Deglaze the pan with the wine, scraping up the browned bits with a wooden spoon. Let the wine reduce slightly and then return the meat to the pot.

Add the chicken stock and tomato sauce. The liquid should come halfway up the sides of the meat; if it doesn't, add enough water (or additional stock) until it does. Bring to a boil, then lower the heat to a simmer. Skim off and discard any scum. Add the bay leaves and thyme. Cover and simmer until the meat is just tender, about 1½ hours. Do not overcook. A good way to tell if the rabbit is done is to pick up a hind quarter and try to bend the knee joint. If it moves easily, it's done.

Remove the meat from the pot and set aside on a platter. When the rabbits are cool enough to handle, remove the meat from the bones. Return the picked meat to the pot, stir, and season with salt and pepper to taste. (At this point the sauce can be cooled and stored in the fridge for up to a week or in the freezer for up to 6 months.)

Bring 8 quarts of salted water to a boil. Add the pasta and cook until al dente (cooked, but still has a bite). Drain the pasta and add to the ragù. Stir.

Stir in the herbs. Serve topped with grated cheese.

GRILLED SQUIRREL WITH LEMON, THYME, AND ROSEMARY

Sometimes I find that the best concepts for squirrel and rabbit recipes come from the chicken recipes of great chefs. You obviously have to adjust the cooking method and cooking times, but the flavor profiles often fit. This particular recipe was inspired by a very simple chicken preparation used by the chef Jamie Oliver. The squirrel meat can stand up to the pungent garlic and lemon, and the overnight marinade and slow cooking help to make the otherwise chewy meat perfectly tender and delicious.

SERVES: 2–4

- 1 bunch thyme, leaves only
- 3 sprigs rosemary, leaves only
- 4 cloves garlic
- 2 tablespoons kosher salt

- Zest and juice of 2 lemons
- 3 tablespoons extra-virgin olive oil
- 2 squirrels, skinned and cut into 4 legs and 2 loins each (about 1 pound total)

In a mortar and pestle (or in a bowl using a wooden spoon), mash the thyme leaves, rosemary leaves, garlic, salt, and lemon zest. Add the juice of 1 lemon and the olive oil and stir.

Using a two-tined fork, pierce the squirrel meat many times. Lay the meat in a glass or ceramic baking dish and coat thoroughly with the herb paste. Pour the remaining lemon juice over the top. Cover tightly and refrigerate for at least 4 hours or overnight.

Prepare a grill for indirect heat. Put the marinated squirrel pieces on the cool side of the grill and roast slowly with the lid closed, turning occasionally, for 20–30 minutes or until tender. Quickly finish them on the direct side of the grill to crisp them up and get nice grill marks. (If you like, when you grill them for this finishing part, lay them on a bed of soaked sprigs of thyme or rosemary, which gives them a little extra smoky herb flavor.)

STEVE'S SPECIAL ROASTED DUCK

In the world of ducks, there are divers and puddlers. Divers often eat more animal matter, such as fish and aquatic invertebrates, and can have an oily and off-putting taste; puddlers tend to have a more vegetarian diet and therefore a more pleasing flavor. Because of its simplicity—there's nothing here to mask any off tastes—I prefer using puddlers for this recipe. My favorites include mallard, teal, canvasback, and pintail ducks. The butchering method is something that I discovered during my grad school years, when I lived near a flyway that usually swarmed with migrating mallards in November and December. It's a very efficient way to remove all the meat from a duck and still have an easy-to-handle product. It gives you a boneless breast that you can slice thin, as well as a bone-in leg that you can eat like a drumstick. And since the halves are nice and flat, it's easy to brown and crisp them in a skillet without a lot of flipping and pressing.

One difference between wild ducks that you hunt and domestic farm-raised ducks is that even after you pluck the wild ducks, you might have to burn off some feathers when you start cooking. So I've put this step in the recipe. After I sear the duck for the first time and the skin shrinks back, if there are any remaining feathers left on the duck they'll appear as little stick-like things poking out of the skin. Then I just take a flame to the skin (a lighter or a kitchen torch, or I just use the burner itself) to get rid of them. Then I proceed with the cooking.

SERVES: UP TO 8 AS AN APPETIZER

- Vegetable or canola oil
- 2 ducks, gutted and plucked, each duck cut into two halves of a boneless breast attached to a whole leg (4 pieces total; see how to butcher on page 308)
- Kosher salt
- Freshly ground black pepper
- Apple Chutney (below, or substitute store-bought)

Preheat the oven to 375°.

Lightly oil a heavy cast-iron pan (I brush mine with oil and remove the excess with a paper towel). Heat the pan on the stovetop over medium-high heat until very hot.

Season the duck on both sides with salt and pepper. Sear the duck halves skin side down, pressing it down so that the duck skin has maximum contact with the hot pan. You want to get the skin crisp and golden; a large duck takes close to 10 minutes.

Using tongs, lift up the duck halves and check to see if there are any feathers poking up from the skin. If so, burn them off with a lighter, a kitchen torch, or the stove burner.

Flip the duck halves so the skin side is up. Set the pan in the oven and roast 5–8 minutes, or until the internal temperature is 135°–140° for medium-rare. The juices should be pink and oily but not bloody, and the breast meat should look pink.

Remove from the oven and let rest for a few minutes. Separate the leg from the breast meat and slice the breast thinly. Serve with Apple Chutney.

APPLE CHUTNEY

I like the idea of making my own apple chutney in the fall when there are so many apples and so many ducks. But you could easily use your favorite store-bought chutney instead and save the apples for a pie.

SERVES: ABOUT 1 QUART

- 2 pounds Granny Smith apples (about 4 apples)
- Lemon juice
- 3 tablespoons vegetable oil

- 1 tablespoon mustard seeds
- 1 teaspoon cumin seeds
- 1 onion, peeled and diced small
- 6 cloves garlic, minced
- 2 tablespoons grated fresh ginger
- 2 tablespoons turmeric
- 1 serrano pepper, seeded and finely chopped
- ¾ cup brown sugar
- ¾ cup apple cider vinegar
- ¼ cup golden raisins
- ¼ cup dried cranberries
- 2 tablespoons honey
- Kosher salt
- ¼ cup lemon juice (optional)

Peel and core the apples, and cut into ⅓-inch cubes. Toss with enough lemon juice to coat the apple pieces and prevent them from browning.

In a large saucepan over medium heat, combine the oil, mustard seeds, and cumin seeds. Cook until the seeds start to toast and pop. Add onion and cook until caramelized, about 6 minutes. Add the garlic, ginger, turmeric, and serrano pepper and cook over medium-high heat until fragrant. Add the brown sugar and stir until it begins to dissolve, about 2 minutes. Add the vinegar and bring to a simmer. Cook for about 10 minutes to combine the flavors.

Add the diced apples, raisins, and cranberries. Cook for about 15 minutes until the apples are softened. Add honey and cook over low heat until thickened.

Adjust seasoning with salt, honey, or additional lemon juice, as needed.

SPATCHCOCKED GAME BIRDS

I fell in love with spatchcocked birds when I used to travel Mexico's Yucatán Peninsula with nothing but a backpack and a fishing rod. After a few days of sleeping on remote beaches and eating little besides beans and rice, I was always eager to gorge myself on the chickens that curbside vendors would split with a machete and then grill over lump charcoal. Since then, I've done pretty much every species of North American game bird in this fashion, always with excellent results. Using kitchen shears, cut along one side of the backbone (you can also cut on both sides of the backbone and remove it completely), then open up the bird, lay it skin side up, and press down on the breastbone so it lies flat. It comes out looking like a butterfly or a Rorschach test—take your pick. (If you cut out the backbone completely, don't forget to save it in your freezer for stock.)

I like to brine game birds to get the maximum juiciness possible. You can brine for as little as 1–2 hours or up to 12 hours. After I brine it, I like to grill it; sometimes I'll set up a quick impromptu smoker on my grill top by wrapping some mesquite or fruitwood chips in aluminum foil and placing the package above a low flame.

- Kosher salt
- ½ cup sugar
- ¼ cup honey
- 2 lemons, halved
- 1 large onion, sliced
- 2 bay leaves

- 2 tablespoons black peppercorns
- Rosemary or thyme sprigs
- 1 game bird, plucked, gutted, and spatchcocked (see note at top of recipe)
- Vegetable or canola oil
- Freshly ground black pepper

To make the brine, combine 1 gallon water with 1 cup salt, sugar, honey, juice of the lemons, squeezed-out lemon halves, onion, bay leaves, peppercorns, and rosemary or thyme sprigs. Lay the spatchcocked bird in a nonreactive baking dish or roasting pan. Pour the brine over the bird. Cover and refrigerate for at least 1 hour and up to 12 hours (the smallest birds, such as quail, could be brined for as little as 15–20 minutes; larger birds, such as turkeys, benefit from 6–8 hours of brining or more).

When ready to cook, remove the bird from the brine, rinse it, and pat it dry. Prepare the grill for indirect heat.

Brush the bird with a little oil and season with salt and pepper on both sides. Lay the bird skin side down on the hot side of the grill. (Leave a little room on the hot side for the impromptu smoker, if using.) Close the lid, checking occasionally; move it off the hotter side if it appears to be burning. Once the skin is golden and crisped, flip the bird over and cook it on the cooler side until done; an instant-read thermometer inserted into the thickest part of the thigh (but not touching the bone) should read 160°.

Note: It's difficult to give precise cooking times when grilling whole upland game birds, including turkeys, as they vary in size, fat content, moisture, etc.—and grill qualities and temperatures vary wildly as well. In short, a safe bet is to cook the bird at medium to medium-high settings until the internal temperature of the thigh is 160°.

PICKLED GIZZARDS AND HEARTS

like to save all of my game bird gizzards and hearts. I'll freeze a few in the bottom of a quart-sized container, and then keep adding more and topping them off with water as I build my stash up to at least 1 pound of meat. Then I defrost them and make up a good pickling brine. You want the hearts and gizzards in bite-sized pieces, so with larger birds like geese or turkeys it's good to slice them down to halves or quarters. With grouse-sized or smaller birds, leave them whole. It's a bit of a process and takes a couple of weeks from start to finish, but it's well worth it. In the end, you can kick back with some friends at the table, poppin' pickled giblets with crackers and beers.

SERVES: 1 QUART

- 1 pound bird giblets (gizzards and hearts), cleaned, trimmed, and if necessary, cut into bite-sized pieces
- Kosher salt
- 1 cup white vinegar
- ¼ cup sugar
- 1 tablespoon multicolored peppercorns

(substitute black if that's what you have)
- ½ teaspoon red pepper flakes
- 1 tablespoon pickling spice
- 3 cloves garlic, peeled and sliced
- 1 onion, peeled and sliced

Place the giblets in a 4-quart pot and cover with water. Add 2 teaspoons salt. Bring to a simmer and cook until tender. Drain the cooked giblets, rinse, and drain again.

In another pot, combine ¼ cup water with the vinegar, sugar, 1½ tablespoons salt, peppercorns, red pepper flakes, pickling spice, and garlic cloves and bring to a boil.

Layer the sliced onions and giblets in a 1-quart canning jar and top with boiling brine. Refrigerate the jar for a couple of weeks while the brine does its work, and then enjoy. For long-term storage, seal the lid according to a standardized, safe canning method. (I use the USDA guide; see below.) Chill the giblets in a fridge before serving, and use within a week of opening.

Note: For more information about canning, go online and look for the *USDA Guide to the Principles of Home Canning*.

This is one of those recipes that you make when you and your buddies are fortunate enough to pile up a couple bag limits of geese. I gut and pluck my geese, saving the skin and fat in order to render it for making goose leg confit (see page 337). The boneless and skinless goose breasts are perfect for corning. The corning process makes them rich and flavorful; it's a very close approximation to traditional corned beef made from brisket. Even if it's not St. Patty's Day, I still pretend that it is and cook this dish with cabbage, carrots, and potatoes. This recipe is fail-safe and extremely easy.

SERVES: 6–8

- 2 quarts water
- 2 cups Morton's Tender Quick
- 1 cup brown sugar
- 2 tablespoons pickling spice (available in most grocery stores)

- 2 boneless, skinless goose breasts, about three to four pounds of meat
- 2 medium onions, peeled and halved
- 1 head garlic, cut in half horizontally
- 2 bay leaves

- 2 pounds small white potatoes, scrubbed and halved or quartered (if very small, leave whole)
- 1 small green cabbage, outer leaves discarded, cut into 12 wedges
- 1 bag (10 ounces) baby carrots
- 1 package (10 ounces) frozen pearl onions
- Grainy or spicy mustard

To make the brine, combine 2 quarts water with the Tender Quick, brown sugar, and pickling spice in a large nonreactive cooking pot or food-safe tub. Bring to a boil to dissolve the Tender Quick and brown sugar, then cool. Add the meat, making sure it is completely covered by the brine. (You can also place the meat in a large resealable plastic bag, pour the cooled brine over it, and seal the bag; this requires less brine to get full coverage.) Cover and refrigerate for at least 4 days and up to 7 days.

When you're ready to cook, preheat the oven to 325°. Remove the meat from the brine. Put the meat in a large stockpot with the onions and garlic and add water to cover. Bring to a boil, lower heat to a simmer, and skim off and discard any scum. Add the bay leaves, cover the pot, and put the pot into the oven. Cook until the meat is fork tender, which could be anywhere from 3 to 5 hours. When the meat is close to ready, add the potatoes, cabbage, carrots, and pearl onions. Cook until the meat and the vegetables are tender.

Using tongs, remove the meat and vegetables and place on a large platter. Break up the meat with the tongs or a meat fork. Serve with mustard.

GOOSE LEG CONFIT

e have far more Canada and snow geese in the United States now than at the time of European contact, and hunters around the country are enjoying extremely heavy harvests. More than ever, people are looking for interesting and novel approaches to cooking these large birds. One of my favorites is goose confit, an ancient preparation in which goose (or duck) legs are cured in a dry brine and then preserved in fat. While pork lard works handily, it's more rewarding to save and render your own duck and goose fat. The ratio is not perfect, though, as it takes the fat from several geese to make confit with the legs of one. So if you do render your own fat, you may still need to supplement with pork lard. Luckily, once the confit is all eaten, the fat can be reused.

HOW TO RENDER GOOSE OR DUCK FAT

Cube the skin and place in a pot. Add any chunks of fat that you find inside the bird's belly. Warm the fat to the melting point, then strain through a wire strainer. Place the strained fat back in the pot and cook over low heat until it quits sputtering. Pour the clear fat off into a freezable container, leaving any solids or residues in the bottom of the pot. It'll keep for a year in the freezer, but use within 6 months for best flavor. (Of course, if you smell rancid odors or see mold, toss it.) It's great for many uses, including frying potatoes.

SERVES: VARIES DEPENDING ON INTENDED USE

- 1 cup kosher salt
- ¼ cup sugar
- 2 tablespoons freshly ground black pepper
- Leaves of 3 sprigs fresh thyme, minced, or 1 tablespoon dried thyme
- ½ teaspoon nutmeg
- ¼ teaspoon allspice
- ¼ teaspoon ground cloves
- 2 geese legs, bone in, skin removed
- 3 cloves garlic, thinly sliced
- 2 quarts rendered goose fat (see above; supplement with store-bought duck or goose fat or even pork lard if necessary)

In a small bowl, make the curing mixture by combining the salt, sugar, pepper, thyme, nutmeg, allspice, and cloves. Place the goose legs in a baking dish and rub them with the mixture, making sure as much of the cure as possible adheres to the meat. Arrange the garlic slices over the meaty parts of the legs. Cover the baking dish with plastic wrap and refrigerate for 2–3 days to cure.

When ready to cook, preheat oven to 225°. Take the goose legs out of the fridge and rinse thoroughly; discard the garlic cloves. Pat the legs dry with paper towels. In a small roasting pan or wide low-sided pot, melt the goose fat over medium-low heat. Add the goose legs. Be sure the fat covers the meat; if it does not, add a little more goose fat or lard. Cover the pot with foil or a lid and place it in the oven. Cook about 3 hours, checking occasionally toward the end of the cooking time, until the meat is fall-off-the-bone tender.

When it's done, allow the goose legs to cool to room temperature while still in the fat. Transfer both meat and fat to a tall, narrow storage container. Make sure the meat is covered with the extra fat, then top it off with about ½ inch of oil, to ensure a good seal against air. Cover with plastic wrap and refrigerate for up to 1 month. As you take out what you need, make sure the remainder is completely covered with fat and oil. (Alternatively, you can freeze in vacuum bags, with the extra fat, for up to 6 months.)

When you're ready to use the goose confit, pick the meat off the bone and either reheat it under the broiler or sear it in a sauté pan. It can be used to top salads, tossed with potatoes or pasta, or used in casseroles. Trust me, it just makes everything better.

WILD GAME PÂTÉ (TERRINE)

This is a fancy dish that turns small odds and ends of meat into pure gold. It's the perfect thing to make as a sophisticated first course when you're hosting a swanky get-together. Your guests will be impressed by your efforts.

SERVES: 12–20 AS AN APPETIZER

- ½ pound game liver
- 2 cups milk
- 8 ounces lean venison and 4 ounces pork fat, ground together through a small-die grinder plate
- ½ cup heavy cream

- 3 cloves garlic, minced
- 1 teaspoon dried thyme
- 2 teaspoons kosher salt
- 2 teaspoons freshly ground black pepper
- 1 teaspoon nutmeg
- 2 leaves fresh sage, finely chopped

- 2 tablespoons unsalted butter

- 2 small shallots, finely minced

- ¼ cup brandy

- 1 pound sliced bacon

- 1 breast fillet from a white-fleshed game bird, such as grouse or pheasant, cut into ⅓-by-⅓-by-3-inch pieces

HOW TO CUT A TERRINE BOARD

A buddy of mine showed me how much easier it was to weight down a terrine if you cut a piece of wood just for the purpose. You need the dimensions of the interior of your terrine. Then go out back and cut yourself a rectangle in those same dimensions minus ¼ inch on all sides, so it will fit snugly. I used wood that was ¼ inch thick. Cleverly, I marked mine with the words "Terrine Board" so that I don't accidentally burn it in the fireplace.

To use the terrine board, I wrap it in foil and place it over the terrine after it comes out of the oven. Then I weight it down with a foil-covered brick or a few 15-ounce cans.

Put the liver in a baking dish or bowl and cover with milk. Cover and let soak in the refrigerator for 2 hours. Remove the liver, pat it dry, and discard the soaking liquid. Cut the liver into 1-inch pieces. Using a food processor, chop the liver finely until it forms a paste.

Preheat the oven to 350°.

In a large bowl, combine the liver, venison, cream, garlic, thyme, salt, pepper, nutmeg, and sage and mix well.

In a sauté pan over medium heat, melt the butter. Add the shallots and cook until translucent and tender, about 5 minutes. Raise the heat to high. Remove the pan from the heat and add the brandy. Using a long-stemmed match or torch lighter, ignite the brandy and allow it to flame. Pour the flaming brandy and shallots into the meat mixture and stir to combine.

Line a 5-cup lidded terrine mold with bacon, laying the slices across the bottom horizontally; the ends of the bacon should hang over the sides of the mold. Put one-quarter of the meat mixture into the mold on top of the bacon slices. Layer one-third of the breast strips on top of the meat mixture. Then top with another one-quarter of the meat mixture and another third of the breast strips. Repeat the layering, finishing with the last one-quarter of the meat mixture. Pat the mixture down firmly and fold the bacon ends over the top of the meat mixture. They should overlap in the middle of the terrine. Cover with the terrine lid (or with foil).

Set the terrine in a roasting pan filled with enough water to come halfway up the sides of the terrine. Bake the terrine about 1–1½ hours, or until an instant-read thermometer inserted into the center reads 160°.

Remove the terrine from the water bath and take off the lid. Cover the terrine with plastic wrap and then place a weighted board on top (see sidebar page 343). Allow the terrine to cool on the counter for 1 hour, then place in refrigerator until thoroughly chilled, about 3 hours.

When chilled, unmold the terrine. Wrap the whole terrine in plastic wrap and foil and let it mellow in the fridge for a day if you can wait—it will be even more delicious. If not, eat with crusty bread, gherkins, and mustard.

TURKEY SCHNITZEL

discovered turkey schnitzel while filming a backcountry turkey hunt in Montana. Our cameraman and director, Mo Fallon, took a look at our supplies, which included a dead turkey, salt, panko breadcrumbs, oil, and a lemon, and he hatched a plan. We sliced the turkey breasts into thick slabs and then flattened them thin as a magazine between two rocks. The result was turkey magic. Since then, I've shown the recipe to several turkey hunting fanatics and they've become total believers; one has foresworn all other turkey recipes in favor of this one. Keep in mind, too, that these breaded wild turkey cutlets are fantastic on sandwiches.

SERVES: 6

- 1 wild turkey breast half, boneless and skinless
- Kosher salt
- Freshly ground black pepper
- 1 cup all-purpose flour

- 2 eggs beaten with a little water
- 2 cups panko breadcrumbs
- Vegetable oil
- 1 lemon, cut into wedges

Cut the turkey breast half crosswise into 6 pieces, roughly 4–5 ounces each. One at a time, place the pieces between two layers of plastic wrap. Using a rock, hammer, meat mallet, or any other heavy solid object, pound the breast pieces until they are about ⅓ inch thick.

Season the turkey breast slices with salt and pepper. Put the flour, beaten egg mixture, and breadcrumbs in separate plates or baking dishes. Dredge the turkey pieces in the flour, then dip them in the egg, and finally coat in the breadcrumbs.

Meanwhile, heat ⅓ inch oil in a heavy-bottomed pot or Dutch oven over high heat. Fry the schnitzel till golden brown on one side, turn, and brown the other side until cooked all the way through. Drain on a plate lined with paper towels. Season with salt.

If eating by the campfire, squeeze a lemon wedge over the meat, then just eat it with your hands. If you're in a more civilized setting, serve with a knife and fork.

FRESH TURKEY BREAKFAST SAUSAGE WITH SAGE

The flavors of wild turkey and sage complement each other perfectly, especially when combined in a spicy breakfast sausage. This mixture can be stuffed into lamb casings to make breakfast-sized links, but I prefer to leave mine bulk and then form it into small patties that are easy to fry next to a couple of eggs. Or better yet, throw a few of these patties on a griddle next to some toad-in-the-holes. It's a memorable start for any day in the outdoors.

SERVES: UP TO 12

- 1½ pounds turkey, cut into 1½-inch cubes
- ½ pound pork back fat, cut into 1½-inch cubes
- 1 tablespoon kosher salt
- 2 teaspoons freshly ground black pepper
- 2 cloves garlic, minced
- 6 sage leaves, chopped
- 2 teaspoons freshly grated ginger
- ¼ cup ice water, or more as needed
- Vegetable oil

Using the large die of a meat grinder, grind the turkey and pork fat into a bowl set over a bowl full of ice. Grind the meat a second time through the small die.

In a large bowl, combine the meat with the remaining ingredients except the oil and mix well with your hands. Cover and refrigerate until ready to use.

Form patties with a slightly wet hand. I like to make 'em 3 inches in diameter, 'cause they are easy to throw on the grill or in a pan that way, but you can make them any size you like.

Preheat a cast-iron pan over high heat. Put a little oil in the pan and sear the sausage patties for 4 minutes per side.

Note: To freeze, separate the patties with a piece of freezer paper or parchment paper between them. Then wrap well with plastic wrap. They will keep in the freezer for up to 6 months.

STUFFED TURKEY BREAST

I love to stuff and roast whole wild turkeys, but it always leaves me wishing that I'd saved some of my bird for the rest of the year as well. This recipe is part of the solution to that problem. You stuff and roast just a single boneless breast, and then save the rest of your turkey for grilling, smoking, or whatever other recipes you enjoy. I make a pocket in the breast with a long-bladed fillet knife, then pipe the filling into the pocket and close it up with skewers or whittled sticks. It goes in the oven on a bed of leeks and comes out dripping with flavor. If you choose to stay true to your whole roasted turkeys, try this same stuffing recipe next Thanksgiving. You'll love it.

SERVES: 6

- 2 tablespoons extra-virgin olive oil
- 1 onion, peeled and sliced thin

- 2 cloves garlic, minced
- 8 ounces mushrooms, sliced thin

- 2 sprigs fresh thyme, minced
- ½ cup dried cranberries
- ¼ cup pine nuts, toasted
- Kosher salt
- Freshly ground black pepper
- 1 boneless turkey breast half, skin on
- 1 apple, peeled, cored, and diced small
- 1 cup shredded sharp white cheddar cheese (or Monterey Jack)
- ¼ cup finely chopped parsley
- 3 large leeks, white parts only, trimmed, cut in half lengthwise, and cleaned well of grit and sand
- 1 stick butter, melted

Heat oil in a 12-inch sauté pan over medium heat. Add the onion and cook until translucent, about 6 minutes. Add the garlic and cook for 1 minute more. Add the mushrooms and cook until browned, about 6 minutes. Add the thyme, cranberries, and pine nuts and cook until fragrant, about 1 minute more. Season with salt and pepper to taste. Set aside to cool slightly.

Make a slit in the side of the turkey breast with a sharp paring knife or a long-bladed fillet knife. The slit should be about 2–2½ inches long. Carefully pivot the knife inside the opening to create an interior pocket in the turkey breast, without making the opening larger. Season well with salt and pepper on the outside and inside of the pocket. Set aside.

Preheat the oven to 375°.

Stir the apples, cheddar cheese, and parsley into the mushroom mixture. Transfer the filling to a pastry bag. (You can also use a resealable zip-top bag as a makeshift pastry bag; snip off a bottom corner of the bag and squeeze the filling out.) Pipe the filling into the pocket, filling it as full as possible without letting it burst. Close the opening with small skewers or whittled sticks.

Lay the leeks in the bottom of a greased roasting pan. Lay the turkey breast on top of the leeks and brush with the melted butter. Baste periodically with more butter while cooking. Roast for 40–45 minutes, or until an instant-read thermometer inserted into the center of the meat reads 160°. Remove from the oven and let rest for 10–15 minutes under a tent of foil.

Cut the meat into ¾-inch-thick slices. Serve with the roasted leeks.

ACKNOWLEDGMENTS

Many biologists and hunters gave freely of their knowledge and photographs in order to make this book as good as could be. It's impossible to list them all, but special thanks to Robert Abernethy, Ed Arnett, Ronny Boehme, Ryan Callaghan, Matt Carlson, Darr Colburn, Chris Denham, Morgan Fallon, Jerod Fink, Joseph Furia, Chuck Hawks, Brody Henderson, Scott Justice, Cody Lujan, Karl Malcolm, James Miller, Cameron Mitchell, Kevin Murphy, Paul Neess, Chip Parkins, Martins Putelis, Steve Reid, Danny Rinella, Matt Rinella, Jay Scott, Hank Shaw, Kent Undlin, Remi Warren, and Mike Washlesky.

At some point or another, at least a dozen or so of my colleagues from Zero Point Zero Production were engaged in the creation of this book. Thanks to Dan Doty and Jared Andrukanis for their general oversight of this project; Helen Cho for cheering us on and spreading the word; Chris Collins, Lydia Tenaglia, and Lou Festa for finding good people and giving them a great place to work; and Joe Caterini for making all of this possible in the first place. Huge thanks also to stylist/producer Krista Ruane and her crew, Ericka Martins and Ashley Berman, for bringing the recipes to life and making them look so beautiful.

Thanks to Marc Gerald, at the Agency Group, for helping to shape the concept of this book and then explain it to the right people. Thanks to Cindy Spiegel and everyone at Spiegel & Grau and Random House, including Annie Chagnot, Carole Lowenstein, Benjamin Dreyer, Tom Perry, and Christopher Zucker.

Finally, I'd like to acknowledge the work of Sam Terrell, Peter Sucheski, John Hafner, Janis Putelis, and Brittany Brothers. Sam contributed significantly with research and writing on firearms, ammunition, and waterfowl. Peter's illustrations can be found throughout this book; thanks to him for enduring endless requests for revisions as we tried to make everything look just right. Thanks to John Hafner for the splendid food photography and also for generously opening up his archives of wildlife photography for our use. Brittany Brothers assumed the roles of photo editor and archivist for this project and helped the book achieve a cohesive look and feel. Janis Putelis worked on literally all aspects of this project from start to finish, including research, writing, and photography. There's hardly a page within this book that has not benefited from his touch as both a hunter and a writer.

PHOTO CREDITS

Peter Sucheski 6, 14, 16, 26, 27, 38, 52, 68–71 (a), 96–99, 103, 105 (a), 106, 108, 109 (a), 110 (b), 116, 129, 138, 140–142 (a), 147 (a), 153, 162 (a), 166, 170, 176, 180, 185, 199 (a), 206 (a), 211, 216, 219, 224 (b), 226 (a), 228 (a), 230 (a), 232, 235, 243, 246, 253 (a), 255 (a), 257 (b), 258 (b), 260 (a), 276, 278, 285, 286, 287 (b), 288, 289 (b), 290, 291 (b), 292

Pictureguy66/123RF.com 204

Randi Berez 22, 81, 94, 117 (b), 119, 142 (b), 298 (c), 299

raptorcaptor/123RF.com 225

Robert Abernethy 135

Robert L. Kothenbeutel/Shutterstock 231

Ronny Boehme 7, 11, 236, 237, 238, 314 (a)

Russell Graves 4–5, 92, 109 (b), 151 (a) 168, 182, 183, 228, 242, 245, 249, 257 (a)

Ryan Callaghan 111, 190 (a), 233

Sam Terrell 251, 255 (b), 264, 265, 274 (b)

Sascha Burkhard/123RF.com 160 (b)

Shoshana Malcolm 66 (b), 104, 187, 188, 207, 224 (a), 230 (b&c)

Steve Byland/123RF.com 234

Steve Oehlenschlager/123RF.com/Shutterstock 254, 258 (a)

Steven Love/123RF.com 223

Steven Rinella 2–3, 4, 28 (a), 50, 100, 124, 167, 190 (b), 199 (b), 206 (a), 208, 213, 244, 247, 272 (b)

Timur Abramoc/123RF.com 218

Tom Tietz/123RF.com 165, 275

Torbjorn Swenelius/123RF.com 184

Tracy Breen 133

Zack Peterman 147 (b)

Zero Point Zero Production 5, 8, 9, 17, 41, 57, 58, 61, 62, 63 (b), 64 (a), 82, 88, 91, 107, 128, 149, 162 (b&c), 177, 191, 196, 206 (b), 220, 226 (b–e), 240, 253 (b), 261, 262, 268, 273 (b), 281, 296-298 (a&b), 300-302, 308 (a–c), 309 (c), 313

INDEX

Page numbers in italics refer to illustrations.

ABOUT THE AUTHORS

STEVEN RINELLA is the author of four previous books: *The Complete Guide to Hunting, Butchering, and Cooking Wild Game: Volume 1: Big Game, The Scavenger's Guide to Haute Cuisine, American Buffalo: In Search of a Lost Icon,* and *Meat Eater: Adventures from the Life of an American Hunter.* His writing has also appeared in *Outside, Field and Stream, Men's Journal, The New York Times, Men's Fitness, Bowhunter,* and the anthologies *The Best American Travel Writing* (2002, 2010, 2014) and *Best Food Writing* (2005, 2013). A native of Twin Lake, Michigan, he now lives with his family in the Pacific Northwest.

stevenrinella.com
Facebook.com/StevenRinellaMeatEater
@stevenrinella

JOHN HAFNER is a Montana-based photographer, writer, and lifelong deer and turkey hunter (johnhafner.photography). He works with many of the top manufacturers, magazines, and retailers in the hunting industry, and travels the globe shooting ad campaigns, catalogs, and stories for an extensive client list.

A Michigan native, JANIS PUTELIS started his hunting career as a teenager chasing whitetail deer in Michigan and Wisconsin. He worked for well over a decade as a professional big game guide in Colorado, Arizona, and Mexico. He is now a producer for the television show *MeatEater.*